Music, Music Therapy and Trauma

of related interest

Constructing Musical Healing
The Wounds That Sing
June Boyce Tillman
ISBN 1 85302 483 X

Music Therapy – Intimate Notes
Mercédès Pavlicevic
ISBN 1 85302 692 1

Music Therapy in Context
Music, Meaning and Relationship
Mercédès Pavlicevic
ISBN 1 85302 434 1

Psychodrama with Trauma Survivors
Acting Out Your Pain
Edited Peter Felix Kellermann and M.K. Hudgins
ISBN 1 85302 893 2

Clinical Applications of Music Therapy in Psychiatry
Edited by Tony Wigram and Jos De Backer
ISBN 1 85302 733 2

Clinical Applications of Music Therapy in Developmental Disability, Paediatrics and Neurology
Edited by Tony Wigram and Jos De Backer
ISBN 1 85302 734 0

Music Therapy Research and Practice in Medicine
From Out of the Silence
David Aldridge
ISBN 1 85302 296 9

Music, Music Therapy and Trauma

International Perspectives

Editor Julie P. Sutton

Jessica Kingsley Publishers
London and Philadelphia

First published in the United Kingdom in 2002
by Jessica Kingsley Publishers Ltd
116 Pentonville Road
London N1 9JB, England
and
325 Chestnut Street
Philadelphia, PA 19106, USA

www.jkp.com

Copyright © Jessica Kingsley Publishers 2002

Library of Congress Cataloging in Publication Data
A CIP catalog record for this book is available from the Library of Congress

British Library Cataloguing in Publication Data
A CIP catalogue record for this book is available from the British Library

ISBN 1 84310 027 4

Printed and Bound in Great Britain by
Athenaeum Press, Gateshead, Tyne and Wear

For Jack, Vi, and Mandy

Contents

ACKNOWLEDGEMENTS   10

Introduction   11
Julie P. Sutton

Part 1 Trauma Perspectives

1. **Trauma**   21
   Trauma in Context
   Julie P. Sutton, Belfast and Dublin; Clinical Adviser,
   Paravotti Music Centre, Mostar, Bosnia

2. **Neurology**   41
   The Brain – its Music and its Emotion: the
   Neurology of Trauma
   Michael Swallow OBE, FRCP

Part 2 Culture, Society and Musical Perspectives

3. **Culture and Society**   57
   The Role of Creativity in Healing and Recovering
   One's Power after Victimisation
   Marie Smyth, University of Ulster and the Initiative on
   Conflict Resolution and Ethnicity

4. **Musical Persepctives**   83
    The Politics of Silence: the Northern Ireland
    Composer and the Troubles
    Hilary Bracefield, University of Ulster

Part 3 International Clinical Perspectives

5. **South Africa**   97
    Fragile Rhythms and Uncertain Listenings: Perspectives
    from Music Therapy with South African Children
    Mercédès Pavlicevic, University of Pretoria

6. **UK**   119
    Music and Human Rights
    *Matthew Dixon, Medical Foundation for the Care
    of Victims of Torture*

7. **Ireland**   133
    See Me, Hear Me, Play With Me: Working with the
    Trauma of Early Abandonment and Deprivation in
    Psychodynamic Music Therapy
    *Ruth Walsh Stewart, Our Lady's Children's Hospital
    Dublin and David Stewart, NOVA Project, Barnardo's
    Northern Ireland*

8. **Bosnia**   153
    A Music Therapy Service in a Post-war Environment
    *Louise Lang and Una McInerney, Pavarotti Music
    Centre Mostar*

9. **UK**   175
    In the Music Prison: the Story of Pablo
    *Helen M. Tyler, Nordoff-Robbins Music Therapy
    Centre London*

10. Israel 193

Trauma and its Relation to Sound and Music
*Adva Frank-Schwebel, Bar Ilan University
and David Yellin College Jerusalem*

Part 4 The Support Perspective

11. Supervision 211

Processes in Listening Together – an Experience
of Distance Supervision of Work with Traumatised
Children
*Louise Lang, Una McInerney, Rosemary Monaghan
and Julie P. Sutton, Bosnia and the UK*

12. The Wounded Healer 231

The Voice of Trauma: a Wounded Healer's
Perspective
Diane Austin, New York University

Afterword 260
Julie P. Sutton

LIST OF CONTRIBUTORS   262

SUBJECT INDEX   265

AUTHOR INDEX   271

Acknowledgements

I would like to thank the following people, who helped in various ways in the publication of this book: the staff involved with my Millennium Award (UK Millennium Commission), which stimulated the idea of the book; Diane Austin, Hilary Bracefield, Matthew Dixon, Adva Frank-Schwebel, Louise Lang, Una McInerney, Rosemary Monaghan, Mercédès Pavlicevic, Marie Smyth, David Stewart, Ruth Walsh Stewart, Michael Swallow and Helen Tyler, who generously contributed their time and energy; Seamus Dunn, for encouragement in the early days; Nigel Osborne for his inspiring work; my colleague Jacqueline Robarts, for sharing ideas and advice; PS for listening; 'Jerry', who taught me more than I realised at the time; and finally, Ray Hunt, for doing the dishes and for showing me how something good could come out of something bad.

Introduction

Julie P. Sutton

The contents of this book originated in a Millennium Award that enabled the editor to make contact with music therapy colleagues throughout the world who were working with those traumatised. The Award year culminated in a conference that was held in Belfast during November 2000. This event drew together a number of international experts who had an interest in or were working with people affected by traumatic events. During the day it became apparent that there were many links between the ideas presented and that this material warranted publication. This book is the result.

The reader will find that there are many different voices in the book, but from the beginning there is a Northern Irish slant. This is because Northern Ireland was the home setting for the Millennium Award. The growing interest locally in the effects of trauma as a result of ongoing conflict reflects worldwide changes in perception and attitude to the subject. A broad range of individual and cultural experiences of different aspects of trauma is also present in the book, with chapters describing trauma relating to developmental aspects, single events and war. It will be shown that the effects of trauma are long lasting and pervasive both in the individual and in society. It is therefore particularly apt that there is a post-conflict context for the book, for at the time of writing there is continued although hesitant progress in the Northern Ireland peace process. This underlines how the trauma process is complex and never clear cut.

In a poem entitled 'Ricochet', the Bosnian poet Fahrudin Zilkić (1998) defined the impact of a traumatic event as a ricochet. A dictionary (Hornby 1974) definition of the word ricochet is 'to rebound, skip or bound off (the bullet ricoched off the wall)', giving the impression of an action where something is ejected at speed and then rebounds. Trauma can affect us in much the same way, intruding explosively into our lives and reverberating unpredictably into the future. In the same poem Zilkić also uses the word 'scar' to indicate not only the physical impact of the event he describes (a bullet hitting a stone), but also the hidden impact upon the psyche of the person (the internal psychic wound). It is this hidden impact of trauma that the following chapters explore, both in more general terms and also in detail through descriptions of music therapy work.

The book is divided into four parts: Trauma Perspectives; Culture, Society and Musical Perspectives; International Clinical Perspectives and The Support Perspective. While there is a deliberate focus upon the clinical work, the broader areas within which trauma work can be seen are also included. Finally, there is space given to the need for external support for those undertaking this work. This support is seen as an essential feature of work with those who are traumatised.

The diverse cultural contexts in the book are presented by different voices that speak to the reader in different styles. This was a conscious decision, to enable the topic to be viewed from a variety of perspectives, including each author's unique theoretical and personal stance. The concept of becoming informed about trauma through a multidisciplinary approach is central to this book and this is a constant theme throughout. There are also clinical themes that emerge from Part 3, International Clinical Perspectives, including the significance of early attachment and the contrasting topics of silence and constant sound.

The book begins with two chapters that offer quite different views of trauma. In Chapter 1 the editor sets the context for what follows. The three strands of the chapter – a perspective for thinking about trauma, a clinical example, and the impact of the work upon the therapist – are echoed throughout the book by different authors. Beginning with the ways in which society views and is affected by trauma, the central section of the chapter tells a single story of one boy's use of music therapy. In this case, violence in the community and a traumatic event had resulted in an experience of silence that operated on different levels, both internal and external. The theme of silence is common to trauma work and is revisited by other authors in the central section of the book. The final section of the chapter considers how the work might affect the therapist; an area that is less commonly found in the literature. Chapter 2, by Michael Swallow, gives a point of view from a neurologist who is also a practising musician. This is an unusual perspective in the music therapy literature, which draws together past and contemporary brain research. The ideas presented are backed up by scientific evidence, for instance, a concept of the healing properties of music in relation to brain damage due to post traumatic stress disorder. There are also thoughts about memory that, while emanating from neurology research, are echoed in the work of developmental psychologists. This chapter is unique in the music therapy literature and should be of interest to any practising therapist.

Part 2 of the book contains two chapters from researchers based in Northern Ireland. In Chapter 3, Marie Smyth presents the outcomes of many years of action research with those affected by the Troubles (the local term for the Northern Irish conflict). Beginning with a comprehensive overview of the impact of the Troubles presented statistically, through her own research findings Smyth also details the effect at the personal level. The concept of trauma is placed in a Northern Irish context, along with a complexity of political, social and cultural influences, and this complexity is also echoed by other authors in the main section of the book. Smyth concludes by considering music therapy, making a case for the importance of creativity in divided societies. In Chapter 4 in the series of broader perspectives, Hilary Bracefield offers a view of how Northern Irish composers have – or have not – used the Troubles in their own work. Describing the use of music in a society experiencing ongoing conflict and based on her own research, the chapter stems from interviews with Northern Irish composers. The theme of silence is discussed, in relation to the ways in which cultural factors have affected composers. Bracefield explores how affected by the

Troubles these musicians were, coming to conclusions that might surprise the reader.

From these broader perspectives, the book moves to the larger, clinical section, Part 3, where therapists from different parts of the world describe their work. As well as descriptions of each setting and theoretical considerations, each chapter focuses on the ways in which the clinical application of music was of use to the clients. Here the reader will find a rich variety of approaches, with different uses of and attitudes to the music. There are also common threads throughout, in particular the impact of early life upon later traumatic experiences and the theme of sound contrasted with silence. A central theme is the care with which each clinician approaches their work with this extremely vulnerable client group.

The main section of the book begins with a South African perspective given by Mercédès Pavlicevic. Chapter 5 contains an account of music therapy with a group and two individual children. Contextualising violence in different ways (with themes of violence in society and violence in childhood), Pavlicevic reveals the underlying complexity of the situation in South Africa. There are also outlines of a range of theoretical thinking relating to early development. In terms of music therapy work, Pavlicevic incorporates the concept of the 'music child', which she states 'integrates all aspects of the child in music therapy'. It is this non-traumatised part of the child that engages in an active healing process.

In Chapter 6, which was stimulated by work at the Medical Foundation for the Care of Victims of Torture in London, Matthew Dixon explores the broader issues of music and violence. He invites the reader to think with him about what being musically active entails, and also asks questions about what music and words can express or represent. Placing emphasis on the interaction itself, he describes the function and role of the music during the sessions with a teenage client. The twin themes of silence and a 'wall of sound' also appear. This is a chapter that describes both the individual and the collective perspectives of music and violence, at the heart of which is a single story.

Chapter 7 is co-authored by Ruth Walsh Stewart and David Stewart and describes the traumatic impact of early abandonment upon a child who was then adopted into a different culture, in Ireland. Using psychodynamic theory and focusing particularly on stages of the earliest life experiences, the chapter traces how the therapist's central task was to provide a safe, containing environment. The therapist's reflecting stance is shown to be significant in enabling the client to experience something 'akin to early care-giving', and this concept is explored in detail through the use of a theoretical commentary. This chapter outlines the approach of music therapists who work in a psychodynamic framework, making clear the importance of careful observation of and further thinking about the vulnerable client. It is essentially cross-modal work and at its root is play. However, music is always present – in musical activity, musical sound and silence, and the timing and expressive quality of what passes between client and therapist.

Chapter 8 is also co-authored, by Louise Lang and Una McInerney, who explore music therapy in post-war Bosnia-Herzegovina. Concerned with experiences of setting up a clinical service in a post-war environment, their work is seen from several perspectives. These include the physical setting (the Pavarotti Music Centre), the development of the service, clinical examples and four major themes emerging from the ways in which the clients used their music therapy. This work is unique in that to date no other music therapists have lived and worked in a different cultural setting during the months immediately after the cessation of war.

Chapter 9 is from Helen Tyler, who gives a moving account of work with a refugee child who had witnessed the torture of his father. Tyler details the progress of the therapy, including the impact of this work upon the therapist. Central features emerge relating to traumatic re-enactment, improvised story or narrative and symbolic use of musical instruments. This is not a neat story, because the therapy process took unexpected turns and – beyond the control of the therapist – the work was terminated unexpectedly. Yet, as Tyler points out, the messy ending did not detract from the child's experiences of a reliable, attentive therapist. This, along with the care with which the therapy space was held safe and secure for what needed to be expressed, was something that could be internalised by the client.

The final chapter of this section of the book comes from Israel. In Chapter 10, describing work with anorexic women, Adva Frank-

Schwebel offers the idea of 'more primary ways of experiencing sound', when the clients avoid playing music themselves. This is linked with the concept of regression in therapy and how significant this is for clients who have experiences of early cumulative trauma. Frank-Schwebel shows that when active music-making is inaccessible, the therapist can provide a creative, symbolic musical space in other ways, thus keeping alive what was felt to be dead. This chapter presents another view of the theme of silence in work with those who are traumatised. It culminates in the significant listening, thinking and reflecting that the therapist takes on behalf of the client.

Part 4 of the book is unusual in that it moves from the impact of trauma upon the client to the therapist's experience of the work. Chapters 11 and 12 provide a view of this perspective, which advises care in the work. There are arguments for grounding one's work theoretically and of continually developing one's awareness of oneself. Space is also given to the potential of the therapist's issues and wounds shared with the client.

Chapter 11 is collaborative and details a shared process of distance supervision. It is an honest account, bringing to light aspects of clinical supervision as well as the realities of work in a post-war environment. Broad theoretical concepts are identified that relate to an overall perspective for trauma work supervision, as seen from the joint viewpoints of supervisee and supervisor. It is unusual in the literature to find both supervisees and supervisors collaborating in this way, and the different perspectives given by each reveal the complexities of this kind of working relationship.

Chapter 12 is longer in length, because of its dual role in completing the book. Diane Austin offers a full theoretical underpinning for the work, along with techniques and examples of work with traumatised adult clients. In addition to this, the impact upon the therapist is examined, with Austin's personal insights adding to the richness of this account of the work. Several important features are included here that relate to the nature of the music itself. First, the setting is seen to offer a containing space within which vocal play can occur. Second, Austin introduces a concept of music as something that can provide both stability and fluidity for the client's self-expression. Third, music is described as 'medial', that is, something that can bridge both conscious and unconscious aspects of life.

Finally, Austin emphasises the care with which the work must be undertaken, particularly because of the intimacy of the music-making and its potential effect upon both client and therapist. Overall, the chapter reminds practising therapists to acknowledge their personal responsibility in the treatment of those who are traumatised.

As stated earlier, this book has evolved out of the editor's experience of clinical work in Northern Ireland and Bosnia-Herzegovina, as well as through collaboration and discussion with colleagues worldwide, stimulated by the findings of the conference that took place in Belfast in November 2000. It is the editor's aim that the different voices and theoretical strands in this publication will stimulate further thought in the reader. The ideas represented here are a starting point from which to explore further the connections between music, music therapy and trauma. It is hoped that what is documented in this book will provide a firm base from which new, informed exploration can continue.

References

Hornby, A. S. (1974) *Oxford Advanced Learner's Dictionary of Current English.* Oxford: Oxford University Press, p.728.

Zilkić, F. (1998) 'Ricochet' (transl. F.R. Jones. In C. Agee (ed.) *Scar on the Stone. Contemporary Poetry from Bosnia.* Newcastle upon Tyne: Bloodaxe Books, p.198.

Part 1

Trauma Perspectives

CHAPTER I

Trauma

Trauma in context

Julie P. Sutton

Over the past decade something has happened to our perception of 'trauma'. We have always reacted with horror to reports of the physical aspect of disasters, but more recently we have become better informed about the psychological shock that takes place. We are now aware not only of the immediate impact of traumatic events, but also of their repercussions. We realise that these repercussions are widespread and affect not only those immediately involved in the event itself. There is a complexity of influences that reaches far beyond the place where the event occurred. As the catastrophic event in New York on 11 September 2001 showed, these influences can reach across community and country boundaries. In today's society it is very likely that we will all experience the impact of single event trauma at some level.

In this chapter the concept of traumatic experience is placed in a historical context, in order to demonstrate how attitudes to the psychological effect of traumatic events have changed over the centuries. These changes in approach have influenced the provision of support and treatment for those who have experienced events beyond the ordinary. There is a further exploration of traumatic experience through a single music therapy case study. A final perspective is then added, inviting the reader to consider the impact of the work with those traumatised upon the therapist.

Contextualising definitions of trauma

For 30 years or more, dictionary definitions of trauma have mentioned a 'shock' (Hornby 1974) or a 'wound' (Wingate 1972) that causes lasting effects and/or damage. These three facets – shock, wound and a lasting effect – remain in the literature and are still central to our understanding of trauma. The task of describing how trauma affects people is more complex. In the medical literature, rather than attempt a single definition, the *Diagnostic and Statistical Manual of Mental Disorders (DSM)* details categories of response and lists of symptoms, including post traumatic stress disorder (PTSD) and related conditions (APA 1994).

The term PTSD was first used in 1980 (APA 1994) and includes three types of symptoms – the re-experiencing of the event, a lack of affect or numbness, and active avoidance of any reminder of what took place. PTSD is a chronic, debilitating condition, with extremely distressing symptoms such as flashbacks, numbing, dissociation and persistent, increased arousal. People who develop PTSD find that these symptoms are present for more than a month and are long lasting and devastating, with impairment in social, occupational and other areas of life. Work with Vietnam veterans, for instance, has shown that all aspects of social functioning were severely impaired and continued so for many years (Goldberg *et al.* 1990, pp.1227–32; Kaylor, King and King 1987, pp.257–71). Later research into Desert Storm troops' experiences replicated such findings, demonstrating the life-changing impact of exposure to experiences beyond the norm (Sutker *et al.* 1994, pp.383–90).

To put this in an overall context, it can be said that for the majority of us encountering trauma, the more acute and distressing symptoms are present during the 48-hour period after the traumatic event itself. We will discover that after two days the effects of our symptoms will lessen. Not every person will develop PTSD, nor will all find that symptoms decrease after the two-day period. Others will develop acute symptoms similar to PTSD (marked anxiety or avoidance, numbing or detachment, derealisation and depersonalisation), lasting between two days and four weeks. With their symptoms beginning to diminish after a month, this group of people will not develop PTSD and, in recognition of this, the term acute stress disorder (ASD) has been added to the *DSM*. Encompassing the whole range of responses and symptoms, from the relatively short lived (up to two days) to the longer lasting (one month onwards), the term ASD separates the commonly experienced, immediate, over-whelming impact of trauma from the chronic condition of PTSD. ASD can also used as a predictor, revealing a process that potentially could lead to PTSD. Most importantly, ASD can be seen as an attempt to acknowledge how high the level of distress can be in the period immedi-ately after the traumatic event.

With a catalogue of symptoms that can change over time, such post-trauma conditions still do not provide a clear-cut picture of how trauma affects the individual. This is further complicated because of the amount of time involved in the development of symptoms that eventually result in PTSD, including the possibility of a delayed onset, perhaps occurring some months or years after an event. This was seen recently in Northern Ireland, following the first IRA ceasefire. Rather than bringing a greater sense of safety in the community, the beginning of the peace process was linked with evidence of a statistically significant increase in psychiatric admissions (Northern Ireland Association for Mental Health 1995). Therefore, the aftermath of a traumatic event can be thought of as a long echo into the future – an echo that can begin to be heard after rescue services have left the disaster scene.

The change to the *DSM* view of trauma is significant, because it high-lights the increasing complexity of conditions emanating from traumatic events. This not only testifies to the severity of the impact of trauma upon a greater number of people, but also acknowledges that the aftermath of a traumatic event will render any of us vulnerable to serious, prolonged illness. Such vulnerability can remain over a considerable time, held within the long post-trauma echo.

To expand upon the traditional definitions and approaches, we can think of trauma in terms of something so far beyond the ordinary that it will overwhelm one's resilience and defences. It becomes impossible to feel the full impact of the trauma, or to function as normal. Reports of survivors and witnesses frequently detail a sense of disbelief and numbness in response to what they have seen and experienced. The result is that what one had previously held safe is no longer reliably so. One's perception of the world changes irrevocably. Garland (1998) has noted that trauma causes a kind of wound, that renders useless the protective filtering processes through which we have come to feel safe in the world. I believe this is a useful context within which to think about trauma, because it links both the inner life and previous life experiences of the individual to the traumatic event. Trauma does not occur due to the external factor of a single event. Trauma is enmeshed in an internal process of an attempt to assimilate how the event has irrevocably affected the individual.

We usually associate the word trauma with single events, such as major accidents, natural disasters and acts of war. While most people said to be 'traumatised' have experienced or witnessed a terrible event, it is not necessary to be present at the site of a disaster to be affected. Our vulnerability to the effects of trauma is increased with the speed of satellite communication, where news reports including pictures and footage of disasters can reach across the world in minutes. Trauma is also not only experienced in relation to disaster or war. Sudden or unexpected news of the violent death or injury to a loved one can also cause a severe, traumatic reaction, including PTSD. In today's society, the impact of trauma is more widespread than ever before.

Contextualising multidisciplinary attitudes to trauma

While contemporary thinking about trauma takes into account the severity of impact upon the population, this has not always been so. A brief overview of the changes in attitude to trauma reveals it was only recently acknowledged that people are indeed acutely affected by exposure to traumatic incidents.

One of the first examples of any mention of trauma is from the 1860s. John Ericson, a British physician, noticed a pattern to the psycho-emotional responses of patients involved in railway accidents. Ericson hypothesised that there was a direct physical cause for this because of the shock to the spine during the accident. This work motivated half a century of further research from authors such as Pavlov, Crile and Cannon (cited in Young 1995, pp.21–6). However, it was the thinking of Freud, Binet, Janet and Breuer that considered the psychological consequences and the idea of a shock or wound to the mind (Leys

2000). This idea was by no means generally accepted. Although during World War I the term 'shell shock' was used to describe what we now understand as post-trauma responses, there was very little support or sympathy for those affected. Only relatively recently – during the past four decades – has widespread interest been shown in the effects that traumatic experiences have upon people. From the 1970s onwards, there has been an increase in multidisciplinary perspectives, and with this came an expansion of the concept of trauma. Notable contributions are found from Herman's 20 years of work on the trauma of abuse and violence (1992), and van der Kolk's focus on mind–body links rather than the mind or body alone (van der Kolk, McFarlane and Weisaeth 1996).

The field of neurology has had a significant role in current thinking, suggesting that during the traumatic event there is a sensory overload, which can result in lasting damage to brain processes (Sutton 2000). This approach has presented a hypothetical overall process relating to the traumatic experience itself. Damasio, for instance, suggested a distinction between two kinds of brain processes, 'primary' and 'secondary' emotions, that are implicated during traumatic experiences (Damasio 1994). 'Primary' emotions relate to ancestral survival responses that can be said to be 'wired at birth', while 'secondary' emotions are linked with the patterns of behaviour set down through early life experiences. 'Primary' emotions are set in place while living through a potentially life-threatening situation (the familiar 'fight or flight' responses), and 'secondary' emotions offer opportunities for finding ways of adjusting to having experienced such situations. These processes are inevitably inter-connected, in the sense that Damasio says: 'secondary emotions utilise the machinery of primary emotions' (Damasio 1994, p.137). Grounded in brain research, the work of neurologists has introduced some new perspectives from which to view the post-trauma process (Swallow 2002).

Experiences of real or perceived threat to survival have roots in our ability as a species to survive. These experiences link with our early perceptions of feeling safe or 'not safe'. As infants we depend on our primary caregivers for our physical and emotional safety and these first relationships colour all subsequent relationships. The impact of these early experiences of threat to survival – or loss of safety – have been another important perspective from which to think about trauma.

Klein related a sense of loss of safety to the early infant experience of the breast (Klein 1940, pp.311–38). Klein suggested that when the feeding breast was removed there was a feeling of abandonment for the baby. Infant caregiver observations have revealed the overwhelming nature of sensations for the infant in these situations (Marrone 1998; Piontelli 1992). The impact of this experience is at such an early stage that neither resources nor language for processing or assimilating the experience are available, with the repercussions reverberating throughout life. Bowlby considered the earliest relationships from infancy into childhood to have had a central survival function, enabling the developing child to feel safe and protected (Bowlby 1988). It would be impossible for the adults in these relationships to have created a constant state of security for the infant. Nor would this cushioned existence be of use to the infant, who would be without a means of developing any resilience to the stresses of everyday life. Bowlby wrote in detail about the result of developmental changes in infant perception, from feeling safe to feeling unsafe, particularly focusing on the sense of loss of safe attachment and its implications for later life.

Stern (1977) also showed how the two participants in the first relationship brought their individual life experiences to the interaction. Here, for instance, through the mother's own developed patterns of response, she passed on to her child her experience of *her* mother. However conscious the adult is of the experience, and however they aim to protect the infant from it, they still have the memory of their own abandonment and losses at the unconscious level. While in altered form, this inherited experience passes through generations.

As shown briefly above, the psychological literature is another area that has informed the work of trauma specialists, based on the realisation that our early experiences are not only carried throughout life but also in some altered form passed on to our children. When faced with perceived or real physical threat to survival during traumatic events later in life, these early survival experiences directly influence the ways in which we respond.

Broadening the perspective further, traumatic events have an impact not only on the individual, but also upon community and society. Northern Irish researchers Dunn (1995) and Smyth (2002) have shown how delicate and complex exposure to such events can be. Taking the example of the New York World Trade Centre collapse on 11 September 2001, the repercussions of a single event can be immense and long lasting. There are many levels at which this occurs and one does not have to be physically close to the event to have become affected. For instance, while those at or near the scene were severely affected, those outside the immediate area and beyond also felt the traumatic shock. The news footage that travelled across the globe rendered countless others vulnerable to the impact of the event. Apart from the observers' responses to news footage, it is easy to forget that those who brought us reports of the event could be affected. Mark Devenport, the BBC Northern Ireland Political Editor, has written about how his experiences of reporting have stayed with him: 'I never liked knocking on the door or picking up the phone to talk for the first time to the family of a terrorist victim. Unlike the doctor, the priest, the neighbour or the social worker, I felt I wasn't offering something for nothing, but looking for something in return' (Devenport 2000, pp.227–8). Devenport's words outline the dilemma that news crews, photographers and journalists ultimately face when they arrive at the aftermath of a disaster.

We should not forget how trauma as news – as in the case of the New York attack – has a powerful effect upon those reporting, those who are interviewed and those who watch the end result on their television sets. Apart from the terrible nature of the film footage, the news reports made public the private grief process. We saw many photographs and interviews during which we came to know the families of victims as familiar faces, watching them grow ever less confident of the return of their loved one. It was difficult to escape this extremely harrowing material during the days immediately after 11 September.

Therefore, the multitude of influences created by a single event are wide ranging at many different levels and affect many people. In the following ways, a single event has a post-trauma echo caused by:

- the impact upon those who survived the trauma (injured or not)

- the impact upon those witnessing the event (the related/friends/passers by)

- the impact upon close family members who were not there
- the impact upon the rescue services
- the impact upon the media (film crews, news editors)
- the impact upon hospital staff (including porters and cleaners)
- the effect upon the immediate community (those in the street or area)
- the effect upon the broader community (county, country and beyond)
- the effect upon those with previous experience of a traumatic event (retraumatisation)
- the effect upon those seeing the TV reports and the newspapers
- the longer term impact on survivors (physical/psychological)
- the longer term impact on family and friends and on ongoing support services
- the longer term effect on the community (the ability of survivors to contribute to their community, their future relationships, etc.)
- the current impact (the reader of these words).

A single event can have long-lasting repercussions at many levels throughout a community and wider society. While the traumatised individual will never be the same again, nor will the immediate community and in this way society itself will be changed.

In summary, the impact of trauma is wide ranging and accessible to all. The concept of trauma has changed over the years and it is now used as a term describing the impact of single events, as well as events from the past that can resurface over time. It is also frequently the case that in the area of trauma practitioners are now informed not only by their own field, but also by that of other multidisciplinary areas. Yet while generalisations can be made about the effects of trauma, each individual will have his or her own unique story. The following brief example of music therapy illustrates how one child coped with life in a community where traumatic events were taking place. In order to highlight the complexity of the therapy process, this is described as it was experienced at the time and then revisited over a decade later, to add the perspective of time passing.

An example of music therapy work in context

Jerry was 8 years old at the time of his 40 sessions of therapy and had been referred because of increasingly aggressive behaviour in the playground and schoolroom (Sutton 1996, 2000). Placed in a setting in Northern Ireland for children with complex speech and language impairment, Jerry had developed such a severe non-fluency that he was unable to produce any words at all during moments of stress. He attended his first session with interest and a willingness to use the instruments. His music was at first unformed, chaotic and intense, and appeared to consist of fragmented attacks upon the instruments. After the first months, there emerged an order in his playing, to the point at which he completely controlled what happened in the room. Jerry made no sounds at all with his voice, but as he was able to make choices and organise what happened in the room, so he began at first to whisper and then quietly to speak.

There was then a gathering intensity in the therapy, culminating in six sessions during which he improvised a story, which he called 'The Trap'. In his story Jerry narrated several scenarios, each of which had an immediacy and felt very real. There were monsters, something lurking in a wood, an army, bombs and bullets. It was only at this point in his therapy that I discovered that Jerry's father was a member of the local army. Jerry was only too aware of the danger his father was in. This was at a time in Northern Irish history a few months after a huge bomb had killed several people and injured many others attending a Remembrance Day ceremony. At the time of these sessions, two British army officers, filmed by news crews, had been taken prisoner and later murdered during a funeral, and many members of the security forces were being targeted by car bombs and ambushes. It was only too clear what Jerry's stories were about.

As Jerry's narrative continued, two opposing voices emerged to give voice to his inner conflict. These two characters would argue with and taunt each other, until in one intense and very long session, beyond words, Jerry screamed in rage and terror. From this cathartic point, the sessions changed again and became gradually more relaxed and playful. His non-fluency disappeared and finally Jerry left the specialist school and was reintegrated into mainstream education.

The readiness with which Jerry came to each session, eager to use the room, the therapist and the music, was a marked feature of the therapy. There was urgency in the work that began when Jerry first crossed the boundary of the therapy room door. The sessions had begun some months after the horrific Remembrance Day bomb attack, at a time when Jerry was perhaps ready to explore the impact upon him of what was happening in his community. From time to time he tested the therapy room and me (his therapist), for instance, hurling beaters off the walls, running full pelt around the room, and crouching in the window, poised right on the boundary of the room. Jerry pushed at the very fabric of the room in these ways, making sure that it could contain what was there to be voiced. It was important for him to make sure that I could survive this, be resilient enough to keep the space safe and to contain what Jerry held inside. This is an essential feature of all therapy, but none more so than in work with those traumatised. If therapists become overwhelmed, they are unable to function usefully or even adequately in the work setting. Having lived with experiences beyond the norm, clients need to know that it is safe to talk and that they can tell their story without damaging the therapist. The therapist's inability to hear what is in the room can be damaging and there is a real danger of retraumatising the client. Therefore, great care must be taken with such work and the therapist should be well informed by theoretical thinking.

It is useful at this point to pause and consider Winnicott's ideas about infant ego development, where needs that at first seem to be environmentally led become associated with inner stimulus. Simply put, we can consider how baby is not able to feed at will, but is reliant on mother's interpretation of his or her need, after which baby is then actually given food. This vulnerable state leaves baby dependent on mother's ability to understand and react to what is required. When basic needs are not met, baby is thrown into a chaotic confusion that may feel as if very survival is at threat. However, quite soon, baby seems able to enter into the process and take an active part in an interaction at the end of which is the desired goal – the food and the accompanying pleasure in having one's needs met. A form of basic negotiation has begun to take place and, in order to do this, baby has had to be able to develop at some level a sense of purpose and responsibility. Baby has assumed some control.

It is this very ability – to experience, act on and re-experience one's own influence in a threatening situation – that is stolen from us when we encounter traumatic situations. The event happens *to* us and we are completely controlled *by* it. There is not only a sense of loss of security, but also loss of the ability to have an influence upon what is happening. There is an intense feeling of powerlessness that leaves one unable ever to feel that the world is quite the same safe place it was before the event. This experience most powerfully resonates with our earliest experiences – as babies – of life under threat. Seen in this context, Jerry's therapy took place in an environment that was felt to be safe enough to hold what he had been holding onto internally. Jerry moved from an initially confused, chaotic state to one of being able again to discover and exercise control over his environment. Jerry checked that I could provide the kind of space he needed and that I could be attentive to his changing needs within this space. This process was 'sounded', through the music I made in response to what he said and did in the room. In doing this I was also representing the early mother role that was such a vital part of what Jerry had experienced as an infant and linked to his earliest sense of feeling safe/not safe. By my attempts at attunement to his current needs, there was a repetition of the early caregiving attentiveness to his needs as a baby. This reflected the security of the early sense of safety, so that Jerry had a firm base from which to begin to explore what was now unsafe in his world.

During this difficult period in his life, it had been impossible for Jerry to voice his extreme anxiety, either at home or at school. He had been silenced because it did not feel safe at home to talk. I believe that this pressure of holding onto how he felt and keeping it secret to himself had culminated in the non-fluency. Almquist and Broberg (1997, pp.417–35) have explored the mutual silencing that can occur between child and parent in the face of overwhelming trauma in families exposed to war. The authors' term 'family survival strategy' described the ways that parent and child collude in order to avoid talking about the trauma or experiencing fully its repercussion. This unresolved state of secrecy is held by each family member, affecting the child in particular. As Almquist and Broberg stated: 'A traumatic event fills the inner life of the traumatised person … and because of this a pressure builds up in the child to verbalise his or her experience' (1997, p.423). This observation fits with the sense of urgency in Jerry's earlier music and his increased non-fluency and provides at least a partial explanation for the constant – at times relentless – pace at which the sessions progressed. During his therapy, Jerry's need to be heard was paramount, as was his inner struggle for words to express the reality of his situation.

Jerry was also silenced in other ways. The community in which he lived was a place where neither the impact nor the reality of what was happening was addressed. In the broader context, mechanisms of denial and minimisation of the severity of the violence were apparent (Sutton 2000). Further silence surrounded the very nature of Jerry's father's occupation, a fact that should be seen in the context of the considerable danger at which members of the security forces were placed during this period of Northern Irish history. In Jerry's file there was a note about his father being a civil servant, a description that I later discovered was a coded reference to his real job. This term was generally accepted and silently colluded with by the whole community; more significantly, this was not even given words in the school staffroom. Such a pervasive silencing only added to Jerry's traumatisation. Yet Jerry's music, while initially not incorporating words, *sounded* what was held inside. His narrative began non-verbally in music at a time when he was mute, but while wordless it was audible, and it could be listened to and heard.

The context of therapist's stance

This was my first case with a traumatised child in Northern Ireland and it had a strong impact upon me. As a newcomer to Belfast, I had felt first hand some of the challenges of life in a community where organised violence had existed within a political framework for 20 years. I became aware of the ways in which the community responded to and coped with this environment. I noticed that there had been no use of the word 'war' to describe what had happened in Northern Ireland. The media had described this long-term, sporadic violence as a 'conflict', and it was known locally as 'the Troubles'. Hidden within these somewhat understated terms is an indication of one of the coping mechanisms available to those living with the threat of violence (Dunn 1995). In order to survive on a day-to-day basis, we tended to minimise the nature of the threat. This was necessary up to a point, because in living with potential, identifiable threat to survival it would be impossible fully to realise and process such experiences every day.

Protective mechanisms also included habituating to and denying the severity of the violence (Sutton 2000). Adults do not to express aloud fears and anxieties in order to protect their children, and in shielding their families they have also shielded themselves. Clearly, we have to protect in order to survive and before long I began to develop similar attitudes. During telephone calls with friends and family on the mainland, I recall minimising the severity of the violence. On more than one occasion I stressed the fact that a bomb had been several miles away, yet failed to mention being woken from sleep by the after-shock, felt through double-glazed windows. While natural responses to threatening situations lie behind these coping strategies, it is important to remember that they have an impact upon those around us. For instance, such strategies can be interpreted as signs that one is not ready or prepared to talk. If this is true for enough people, the subject becomes taboo and the community becomes silenced and silent about the reality of life in such situations.

It also became clear during my first year of work in Northern Ireland that I was not being referred any clients who were directly affected by the conflict. Anyone significantly traumatised by violence had found their way to the therapy room for other reasons, as in Jerry's case. Given the atmosphere of fear and suspicion, the fact that I was an 'outsider' from another culture could have influenced the lack of referrals. Could I be trusted? Would I really be able to understand what was happening? Having spent my formative years in England, how could I know what it was really like? Less likely was that my 'outsiderness' could also have had the opposite effect, and I could be seen as less involved in the situation. At the time I had the impression that the protective mechanisms within the community would have prevented such referrals, to whatever agency. I was aware that only a small number of children had found their way to child psychiatry services as a result of identifiable, violence-related trauma. It was likely that the mood of suspicion within the most vulnerable communities made it difficult to approach statutory (i.e. government) agencies, and in this way support services, amongst many other aspects of life, became politicised. In retrospect, I was feeling the impact of these broader issues as well as of the work itself.

My own history also had echoes of some aspects of Jerry's story. This heightened the impact of the work upon me, but also provided personal reference points from which I could reflect upon the content of the sessions. Clinical supervision and personal therapy work were essential in giving a space that offered perspective for this reflection. It also ensured that I did not overidentify with my client and kept my personal material separate from his. I have come to recognise that amongst other things, my own experiences as a silenced child, while different in context from Jerry's, were invaluable. The insights gained in supervision and personal work enabled me to visit some of the difficult places to which Jerry had to travel. This process was kept safe through the support I obtained outside the sessions. I feel that without this, Jerry would have sensed a reticence in his therapist to accompany him where he had to go. This work was possible only because of these external factors and it would have been dangerous to proceed without them. As I have written earlier, in work with those traumatised 'our own histories can be particularly exposed' (Sutton 2000, p.57). Austin (2002) has also stated that 'the threshold between self and other can become slippery when therapist and client have overlapping issues'. Great care must be taken by anyone working in this area and external support networks with space to reflect are essential.

In terms of the usefulness of music therapy, in this and other work with traumatised children I have come to believe that there is a strong case for the application of music in the clinical setting, which impinges upon states of feeling at a pre-conscious level. This idea is explored further by a number of international authors in Part 3.

As with Jerry's story, a central theme with these clients is frequently one of silence and of being silenced, whether actual or perceived. In work with two clients, Woo looked at the ways in which silence impinged particularly powerfully in psychotherapy sessions (Woo 1999, pp.93–114).

In different ways, Woo's clients found great difficulty in experiencing the therapist as 'other' in the sense that the therapist could be there/not there. Tracing backwards in time from verbal to non-verbal sound experience and across the divide between post- and pre-natal existence, Woo developed a hypothesis deriving from an essential body experience of 'being' in sound. From this primary bodily sense, other experiences evolve. Significantly, Woo used a musical metaphor to apply to the clinical work, stating:

> The use of a 'musical vertex' of analytical attention sheds light on the developmental processes that are set in motion before birth. Although the means of communication in our analytic work is verbal language, nevertheless the understanding of primitive mental states involves both the use of 'symbol and sound' ... by our patients and ourselves. (Woo 1999, p.112)

Woo recognised what music therapists know about the levels of states of being that are accessible in music. In Jerry's therapy, the immediacy of his music and its sense of coming into form (or order) reflected an unfolding emotional experience of himself. Perhaps the pre-symbolic – some would say pre-conscious – level at which we experience music in the body as emotion has a special role in work with those traumatised. Feeling grounded in one's own body while processing and assimilating the emotional impact of traumatic experience is accessible when one is musically engaged with a therapist. Music is also a means of experiencing oneself in time, from moment to moment. Pavlicevic's concept of dynamic form is useful here: 'dynamic form is ourselves, portrayed in relation to another, in sound' (1997, p.129). Put this way, music offers experiences of ourselves as embodied and in sound and silence. Traumatic experiences disturb this sense of bodily connectedness. It follows that music therapy can be of use to those vulnerable to the effects of trauma because of these qualities of musical embodiment, but that it should be offered with great care.

In this way, access to the medium of music in a spontaneous yet boundaried environment can be of use to those traumatised. Music exists in time, is felt physically and as emotion in the body. As such it can be a powerful resource for finding a form within which to begin to adjust to extreme experiences – where very existence itself is threatened. Such experiences can in themselves be explosive and fragmenting, enforcing change and requiring considerable adjustment. In music, a primarily pre-symbolic art form, there is opportunity for expressing such fragmentation and chaos. There is also space for the traumatic experience itself to begin to find form, or 'come into form', as in the example of Jerry. When this musical–emotional experience comes into form, there can also be an emerging process of loss and mourning, one that is central to adapting to the experience of trauma. The client will need to mourn the loss of the person they were before the trauma, with deeper work touching on the earlier life experiences of abandonment.

Most significantly, and as other chapters in this book reveal, the environment for this work needs to be safe. The therapist must survive the experience with the client and the need for good-enough support is paramount. Apart from the challenging nature of the clinical material, therapists also live within the communities in which they work. Therefore, both clinical supervision and one's own therapy work are recommended. Anecdotal evidence from colleagues in New York has provided further confirmation of the post-trauma echo upon a community. For some time after the 11 September event, experienced clinicians have noticed how widespread and pervasive the sense of no longer feeling safe has been, along with the ongoing process of mourning those who died. Without the perspective of personal insight and the supervisory space, the therapist is made extremely vulnerable to traumatisation through their work in such communities.

We must also be able to come to an awareness of how, as individuals, we all respond to hearing about traumatic events. This includes an acknowledgement that our own histories contain the early traumatic experiences described earlier. We need to recognise the impact of this at both conscious and unconscious levels upon work with traumatised, vulnerable clients. Amongst those documenting the necessity of this awareness in therapists is the Jungian analyst Sedgewick, who commented: 'Not just the patient but the *therapist* brings his entire "self" – neuroses, wounds, needs, soul, etc. – to the analysis' (1994, p.42). This is, of course, central to all therapy work. However, in working with and thinking about those who have lived through events where survival has been at threat, we are also vulnerable. As clinicians we know that we should become aware of this in order to safeguard our clients and ourselves. As Sedgewick wrote: 'the analyst should note both *how* he is interpreting and where he is interpreting *from*' (1994, p.37).

Finally, in summary, the aim of this chapter has been to place the concept of trauma in a variety of contexts, many of which are echoed in following chapters. As the rest of the book will show, this is a new and expanding area of work, as well as one where theoretical thinking is constantly reassessed. I believe that it is important for music therapists undertaking clinical work with those traumatised to become informed from a variety of perspectives, and to be aware that these perspectives will change over time. Traumatic events are by definition beyond the ordinary life experiences, yet they can and will happen. In today's society, trauma is more pervasive and widespread than ever before and, as well as anyone else, clinicians are vulnerable to its effects.

References

American Psychiatric Association (APA) (1994) *Diagnostic and Statistical Manual of Mental Disorders*, 4th edn. Washington DC: American Psychiatric Association.

Almquist, K. and Broberg, A. G. (1997) 'Silence and survival: working with strategies of denial in families of traumatised pre-school children.' *Journal of Child Psychotherapy 23*, 3, pp.417–435.

Austin, D. (2002) 'The voice of trauma. A wounded healer's perspective.' In J. P. Sutton (ed) *Music, Music Therapy and Trauma: International Perspectives.* London: Jessica Kingsley Publishers.

Bowlby, J. (1988) *A Secure Base.* London: Tavistock.

Damasio, A. R. (1994) *Descarte's Error. Emotion, Reason and the Human Brain.* London: Picador.

Devenport, M. (2000) *Flash Frames. Twelve Years Reporting Belfast.* Belfast: Blackstaff Press.

Dunn, S. (1995) *Facets of the Conflict in Northern Ireland.* London: Macmillan Press.

Garland, C. (ed) (1998) *Understanding Trauma. A Psychoanalytical Approach.* London: Tavistock Clinic Press.

Goldberg, J., True, W. R., Eisen, S. A. and Henderson, W. G. (1990) 'A twin study of the effects of the Vietnam War on post-traumatic stress disorder.' *Journal of the American Medical Association 263*, pp.87–96.

Herman, J. (1992) *Trauma and Recovery*. London: Pandora.

Hornby, A. S. (1974) *Oxford Advanced Learner's Dictionary of Current English*. Oxford: Oxford University Press.

Kaylor, J. A., King, D. W. and King, L. A. (1987) 'Psychological effects of military service in Vietnam: a meta-analysis.' *Psychological Bulletin 102*, pp.257–271.

Klein, M. (1940) 'Mourning and its relation to manic-depressive states.' In M. Klein *Love, Guilt and Reparation and Other Papers, 1921–1946*. London: Hogarth Press (1947).

Leys, R. (2000) *Trauma. A Geneology*. Chicago: University of Chicago Press.

Marrone, M. (1998) *Attachment and Interaction*. London: Jessica Kingsley Publishers.

Northern Ireland Association for Mental Health (1995) *Public Health Matters 1995*. Belfast: Department of Public Health Medicine.

Pavlicevic, M. (1997) *Music Therapy in Context. Music, Meaning and Relationship*. London: Jessica Kingsley Publishers.

Piontelli, A. (1992) *From Fetus to Child. An Observational and Psychoanalytic Study*. London: Routledge.

Sedgewick, D. (1994) *The Wounded Healer. Countertransference from a Jungian Perspective*. London: Routledge.

Smyth, M. (2002) 'The role of creativity in healing and recovering one's power after victimisation.' In J. P. Sutton (ed) *Music, Music Therapy and Trauma: International Perspectives*. London: Jessica Kingsley Publishers.

Stern, D. (1977) *The First Relationship*. Cambridge, MA: Harvard University Press.

Sutker, P. B., Uddo, M., Brailey, K., Vasterling, J. J. and Errera, P. (1994) 'Psychopathology in war-zone deployed and nondeployed Operation Desert Storm troops assigned graves registration duties.' *Journal of Abnormal Psychology 103*, 2, pp.383–390.

Sutton, J. P. (1996) 'Jerry's story.' *Journal of Therapy and Rehabilitation 3*, 4, 215–217.

Sutton, J. P. (2000) 'Aspects of music therapy with children in areas of community conflict.' In D. Dokter and J. Glasman (eds) *Exile: Refugees and the Arts Therapies*. Hertford: University of Hertfordshire, Faculty of Art and Design Press, pp.54–73.

Sutton, J. P. (ed) (2002) *Music, Music Therapy and Trauma: International Perspectives*. London: Jessica Kingsley Publishers.

Swallow, M. (2002) 'The brain – its music and its emotion. The neurology of Trauma.' In J. P. Sutton (ed) *Music, Music Therapy and Trauma: International Perspectives*. London: Jessica Kingsley Publishers.

Van der Kolk, B. A., McFarlane, A. C. and Weisaeth, L. (eds) (1996) *Traumatic Stress. The Effects of Overwhelming Experience on Mind, Body, and Society.* New York: Guilford Press.

Wingate, P. (1972) *The Penguin Medical Encyclopedia.* London: Penguin.

Woo, R. (1999) 'Sounds of silence: the need for presence in absence.' *Journal of Child Psychotherapy 25,* 1, pp.93–114.

Young, A. (1995) *The Harmony of Illusions: Inventing Post-Traumatic Stress Disorder.* Princeton, NJ: Princeton University Press.

CHAPTER 2

Neurology
The Brain – Its Music and its Emotion: The Neurology of Trauma

Michael Swallow

Music is the harmony of the universe in microcosm; for this harmony is life itself; and in man, who is himself a microcosm of the universe, chords and discords are to be found in his pulse, in his heart beat, his vibration, his rhythm and tone. His health or sickness, his joy or displeasure show whether his life has music or not.

(from the Sufi Message of Nazrat Inayat Khan, quoted by Hamel 1976)

This chapter is an introduction to the nature of music, exploring the neurophysiological changes that occur when we listen to or take part in musical activity, and the relationship between music and the emotions. Following this is a discussion of recent work on the way the nervous system responds to psychological stress and trauma.

No one really knows when homo sapiens first started to use, understand and enjoy music. Some believe that music, song and dance preceded language as a means of communication and in evolutionary terms many animals have used musical utterances to establish territory, attract mates and maybe just for the satisfaction of making pleasant sounds. Birds have an inbuilt capacity for song but their music is refined by environmental factors and practice, and is thus to some extent a learned experience. The male sings to attract a mate but he who sings best wins the girl.

Evolution would suggest that man has also inherited a capacity for processing music and the relatively recent discipline of ethnomusicology has confirmed that music has been of importance throughout history and in all societies. In *A Commonsense View of All Music*, John Blacking (1987) puts forward a persuasive argument for the innate musicality of man. This was based on Percy Grainger's concept of folk music as a universal language, and his own studies in ethnomusicology along with several years' work with the Venda people in South Africa.

Further evidence of the capacity of all human beings to react to music is to be found in observations on the unborn child, when motor responses to rhythmical stimuli or even specific pieces of music are commonly reported by the mother (Verny and Kelly 1982). In the neonatal period the vocalisations of the young child are musical responses and the rise and fall of the mother's cooing patterns are very similar in all societies and cultures. The musical qualities of rhythm and pitch, which are important ingredients of 'proto-conversation', as described by Trevarthen *et al.* (1998), are gradually subsumed into the development of speech. It is notable that these qualities are subsequently localised mainly to the left side of the brain (the 'language side'), which is subject to a significant growth spurt between two and four years of age. This innate capacity of the brain to interpret musical information suggests that the process has some biological survival value. Blacking (1976) suggests that this lies in the potential that music has for stimulating and cementing social integration and personal relationships.

Music and movement

Considerable research over the past few decades has shown that there are, indeed, neurophysiological mechanisms which appear to have an inherent capacity to analyse musical patterns. For example, the relationship between the rhythms of the body and those of music have been studied by many researchers. Among these Harrer and Harrer reported changes in pulse rate, respiration, galvanic skin responses and muscle activity in response to a variety of musical and non-musical stimuli (Harrer and Harrer 1977, pp.202–16). They noted that changes in speed of a piece of music could act as a pacemaker on the pulse rate 'within certain limits', but observed that emotional involvement in the music seemed to be more important than simple changes in speed. However, Saperston (1995), in a neat bit of physiological research, showed that the heartbeat could be slowed if the speed of the music was one beat per minute slower than the ongoing pulse rate, suggesting an entrainment effect between the speed of the music and the pulse.

Another area of research has been the relationship between music and movement. Harrer and Harrer (1977) again looked at this and recorded muscle potentials in the leg and in the forehead (using surface electrodes) in response to various types of music and other non-musical tasks. They demonstrated a striking increase in muscular activity in the legs in response to dance music, in the forehead in response to an arithmetical task, and in both when loud music was played. During the recording there was no observable movement in the limbs, even at the height of the electrical activity. Rhythm has to be regarded as the fundamental process of music, the beginning of order at prenatal and infant level and 'the most primitive, yet complex, structure of the human mind' (Lehtonen 1995).

A striking relationship between music and movement can be seen in people suffering from Parkinson's disease (PD). These patients experience a slowing of movement (bradykinesia) and great difficulty in sustaining semi-automatic movements such as walking and repetitive upper limb movements as in arm swing and alternating pronation and supination. Steppage becomes irregular and sudden 'freezing' interrupts the regularity of pacing. Sacks (1982) observed that many of his patients with post-encephalitic parkinsonism were released from their bondage by music; one maintaining that the disease 'unmusicked' her and that she had to be 'remusicked'. In her 'frozen' state this patient would remain motionless and helpless, *until music came* (Sacks' italics). Even the imagining of music, her own inner music, would suddenly restore her to a free and graceful moving being. Our own observations on patients with PD confirmed that playing music while they are trying to walk has a remarkable effect (Sutton and Swallow 1992). Many of these patients appear to have an inbuilt speed of steppage which they are unable to vary at will, but when their personal rhythm is picked up on the piano the stride becomes regular, freezing episodes disappear and the speed of gait will follow that of the music by the process of entrainment.

The pathological process in PD is located in the basal ganglia, specifically the nigro-striatal pathways, where the reduction in concentration of the neurotransmitter dopamine results in a complex impairment of semi-automatic motor activity. These clinical observations and the common presence of a regular tremor in this condition suggest that a rhythmical pacemaker of some sort is located in relation to this part of the brain. Freeman *et al.* showed that people with PD performed poorly compared to a control group in a test of sustained finger tapping, and that when external cueing was withdrawn the patients showed 'marked impairment of rhythm generation' (Freeman, Cody and Schady 1993). Gibbon (1996) postulated the presence of a neurobiological clock system within the striato-cortical loop which was dependent on dopamine-mediated pathways, and demonstrated that in patients with PD treatment with L-Dopa improved the performance of rhythm-related tasks.

Other forms of external pacemakers, particularly visual cues (stripes painted on the floor or blocks of wood to walk over) are also effective as aids to walking, but music seems to be extremely helpful. This is especially true if the music is familiar or has some special emotional appeal to the patient. A striking example of this was seen in one of our patients with fairly mild PD, but who was experiencing difficulty in executing the regular rotational movement required in the process of shaving with an electric razor. One morning while making a determined effort to overcome this frustration, he heard on the radio the Blue Danube Waltz by Strauss (a favourite of his) and immediately found that he could perform this hitherto difficult task with ease and fluency by following the rhythm of the music.

Music and communication

Such observations help us to understand how music might be related to certain basic physiological processes. But music is, above all, a means of communication. Music 'speaks' to us and the phrase 'the language of music' is in common use, reminding us of the Deryck Cooke book (1959) of that title. There are indeed ways in which the structure of music can be compared to that of spoken and written language. The study of disturbances of musical function in relation to focal brain damage from strokes, tumours and injury has led to the use of the term *amusia*, to denote impairment of musical skills and understanding associated with a lesion of the cerebral hemishpere. Like *aphasia*, amusia can be divided into expressive and receptive types. Musical dyslexia and dysgraphia have been used to describe the inability to read or write musical notation respectively.

These clinical observations have been extensively reported in the literature and reviewed by Hodges (1996). Together with recent scanning techniques, this has enabled Warren (1999) to construct a musical map of the brain, which attempts to localise various musical functions to specific areas of the cerebral cortex. It is generally accepted that the left ear is 'dominant' for melody and timbre, and that these functions are processed primarily in the right auditory cortex. Pitch and rhythm seem to be more a function of the left side of the brain and this is perhaps correlated with the importance of these two factors in the prosody of speech. However, music is an extremely complex auditory stimulus and Corballis (1983), writing on hemispheric specialisation, commented that in tasks such as musical perception both cerebral hemispheres are involved. The differences between the two hemispheres are slight compared to the co-operation that exists between them.

These researchers are concerned with the localisation of perceptive and executant aspects of music and these features are important in relation to music education and performance. However, to most people music is felt and expressed as an emotion and it is in this area that we should be looking for an understanding of its healing power. Lehtonen quotes an ancient Chinese saying: 'Music comes from the heart of the human being. When emotions are born they are expressed by sounds and when sounds are born they give birth to music' (Lehtonen 1995, p.20). We might now question whether music comes from the heart rather than the brain, but the quotation acknowledges a recognised definition of music as organised sound, an important concept in relation to music therapy.

Emotion and the limbic system

The anatomical basis of the emotions has been the subject of considerable debate since the nineteenth century, and still is. It was initially thought to be a function of the cerebral cortex, where all feeling was located. The early description from 1878 of the limbic mode by Broca (as a 'rim' of tissue situated deeply in the cerebral hemispheres in man, but constituting a major part of the brain in more primitive animals) drew attention to the importance of this part of the brain in relation to the control of body processes and maintenance of the species (Broca 1987/1861). In 1929 Cannon and Bard isolated the hypothalamus as an important structure in the control of emotion (Cannon 1929). In 1937 Papez postulated a circuit involving the hypothalamus, hippocampus and cerebral cortex as the anatomical basis for emotion and feelings. Kluver and Bucy (1939) found that ablation of the temporal lobe in monkeys abolished the sense of fear or danger, which was subsequently shown to be due to involvement of the amygdala nucleus.

During the 1950s MacLean focused on the limbic lode as the most important structure in the genesis of emotions and in 1970 introduced his theory of the 'triune brain' (MacLean 1970). This proposed a hierarchical system in which the reptilian brain represented the earliest (in evolutionary terms) stage of neural control; the paleomammilian brain was the next stage of development; then the rhinenecephalon and the neomammilian brain represented the highest level of the cerebral cortex. The validity of MacLean's ideas have been seriously questioned by LeDoux (1998) and others. At the same time the work of Goleman (1996) on the concept of emotional intelligence suggests once again that the neo-cortex is important, not only in cognitive efficiency but in the way we feel about things going on around and within us. Goleman has also focused our attention on the importance of a robust emotional life and the way in which this may be disturbed in the face of psychological trauma.

Limbic system and memory

Although doubt has been cast on the integrity of the limbic lode as an anatomical entity, certain structures within this broad area of brain do merit special mention, because of their importance in relation to emotional life. The structures of the limbic system lie deep within the temporal lobes and are sometimes collectively known as the rhinencephalon or 'nose brain'. This draws attention to the strong relationship between this area and the olfactory system (in evolutionary terms the oldest of the five senses), so that familiar smells may trigger memories and emotions in a similar way to familiar music, even in people with brain damage. These memories take origin in the hippocampus (the 'seahorse'), lying deep in the temporal lobe and the final destination of sensory modalities that have been refined into experiences, which in turn are built into long-term memory. The regular arrangement of cells in the hippocampus prompted MacLean (1970) to describe it as an 'emotional keyboard', and LeDoux (1998) puts it thus: 'Even when the elements of the sensory world activate these cells, the tunes they play are emotions.'

Another important limbic structure is the hypothalamus which is, among other things, concerned with the maintenance of homeostasis. This occurs through its connections with the autonomic nervous system and, via the pituitary gland, the endocrine and hormone systems of the body. The amygdala nucleus (an 'almond' due to its shape) lies near the hippocampus and is part of the memory system of the brain. Recent experiments on electrical stimulation of this structure (in patients undergoing operations for epilepsy) suggest that it is also particularly concerned with reactions to fear and is discussed below. The amygdala also has strong connections with the motor system via the basal ganglia and is thus concerned with body posture and movement, changes in which are an integral part of the 'language' of the emotions (witness the lack of facial expression and stooped posture in depression and the hyperactivity associated with manic states).

Although these structures in the limbic system appear to have specific functions in relation to memory, survival and the maintenance of the internal balance of the body, it does not seem reasonable to continue to consider them the sole – or even most important – structures concerned with emotions. These are so varied and individual that detailed cognitive processes and learning must be part of 'the feeling of what happens' (Damasio 1999). It seems likely that different emotions are subserved by different neuronal networks involving many parts of the brain (including the neocortex) which are laid down over time as explicit memories resulting from personal experiences of life.

There are a number of ways of classifying and describing memory. Most people would accept the difference between explicit – or declarative – memory (which is of things, events, everyday activities and experiences that have to be learned as time goes by) and in contrast implicit – or non-declarative – memories (which are of threats and dangers, pleasure and pain, gratifications, and are largely automatic and inbuilt). The former involve conscious perception whereby recent experiences or facts are slotted into a relevant network, a process which involves the hippocampus, and in which any associated emotion may be expressed as feelings. This type of memory is more easily forgotten, or at least has the potential for deconditioning. Non-declarative or implicit memory may not be felt at conscious level, is not easily forgotten or erased and may be reactivated by an appropriate stimulus after many years. Any emotion associated with this type of memory may appear to be illogical and surface for no apparent reason. Much of the recent research on emotions and memory has been concerned with fear conditioning, which is relatively easy to study in experimental animals. It has been shown that the amygdala is the structure which is most concerned with this particular stress.

Trauma

With this background we can perhaps begin to understand the biological basis of the brain's response to trauma – for example, a sudden and unexpected physical or psychological event which is appreciated as a threat and often associated with profound emotional disturbance. LeDoux (1998) described the amygdala as the 'hub of the wheel of fear' and speaks of the *high road* and the *low road* response to the stimulus.

In the low road response, sensory stimuli pass directly from the thalamus (the main sensory pathway to the brain) to the amygdala, provoking an instantaneous response. This is mediated largely through the hypothalamus and activates the autonomic nervous system resulting in the clinical manifestations of shock (that is, preparing the body for fight or flight). This happens at an unconscious level and the subject often has no recollection of the exact circumstances surrounding the event.

The high road response is slower and involves the hippocampus and the cerebral cortex, wherein the events surrounding the trauma are related to past experience and an appropriate response can be planned and executed. This process is accompanied by profound emotional reactions and feelings which will vary to some extent between different people, but will be laid down as declarative memories for the events.

The outpouring of noradrenaline, which is part of the low road response, has been shown to heighten emotional awareness. It may thus play a part in consolidating the explicit memory traces that result from the traumatic event. Immediate and unexpected assault on the amygdala (low road response) may actually result in damage to the cells in this structure, so that subsequent processing functions are impaired with a limited potential for recovery. The amygdala has also been implicated in the genesis of panic attacks, a common clinical feature of stress disorders. Unlike post traumatic stress disorder (which is a direct consequence of a threatening external event), panic attacks are more likely to arise as a result of internal dysfunction, the features being those of activation of the autonomic nervous system, rise in blood pressure, pulse rate, over-breathing, sweating, dizziness and a sense of foreboding. These physical manifestations of panic attacks are often precipitated by over-breathing (I have seen it in woodwind players) and may themselves trigger a conditioned response in the amygdala resulting in a resurgence of the post-traumatic experience.

The subsequent progress of the cerebral processes which have been disturbed by trauma are, of course, extremely variable. It is recognised that explicit memories are forgotten more easily than implicit ones. Lazarus wrote of emotional 'coping' which must depend on many variables, some of which are inbuilt (for example, personality traits), and some environmental (family support, related stresses, general health and so on), also including treatment and management strategies (Lazarus 1966).

Music, music therapy and trauma

Management strategies are what the rest of this book are about. Those who are involved in this work will have different approaches, and for some the possible physical basis for the clinical manifestations of trauma may be of little importance in planning a treatment regime. To some extent the music therapists are in a privileged position. They possess a tool which gives them direct access to the emotions and the inherent dangers of provoking and consolidating unpleasant and threatening memories. However, used appropriately and with care, music also has the power to heal by helping people to understand and rationalise emotions. When these ideas are expressed and shared by the client, the therapist will concentrate on encouraging the deconditioning of explicit memories while accepting that implicit memories will surface from time to time. The therapist helps the client to understand and rationalise this.

Fear conditioning can occur easily and suddenly, perhaps in response to a single traumatic event. Recovery – or deconditioning – is an active but lengthy process and may never be completely achieved. However, any process which inhibits activity in the brain, or a specific area of the brain (in this case the amygdala nucleus) can, by raising the threshold for anxiety, reduce the likelihood of resurgence of traumatic memories. Drug treatment is an obvious example of such an inhibitory mechanism and Valium is a drug for which there are specific receptor sites in the amygdala. Limbic structures also contain specific opiate receptors and music (amongst other things) may stimulate the release of endorphins and similar substances which may act in the same way as exogenous drugs. Dawkins (1998) writes somewhat fancifully of Keats' comparison, in the 'Ode to a Nightingale', of the song of the bird with the drowsy numbness induced by the drug hemlock. Is the bird arousing emotions in his own brain with his song and manipulating the female, as if his song were a drug?

Adrenocoticotrophin (ACTH) is a hormonal substance which also may be released in response to music and have a specific therapeutic action on the 'damaged' amygdala. Since the original work of Hans Selye (1978) on the responses of the endocrine system to stress, there is evidence that a large number of other neurotransmitter substances may be involved in the development of stress disorders. These include serotonin, noradrenaline, dopamine and the neuropeptides, which are particularly concerned with the immune system of the body. Disturbances in the balance of these substances in the brain are likely to play a part in the clinical manifestations of stress and are reviewed by Herbert (1997).

From the physical point of view we have difficulty in explaining just how music works as a therapeutic agent. Our response to music lies most obviously in the perception and processing of a series of complex sound waves with powerful emotional overtones. However, music is more than sounds, as deaf musicians will testify. Performance (even at the simplest level) is accompanied by movement and body language, both of which have to be an important aspect of communication. Deaf musicians are – or become – acutely aware of the sensation of vibration, which accompanies all music. Evelyn Glennie describes a remarkable sensitivity in this respect which, depending on the part of the body that is felt to be vibrating, determines pitch for her almost as accurately as does sound. We do not yet know how the central nervous system registers and reacts to vibrations and particularly those above and below the range of human hearing. The considerable interest and increasing amount of literature on vibro-acoustic therapy (VAT), which uses pulsed frequencies of a very low order as well as musical vibrations, again suggests that the physical effect of vibration on the nervous system may contribute to the therapeutic potential of music. Skille and Wigram (1995) review the clinical applications of VAT and some of the theoretical considerations which may underlie this treatment. They draw attention to the suggestion that certain frequencies vibrate the brain cells and that this process might – in some way – 'wash' the cells, so that the cerebrospinal fluid may more effectively carry away the metabolites and waste products of neuronal activity. Maybe this is the modern equivalent of the ancient belief that the human body and brain 'resonate' with music.

For whatever reason, the successful music therapist has the unique opportunity of gaining access to the microcosm world of the traumatised person. There may be found evidence of discord, displeasure and sickness, but also the prospect of converting these negative feelings to the positive benefits of a life with music.

References

Bard, P. (1929) 'The central representation of the sympathetic system: as indicated by certain physiological observation.' Archives of *Neurology & Psychiatry 22*, 230–246.

Blacking, J. (1976) *How Musical is Man?* London: Faber & Faber.

Blacking, J. (1987) *A Commonsense View of all Music.* Cambridge: Cambridge University Press.

Broca, P. (1987, first published 1861) 'Perte de la parole, ramollissement chronique et destruction partielle du lobe antérieur gauche de cerveau.' *Bulletin de la Société Anthropologique 2*, 235.

Cannon, W. B. (1929) *Bodily Changes in Pain, Hunger, Fear and Rage,* Vol. 2. New York: Appleton.

Cooke, D. (1959) *The Language of Music.* Oxford: Oxford University Press.

Corballis, M. (1983) *Human Laterality.* New York: Academic Press.

Damasio, A. (1999) *The Feeling of What Happens.* London: Heinemann.

Dawkins, R. (1998) *Unweaving the Rainbow.* London: Penguin.

Freeman, J. S., Cody, F. W. and Schady, W. (1993) 'The influence of external cues upon the rhythm of voluntary movements in Parkinson's Disease.' *Journal of Neurology, Neurosurgery and Psychiatry 56*, 1078–1084.

Gibbon, J. (1996) *Science 271*, 905–906.

Goleman, G. (1996) *Emotional Intelligence.* London: Bloomsbury.

Hamel, P. M. (1976) *Through Music to the Self.* Berne, Munich and Vienna: Scherz Verlag. (English translation, Lemessuier, P. (1978) Dorset: Element Books.)

Harrer, G. and Harrer, H. (1977) 'Music, emotion and autonomic function.' In M. Critchley and R. Hewnson (eds) *Music and the Brain.* London: Heinemann.

Herbert, J. (1997) 'Stress, the brain, and mental illness.' *British Medical Journal 315*, 530–533.

Hodges, D. (1996) 'Neuromusical research: a review of the literature.' In D. Hodges (ed) *Handbook of Music Psychology,* 2nd edn. San Antonio, TX: IMR Press, pp.197–284.

Kluver, H. and Bucy, P. (1939) 'Preliminary analysis of the functions of the temporal lobes in monkeys.' *American Journal of Physiology 119*, 352–353.

Lazarus, R. S. (1966) *Psychological Stress and the Coping Process.* New York: McGraw Hill.

LeDoux, J. (1998) *The Emotional Brain.* London: Weidenfeld and Nicolson.

Lehtonen, K. (1995) 'Is music an archaic form of thinking?' *British Journal of Music Therapy 9*, 20–26.

MacLean, P. D. (1970) 'The triune brain, emotion and scientific basis.' In F. O. Schmitt (ed) *The Neurosciences: Second Study Programme.* New York: Rockerfeller University Press.

Papez, J. W. (1937) 'A proposed mechanism of emotion.' *Archives of Neurology and Psychiatry 79,* 217–224.

Sacks, O. (1982) *Awakenings.* London: Pan.

Saperston, B. (1995) 'The effect of consistent tempi and physiologically interactive tempi on the heart rate and EMG responses.' In T. Wigram, B. Saperston and R. West (eds) *The Art and Science of Music Therapy.* Switzerland: Harwood Academic Publishers.

Selye, H. (1978) *The Stress of Life.* New York: McGraw-Hill.

Skille, O. and Wigram, T. (1995) 'The effects of music, vocalisation and vibration on brain and muscle tissue.' In T. Wigram, B. Saperston and R. West (eds) *The Art and Science of Music Therapy.* Switzerland: Harwood Academic Publishers.

Sutton, J. P. and Swallow, M. (1992) 'Music therapy in Parkinson's disease.' *Abstracts, VII World Congress of Music Therapy.*

Trevarthen, C., Aitken, K., Papoudi, D. and Robarts, J. (1998) *Children with Autism.* London: Jessica Kingsley Publishers.

Verny, T. and Kelly, J. (1982) *The Secret Life of the Unborn Child.* London: Sphere.

Warren, J. D. (1999) 'Variations on the musical brain.' *Journal of the Royal Society of Medicine 92,* 571–575.

Part 2

Culture, Society and Musical Perspectives

CHAPTER 3

Culture and Society
The Role of Creativity in Healing and Recovering One's Power after Victimisation

Marie Smyth

This chapter will provide an overview of the human impact of the conflict (referred to as 'the Troubles') using the research undertaken by the 'Cost of the Troubles Study', which is also used to locate Northern Ireland in an international context. A discussion of the concept of trauma shows the need to consider the economic, social and cultural factors that impinge on the lives of those most affected by the conflict. Stimulation and encouragement of creativity is one way of promoting healing and the recovery of one's power after traumatisation. Finally, the use of music therapy in the context of Northern Ireland in order to achieve healing and increase mutual understanding is discussed.

An overview of the human impact of the conflict

The challenge of providing an overview of any conflict is that of achieving a comprehensive and balanced account. For this reason, the description of the Northern Ireland conflict provided here will be largely quantitative, drawing on two main sources of data: a database of deaths in the Troubles, and the results of a survey of the population of Northern Ireland.

The first part of the overview is derived from a comprehensive database of deaths due to the Troubles between 1969 and 1998. While this depicts the most extreme consequences of the conflict, it is also a good surrogate for violence in general and for other effects of the Troubles. A comparison of the numbers of deaths each year and the number of injuries associated with political violence shows a correlation coefficient of 0.93. Injuries outnumber deaths by just over ten to one but have exactly the same cycle. The combination of deaths and injuries represents the primary human cost of the Troubles, although these do not encompass the trauma of grief, imprisonment and intimidation. Nevertheless, the deaths have been taken as an appropriate reflection of the overall costs. There has not been one uniform conflict in Northern Ireland, rather the Troubles are a mosaic of local conflicts, each with its own set of characteristics. Thus, the 'reality' of the Troubles is different for people in different locations and in different occupations.

When did the deaths occur?

The intensity of killing between 1971 and 1976 was more than twice that for the whole period of the Troubles, and more than three times that for all the subsequent years. This means that those old enough to have lived through the 1970s are likely to have more extreme experiences of the Troubles, and cumulatively much more experience than younger people.

Explosions and shootings were the predominant cause of death. Almost 91 per cent of victims died from these causes. Deaths caused by explosions were more characteristic of the 1970s, with shootings more evenly distributed across the period. As the conflict moved into the 1980s, the numbers dying dramatically reduced. It took on the form of a 'low intensity' conflict with around 100 deaths each year.

Where did the deaths occur?

The deaths that have taken place in each district council area in Northern Ireland can be examined according to district council populations in 1991 (see Fay, Morrissey and Smyth 1999, p.142). Deaths can be recorded in two ways: the first is to record the number of violent incidents in which someone died (fatal incidents) occurring within the district; the second is to record the number of district residents who have been killed (victims). A number of deaths occurred outside Northern Ireland, and a large number of non-Northern Ireland residents were victims, so examining deaths within district councils in Northern Ireland will not encompass all deaths. If the number of deaths in each council area is divided by the 1991 figure for the resident population, a comparable death rate per 1000 population is produced and these can be ranked.

In terms of absolute number of incidents, the areas of Belfast, Newry and Mourne, Derry, Armagh, Dungannon and Craigavon stand out. In both absolute and relative terms, Belfast has seen the greatest intensity of violent deaths. Indeed, the rates per 1000 population have been almost twice as high as the next district, Armagh. In some districts, the number of incidents and the number of resident deaths almost tally. In others, the number of incidents was substantially greater than the number of resident deaths, for example, Newry and Mourne. In such cases, a high proportion of casualties were members of the security forces who did not live in the area. It is clear that the Troubles have not affected all regions equally with some, like Belfast, experiencing a high level of death, while other areas remain relatively unscathed.

The possible association between the level of violence in a community and the level of deprivation was examined. The Irish Congress of Trade Unions argued that 50,000 jobs would do more to end the conflict than 50,000 guns. 1 In the early 1990s an exercise in plotting spatial deprivation was undertaken by the Micro Statistics Centre at the University of Manchester[2]. Death rates for particular places are compared with their deprivation scores according to this method. The six district council areas that were ranked highest for fatal incident rate, the ranks for the rates of resident deaths and each council area's deprivation score can be analysed (see Fay *et al.* 1999, p.146).

Of the six districts ranked highest on fatal incidents (Belfast, Newry and Mourne, Dungannon, Derry, Armagh and Cookstown), four were among the six worst deprived with the exceptions of Armagh and Cookstown. Strabane, which ranked highest on deprivation, was ranked eighth on the rate of fatal incidents. There would appear to be some relationship between deprivation and violence, but it is not a simple one. Overall, high levels of Troubles' related violence and deprivation do seem to be positively associated. So, communities that have the worst experience of the Troubles also tend to be the poorest.

In the period up to 1998, 37 per cent of those who died were civilians, a similar percentage members of the IRA and only 26 per cent were security personnel. The Troubles has thus taken a relatively greater toll on civilians and security force members while deaths amongst paramilitary organisations has been remarkably low.

Victim characteristics

By far, the victims of the conflict have been overwhelmingly male. More than nine out of ten of all those killed were men – a total of 3279 male deaths, compared to 322 deaths of females. However, whilst men have been the most direct victims of the conflict in terms of the numbers killed, women's experience of the Troubles is different rather than lesser. Regular prisons visiting and standing at gravesides, or holding the hands of children following coffins are the kinds of indirect effects on women.

Those who died were also skewed towards the younger age groups (see Fay *et al.* 1999, p.181). More than a third of victims were in their twenties. More than half were in their twenties or thirties and one in six victims were aged 19 or less. This can be plainly seen if death rates for each age group are calculated by comparing the ages of those in the database with the age distribution of the general population.

The religious breakdown of victims was also examined (see Fay *et al.* 1999, p.164). Religious affiliation was attributed to all those killed, where such attributions were known. However, this information was not always available, thus the analysis produced a 'Not Known' category which contained a high proportion of deaths of Northern Ireland security forces, and victims from outside Northern Ireland (NNI) for whom, in any case, religion was less associated with the reasons they were killed. The first analysis showed 1065 (29.6%) of deaths as Protestant; 1548 (43%) of deaths as Catholic); 655 (18.2%) of deaths as of those from outside Northern Ireland, many of whom were British soldiers; and 333 (9.2%) of deaths as 'Not Known'.

A breakdown of deaths by religion exposes the basis for grievance and perceptions about what the 'other side' has done. The absolute numbers show that more Catholics than Protestants have died. The smaller proportion of Catholics in the general population suggests a significantly higher death risk for this religion. However, this tends to ignore the very high proportion of 'not known' religious affiliation among local security deaths. It is known that the local security forces are 92 per cent Protestant and this fraction can be used to distribute the 'not known' between the two religious groups. Redistributing the 'not known' and taking into account the time period involved, led to the production of three death rates for Protestants and Catholics. The first rate, calculated on the 1991 census data, showed a death rate for Protestants of 1.49 per thousand population and 2.55 per thousand for Catholics. This rate was recalculated, with the 92 per cent of the 'Not Known' deaths redistributed into the 'Protestant' category. This gives a rate of 1.92 per thousand for Protestants and 2.60 per thousand for Catholics. However, the relative proportions of Catholics and Protestants in the population changed over the period of the Troubles, so three other rates were calculated. Deaths in the period 1969 to 1976 were used on the base of the 1971 census, and this gave a Protestant death rate of 0.69 per thousand and a Catholic rate of 1.88 per thousand. A similar exercise for 1977 to 1986, using the 1981 census data, produced a rate of 1.35 per thousand for Protestants and 0.73 for Catholics and the calculation for 1987 to 1998, using the 1991 census data, showed a Protestant death rate of 0.42 per thousand and a Catholic rate of 0.61 per thousand.

Thus, even when the deaths of local security forces are included almost totally within the Protestant category, Catholics were at greater risk in both absolute and relative terms, in the total period of the Troubles. The figures would suggest that this pattern did not hold in the period 1977 to 1986. However, the 1981 census figures are generally regarded as unreliable and this may cast doubt on this result.

Deaths by religion can also be examined according to the organisations responsible for deaths. To some degree, these data confirm the 'common sense' fears of the Northern Ireland population. The biggest cause of deaths amongst Protestants has been Republican organisations, accounting for 70 per cent of the total. If the 'Not Known' category is treated as before (namely that 92 per cent are regarded as Protestant), then Republican paramilitaries have killed over 80 per cent of Protestant victims. Similarly, almost half of Catholic deaths can be attributed to Loyalist paramilitaries. At the same time, over a fifth of Catholic deaths can be attributed to security force activity, mainly accounted for by the British army. However, there are also some less expected findings. Almost a fifth of Protestants have been killed by Loyalist paramilitaries and over a quarter of Catholics by Republican paramilitaries. The latter is partially explained by the Republican bombing campaign, particularly in city centres where causalities were random. Both Loyalist and Republican paramilitaries killed people in their own communities during feuds and on suspicion of them being informers.

Effects of the Troubles

Using data on death rates in each of the 566 wards in Northern Ireland, all wards were stratified into three categories according to death rate. A random sample of 1000 respondents was drawn from within each of the three categories, wards with high, medium or low death rates – a total sample of 3000. Interviewers administered a questionnaire eliciting information on experiences and effects of the Troubles. The results present a picture of the effects of the Troubles on the population.

Table 3.1 shows responses to a question about experience of a range of psychological reactions. Whilst the majority of respondents had not experienced the listed effects, between 29.6 per cent and 44.3 per cent had experienced each of them at some stage, with the exception of 'felt ashamed or guilty about surviving events in the Troubles'. The most common after-effects experienced on a frequent basis are 'feeling more jumpy or startled than usual' with 14.8 per cent and 44.3 per cent of respondents having had this experience at some point. A further 38.9 per cent of respondents had painful memories of experiences of the Troubles with 7.9 per cent of respondents frequently having painful memories. Some 34 per cent of respondents had the experience of 'having trouble sleeping', with 10.5 per cent having had this experience on a frequent basis. A further 32.1 per cent of respondents 'found [themselves] in a situation which made you feel as though it was happening all over again', and 5.7 per cent of respondents had this experience frequently. Finally, 30.3 per cent of respondents indicated that they had 'lost interest in activities which meant a lot to [them] before', and 5.1 per cent had frequently had this experience.

Table 3.1 Can I ask if you have had after effects as a result of your experiences of the Troubles?

Have you had a period of time when you ...	Frequently (%)	Occasionally (%)	Rarely (%)	Never (%)	Don't remember (%)	Total (100%)
Kept having painful memories of your experiences	106 (7.9)	213 (15.9)	200 (14.9)	779 (58.0)	45 (3.4)	1343
Had repeated dreams or nightmares	80 (6.0)	146 (10.9)	169 (12.6)	904 (67.4)	43 (3.2)	1342
Found yourself in a situation which made you feel as though it was happening all over again	77 (5.7)	191 (14.2)	164 (12.2)	860 (64.1)	49 (3.7)	1341

Lost interest in activities which meant a lot to you before	68 (5.1)	157 (11.7)	181 (13.5)	891 (66.4)	44 (3.3)	1341
Were very jumpy or more easily startled or felt that you had to be on your guard all the time	198 (14.8)	246 (18.4)	149 (11.1)	718 (53.6)	29 (2.2)	1340
Had more trouble than usual with sleeping	141 (10.5)	169 (12.6)	146 (10.9)	843 (63.0)	39 (2.9)	1338
Felt ashamed or guilty about surviving events in the Troubles	32 (2.4)	60 (4.5)	121 (9.0)	1044 (78.0)	82 (6.1)	1339

Of those who had suffered any of the effects, 14.8 per cent had suffered the effects within the last six months, and 12.6 per cent had some of the symptoms for up to five years.

Table 3.2 shows the extent to which the Troubles have affected respondents' health and well-being. There was most agreement with the statement that the Troubles 'had provoked strong feelings of rage in me', with 57.4 per cent of respondents agreeing overall with this statement and 19.5 per cent agreeing strongly. A further 47.2 per cent of respondents agreed overall with the statement that the Troubles 'had made violence a part of [their lives]' with 11.8 per cent agreeing strongly. Some 44 per cent of respondents agreed that the Troubles 'had caused [them] a great deal of distress and emotional upset', and 14.3 per cent agreed with this strongly.

Table 3.2 Do you agree/ disagree that the Troubles have...

	Strongly agree (%)	Agree (%)	Neither agree nor disagree (%)	Disagree (%)	Strongly disagree (%)	Total (100%)
Caused me a great deal of distress and emotional upset	192 (14.3)	399 (29.7)	248 (18.5)	388 (28.9)	115 (8.6)	1342
Made violence more a part of my life	158 (11.8)	476 (35.4)	156 (11.6)	383 (28.5)	170 (12.7)	1343
Made it difficult for me to trust people in general	96 (7.2)	391 (29.2)	240 (17.9)	470 (35.0)	144 (10.7)	1341
Left me feeling helpless	110 (8.2)	421 (31.4)	255 (19.0)	455 (34.0)	98 (7.3)	1339
Provoked strong feelings of rage in me	262 (19.5)	508 (37.9)	222 (16.5)	290 (21.6)	60 (4.5)	1342
Shattered my illusion that the world is a safe place	158 (11.8)	430 (32.0)	284 (21.2)	345 (25.7)	125 (9.3)	1342

Caused me not to want to have anything to do with the other community	49 (3.7)	163 (12.2)	224 (16.7)	606 (45.2)	299 (22.3)	1341

Some 43.8 per cent of respondents agreed overall that the Troubles 'had shattered [their] illusion that the world is a safe place', and 11.8 per cent agreed strongly with this. A further 39.6 per cent of respondents said that the Troubles 'left [them] feeling helpless' and 8.2 per cent agreed strongly with this statement. Overall, 36.4 per cent of respondents agreed to some extent that the Troubles had 'made it difficult for [them] to trust people in general' and 7.2 per cent of them agreed strongly that this was the case. Finally, 15.9 per cent of respondents agreed that the Troubles had 'caused [them] not to want to have anything to do with the other community', and 3.7 per cent of those agreed strongly that this was the case. This data demonstrates the widespread impact of the Troubles on the population, with over 40 per cent reporting a shattered belief in their safety, and almost 40 per cent describing feelings of helplessness. That such a large proportion of the population should report such feelings illustrates the extent to which the Troubles have impacted on general expectations of well-being, safety and the capacity of members of the population to protect themselves from danger.

Help and support

This section of the questionnaire asked about the type of help and support which respondents have sought and received as a result of the effects of the Troubles on them. Table 3.3 lists the types of trained help which have been received by the respondents.

Table 3.3 Have you ever seen a trained helper about the effects of the Troubles on you or on a member of your family?

	Yes (%)	No (%)	Total (%)
Psychiatrist	63 (4.8)	1238 (95.2)	1301
Clinical psychologist	18 (1.4)	1282 (98.6)	1300
GP and local doctor	268 (20.5)	1042 (79.5)	1310
Community nurse	77 (5.9)	1222 (94.1)	1299
Alternative health practitioner	10 (0.8)	1290 (99.2)	1300
Chemist/pharmacist	174 (13.4)	1129 (86.6)	1303
Social worker	51 (3.9)	1249 (96.1)	1300
Child guidance	10 (0.8)	1287 (99.2)	1297
Support through school welfare	17 (1.3)	1280 (98.7)	1297
Teacher	41 (3.2)	1257 (96.8)	1298
Counsellor	36 (2.8)	1262 (97.2)	1298
Self-help group	47 (3.6)	1252 (96.4)	1299
Marriage/relationship counsellor	5 (0.4)	1294 (99.6)	1299
Social security agency	108 (8.3)	1192 (91.7)	1300
Citizen's Advice Bureau	74 (5.7)	1225 (94.3)	1299
The Samaritans	6 (0.5)	1293 (99.5)	1299
Minister or priest	116 (8.9)	1185 (91.1)	1301

Faith healer	8 (0.6)	1285 (99.4)	1293
Lawyer or solicitor	135 (10.4)	1160 (89.6)	1295
Personnel department within my employment	16 (1.2)	1278 (98.8)	1294
Accountant	4 (0.3)	1289 (99.7)	1293
Local politician	146 (11.3)	1145 (88.7)	1291
Community worker	130 (10.1)	1163 (89.9)	1293
Other voluntary organisation	100 (7.7)	1193 (92.3)	1293

Although the majority of respondents have not seen any of the help listed, 20.5 per cent of respondents have sought help from their GP or local doctor. Other sources of help have been from: chemist/pharmacist 13.4 per cent; lawyer or solicitor 10.4 per cent; local politician 11.3 per cent; community worker 10.1 per cent. Only 0.8 per cent sought help from child guidance; 1.3 per cent sought help from child welfare; 3.9 per cent sought help from a social worker; 5.9 per cent sought help from a community nurse. More respondents sought help from their minister or priest (8.9%), community worker (10.1%), or local politician (11.3%). The least popular or applicable sources of help were: accountants 0.3 per cent; The Samaritans 0.5 per cent; marriage or relationship counsellors 0.4 per cent. Overall, respondents who sought help were most likely to look to immediate family members. Family doctors were the most likely to be consulted of all professionals, and other statutory help was not sought on any widespread basis. This is perhaps partly because of the lack of trust in statutory agencies in some communities, but also perhaps because of the 'normalisation' of the Troubles that took place and the belief reported by some that nothing could help.

How does Northern Ireland compare to other conflicts?

Two comparative measures designed to reflect death rates (per 1000 head of population), the first referring to the intensity, and the second the duration of the conflict, are shown in Table 3.4. The first ranks years in which the death rates were highest and compares these across countries. A Northern Ireland base of more than one death per 10,000 population per year (or 0.1 per 1000) was employed to the highlighted six years. A number of countries, selected according to the availability of sufficiently robust population and deaths figures, were then compared to Northern Ireland.

Table 3.4 Comparison of intensity of international conflicts

Northern Ireland		Salvador				Cambodia	
Year		Year	Official	Year	Estimated	Year	
1972	0.32	1981	0.48	1982	4.67	1976	50.25
1976	0.20	1982	0.28	1981	3.60	1977	48.82
1974	0.20	1983	0.21	1986	2.18	1978	47.44
1973	0.18			1983	1.92	1979	46.10
1975	0.17			1984	0.90	1980	44.80
1971	0.12			1985	0.46		
				1990	0.31		
				1987	0.27		
				1989	0.23		
				1991	0.21		
				1988	0.20		

Source: Smyth (2000d)

In Northern Ireland, the first half of the 1970s saw the most intensive killing reaching just over 3 per 10,000 population in 1972. The official Salvadoran figures give three years in which killing rates were higher than in Northern Ireland although the lowest year (1983) is exceeded by Northern Ireland's 1972. The estimated figures for Salvador were much higher reaching 46 per 10,000 population in 1982. The Cambodian figures show that nearly a quarter of the population died between 1976 and 1980. Other comparisons, for example with Turkey (0.07 per 1000) and Argentina (0.04 per 1000), do not demonstrate an intensity of killing matching that in Northern Ireland. In these cases, the greater populations compared to Northern Ireland reduce the relative death rates. In other states, the intensity of violence has been greater. There are examples of states with small populations (thus more like Northern Ireland) but with intensive conflicts that tend to have higher annual death rates.

A death rate based on the total number of deaths and the average population for the period of conflict can also be constructed. This gives greater weight to the duration of any conflict. The comparisons on this basis are shown in Table 3.5.

Table 3.5 International comparison of intensity of conflict

Northern Ireland	Salvador (Smyth 2000d)		Cambodia	Turkey	Argentina
2.25	1.17	20.25	237.02	0.57	0.32

Over 25 years, the total Northern Ireland deaths have amounted to just over two per 1000 of the average population. This is greater than the official Salvadoran figure, though considerably less than for estimated deaths. The Cambodian figure remains startling because of the overwhelming scale of the conflict there. Northern Ireland is about four times worse than Turkey and seven times worse than Argentina. In international comparative terms, Northern Ireland's death rates do not compare with the most intensive killing characteristic of other conflicts, and are described as 'low intensity conflict', yet they are sufficiently serious to merit international concern.

The concept of trauma

Until the advent of the Bloomfield report (1998), little official attention had been paid to those bereaved or injured in the Troubles in Northern Ireland. This was in large part due to the fact that physical survival, rather than psychological well-being, is often the priority in situations of ongoing violence. Yet, even when the violence was at its peak, there was a Criminal Injuries Compensation Scheme (also reviewed by Bloomfield) and a Criminal Damages Scheme for compensation for damage to property. These schemes aimed at providing financial compensation for physical or psychological injury, with important restrictions. For example, no one convicted of offences under emergency legislation in Northern Ireland could be compensated unless under special circumstances. Under the Criminal Injuries Compensation Scheme, eligibility for financial compensation due to emotional distress depended on the opinions of psychiatrists who applied the diagnostic criteria for post traumatic stress disorder (PTSD). There have been suggestions that regional differences in diagnostic practice indicate that psychiatrists in Northern Ireland avail of the PTSD diagnosis much less than their counterparts elsewhere in the UK.

Overall, it is likely that only a fraction of those affected by the Troubles received financial compensation: we have already established that few received therapeutic help beyond medical treatment for physical injury, and even then there are widespread reports of difficulties with accessing appropriate prosthetic and pain control services.

Political, social and cultural factors

Elsewhere, the issue of who 'qualifies' as a 'victim' in Northern Ireland has been discussed (see Smyth 1998a). These matters are far from simple and meaning is often contested. Furthermore, certain categories of people who have sustained loss or injury have not always been regarded as 'deserving', and indeed may continue to be regarded as such by certain service providers. Within certain groups of people such as the armed forces, active disincentives (such as compromising chances of future promotion, or damage to a macho image) exist, which inhibit the declaration of psychological difficulties. Thus, the determination of the existence of 'trauma', its recognition, its manifestation in particular forms or, conversely, the lack of attention paid to such issues are influenced by fiscal, social, professional and political factors.

However, there are more fundamental problems with the concept and specifically with the use of PTSD diagnostic criteria in Northern Ireland and in other low intensity conflicts. The use of the term 'trauma' presupposes a universality of definition of traumatic experience and effects. Yet, as mentioned above, what is described as traumatic in one set of circumstances (for instance, viewing a Batman movie) might be regarded as inconsequential in another. Attempts to standardise such definition and diagnosis, through the use of the International Classification of Diseases (ICD) or the *Diagnostic and Statistical Manual (DSM)* have raised a further set of problems. Indeed, the origins and history of the PTSD diagnostic category is an illustration of this (see Smyth 2000a).

PTSD is a framework that was originally developed to deal with the reactions of soldiers who saw between 12 and 39 months of combat in Vietnam. It was also developed according to symptomatology that appeared after the soldiers were removed from the war zone, and where such symptoms and behaviour were clearly outside the norm for the general population. This raises questions about the suitability of the PTSD framework for work with civilians, and its usefulness in a conflict such as that in Northern Ireland. Unlike the average tour of duty in Vietnam, exposure to conflict has been ongoing in Northern Ireland for almost three decades, raising questions about the applicability of PTSD as a framework in long-standing civil conflicts. Straker (1987) holds the view that post-traumatic stress disorder is a misnomer in situations of ongoing violence and proposes instead the term *continuous* traumatic stress syndrome to encompass the continuing nature of the violence and stress.

The more recent differentiation between type one and type two trauma remains inadequate in the face of experience of ongoing war, because war by its very nature involves repeated and ongoing exposure to traumatic events. Furthermore, and perhaps more significantly, the population of Northern Ireland (particularly those in the security forces, combatants and those who live in militarised areas) have not left the war zone, so the concept of 'post' trauma is not applicable. Voluntary organisations offering support to those affected by the Troubles experienced a rapid increase in the number of requests for help following the 1994 ceasefires in Northern Ireland and on subsequent occasions where the level of violence has diminished. This may tend to suggest that it is only in the post-conflict phase that the true extent of the psychological and emotional effect of armed conflict can emerge.

There are also divided opinions about the value and efficacy of various kinds of intervention, such as storytelling, counselling, EMDR and other forms of 'help'. Eye Movement Desensitisation and Reprocessing (EMDR) is a routinised treatment requiring the patient to follow objects held by the therapist, thus eliciting certain eye movements which, it is claimed, have the effect of extinguishing or reducing traumatic symptoms. As on numerous other subjects, mental health professionals have been divided in their approach to trauma from the outset. The competition between the 'talking cure' of W.H.R. Rivers, and the shock treatment of Yealland is still reflected in debates today, albeit in a less extreme form (For an excellent fictionalised account of this era, see Barker (1991)). Psychodynamically inclined therapists tend to advocate the exploration of the experience through talking or telling and retelling the story of the trauma in order to 'wear it out', whereas the behaviourally inclined therapist would tend to favour the 'reprogramming' approach, where the goal is the extinction of unwanted or dysfunctional response or behaviour. Recent evidence would indicate that EMDR and cognitive behavioural therapy produce good results in traumatised patients, whilst some other treatment regimes such as debriefing seem to compromise recovery.

Since the emergence of concern about victims of the Troubles, public discussion of these issues have often involved those who have been bereaved and injured in 'telling their stories' in order to educate a wider public about their suffering. Since the consolidation of the peace process in Northern Ireland, there is an emerging 'market' for storytelling. This is also apparent in the proliferation of 'fight and tell' biographies of former IRA, SAS and other combatants. Whilst 'storytelling' can be therapeutically useful and often socially valuable, there is also cause for concern. Causing one's story to become a matter of public record has important effects on identity that may subsequently inhibit personal resolution and healing. In addition, by publishing a personal account in the public domain, the storyteller is vulnerable to political appropriation of the story. The difficulty in maintaining the focus on humanitarian aspects of such stories to the exclusion of the political implications can mean that the storyteller may be caught up in controversy and contest about the story itself, which is not often conducive to good mental health.

Psychotropic drugs are also extensively used in 'treating' trauma. Many were shocked by a scene broadcast from Russia in 2000, where a woman whose son was killed in a nuclear submarine accident publicly expressed her anger at a senior politician and was consequently injected with a tranquilliser in full view of television cameras. Yet more subtle forms of medication have been ongoing in Northern Ireland for almost three decades. The wholesale medication of people living with the consequences of the Troubles may not seem a socially or morally attractive scenario, yet it is ongoing. The legal and illegal use of psychotropic medication and the heavy use of alcohol – including children – is endemic in many of the communities that have seen the worst effects of the Troubles.

Human service professionals in Northern Ireland have been ill-equipped to deal with the challenges of work in this field and are often distrusted by those in communities, partly because of their role in child protection and administering the Mental Health Act. Little in the way of new and creative methods of support has been explored by the mainstream professions, who were also caught in the culture of silence that characterised discourse about the Troubles until well into the peace process. It is in this context that music therapy's potential contribution can be seen.

The effect of psychological traumatisation on individuals may be manifest in a range of well-documented effects: a shattered belief system; disempowerment and deskilling; feelings of helplessness and dehumanisation; loosened grasp of 'reality'; mind/body alienation; disturbed sleep; acute attacks of fear; inability to engage in pre-trauma relationships and lifestyle; inability to trust or to feel safe. Those affected by the Troubles in Northern Ireland, and other conflicts where enmity between factions continues and where there is an ethno-national or racial dimension, also experience additional difficulties. However, there is often not a consensus about their loss or injury in the wider society. Some fellow citizens may see the attack on them as justified, some may even rejoice in their suffering. As a result, the rage and sense of injustice that may be experienced by all those experiencing trauma can be complicated by these factors, which may be more marked in situations like Northern Ireland.

Furthermore, the wider divisions within the community and the political and media interest in the conflict may create a new public victim identity for those bereaved or injured, with all the attendant media attention that such an identity involves. This may require those bereaved or injured to rehearse their situation over and over again for public consumption. The effects on their emotional well-being are not often considered. This new identity may also alter individuals' relationships with their wider community. Their association with the traumatic loss may overwhelm and subsume their individual identities. Individual losses or suffering may become representative of wider community grievances, and this may have implications for individual healing and closure. There are numerous examples of families who lost members several decades ago, such as those bereaved on Bloody Sunday. Such events can become icons of grievance for an entire community, thus rendering a private loss into public property. Continued political or legal attempts to ascertain the circumstances surrounding contentious killings, for example, may inhibit emotional closure and personal resolution at an individual level.

One further aspect of traumatic loss takes on a sinister dimension in the context of divided societies. The desire for revenge which is reported by many of those experiencing trauma or loss may take on a dangerous aspect in ethno-national or racial conflicts, particularly when there are militant groups anxious to act out such desires. The cycle of retaliation can escalate conflict in the most bloody manner, as was the case in the 1980s and 1990s in Northern Ireland and continuing into the twenty-first century in the Middle East.

Finally, and most dangerously, victimhood and suffering have two main political functions in such conflicts. First, the suffering of one faction is used politically as evidence of the brutality and inhumanity of the other, and can thus be turned into propaganda. Second, the suffering of all factions may become a justification for further violence, as 'retaliation', 'defence of the community' or 'deterrence'. (See Smyth 2000b,

2000c for a more in-depth discussion of the politicisation of victims of Northern Ireland's Troubles.)

Thus it becomes crucial, not only at the individual therapeutic level, but also at the communal and societal level, that means of supporting healing are found. In such circumstances, healing is not a neutral professional act – if it ever is. Rather, healing is a contribution to diminishing the impact of violence and to inhibiting its proliferation. Healing can offer a 'third way' in the face of polarisation and deep division. This can mean the removal of attention and focus from the external 'enemy' and paying exclusive attention to the subjective and internal processes of those who have been hurt.

Central to this process of healing is the rediscovery and re-establishment of the creativity of the 'victim'. Victimhood is associated with helplessness, silence and dependence. In order to heal, the victim must overcome helplessness, to become an active participant in his or her own healing. Creativity is resistance to oppression: it is the refusal of victimhood and helplessness. Creating something new is an act of defiance in the face of destruction. Survivors of devastating experiences often talk about recovering or finding their voice and their power. Some of those who have successfully negotiated such transitions describe arriving at new understandings and insights by processing events creatively. Creativity is central to the process. The ability to recreate a positive role and sense of future is essentially an act of creativity, of turning misfortune to advantage – of alchemy.

Creativity is necessary in the process of rebuilding a new schema after the shattering of one's belief system, of reconnecting with a changed 'reality' and of rediscovery of the mind–body connection. Anxiety and panic must either be understood and transformed, or new responses learned. Nightmares, disturbed sleep and the symbolic images of the trauma must be transformed into more benign and tolerable forms. The ability to engage in relationships and resume a healthy lifestyle requires the creative struggle to triumph over fear, mistrust and the other sequelae of trauma. Even rage and a sense of injustice can be creatively used to fuel energy and work for human rights or justice. The desire for revenge can become transformed into what Garbarino and Kostelny (1997) described in Cambodian refugees as positive revenge: the refusal to let the perpetrator 'win' by recovering and moving on in life in a positive direction.

Even when 'recovery' is not achieved or indeed possible, the process of making one's way in the world whilst accommodating the losses and changes is essentially a creative one. Adaptation, problem solving to find solutions to new problems, relies on creativity. This is true, even if the solutions are not always health promoting. The practice of self-medication through the use of alcohol, for example, can be seen as problem-solving behaviour. However, it may be necessary to find an equally effective but less dangerous solution to the problems of sleep disturbance, anxiety or painful thoughts. Traditional therapeutic methods have their role to play. However, some people find the idea of therapy threatening or stigmatising, so caution and sensitivity is called for. Furthermore, some of the effects of trauma may mitigate against the use of therapy.

Turner, McFarlane and van der Kolk (1996) point out that traumatisation may lead to problems in tolerating intimacy, the impulse to avoid the suffering caused by the traumatic situation, and shame and guilt, all of which are factors that may impede therapeutic engagement (see Sparr, Moffitt and Ward 1993). The sense of alienation and being misunderstood that can result from traumatisation may be a further barrier to seeking help (Turner et al. 1996); as are cultural factors such as stoicism or cultures of denial and silence which prevailed in Northern Ireland (Smyth 1998b) until relatively recently. Non-verbal methods, such as music therapy, art therapy (see Malchiodi 1999; Rackstraw 2000), interactive image work (see Plummer 1999), and other techniques such as hypnosis (Putnam 1992), VK/D3 and EMDR (Jensen 1994) have an important role to play in offering a diversity of paths to integration and potential resolution to those who have been traumatised. Their importance may well lie in their capacity to provide a vehicle for exploring the traumatic experience without requiring a tolerance for intimacy or other factors associated with more traditional therapies.

The use of music therapy in Northern Ireland

It is clear from other chapters in this volume and documentation elsewhere (see Murray 2000; Pavilicevic 2000) that music therapy can be a powerful and healing intervention in violently divided contexts. The non-verbal nature of music can allow the therapist and patient to transcend the many traps that language can set in the path of expressiveness and thus recovery. The expressive nature of music can facilitate expression of difficult emotions, and music can help break the silence of isolation.

However, the music therapist faces a specific challenge in violently divided societies where national identity and sovereignty are contested, and where such contests lie at the heart of the conflict that has traumatised people. In such contexts, nothing, including music, is neutral. Certain melodies are associated with the triumphalism of one side or the other; certain popular tunes have had lyrics rewritten into derogatory ditties about one or other faction. The playing or not playing of music may be a contested issue. Musical instruments have political identities and associations. There are two kinds of pipes played in Northern Ireland – the Scottish bagpipes associated with Unionism and the Irish Uileann pipes associated with Irish traditional music and identity. The Lambeg drum is similarly associated with Orangeism and Unionism and the bodhrán with Irish traditional music. Similar associations exist in relation to musical forms, with gospel and certain forms of country music associated with Protestant fundamentalism, and classical and orchestral music associated with the ascendancy.

In violently divided societies, neutrality is non-existent and in such contexts neither can music as a language be neutral. If the music therapist is not aware of and sensitive to these issues, music therapy not only risks further alienation of the patient, but loses a golden opportunity to explore, through such associations, the divided and polarised contexts of the patient's life. Indeed, music and instrumentation have begun to be used in the context of reconciliation in Northern Ireland through the work of such initiatives as Different Drums, a group who use both Lambegs and bodhráns in perfomance.

In the emerging and diverse field of therapeutic intervention with those affected by the Troubles, the incorporation into music therapy practice of an understanding and open recognition of the political associations that music and instrumentation have in Northern Ireland offers exciting possibilities, not only for therapeutic work with traumatised patients (Smyth 2000d), but also in developmental work in schools and elsewhere. Exploring with a patient how it might feel to play a 'different drum' may open up a range of therapeutic possibilities. Music therapy as a whole-school activity in divided societies might use such approaches to contribute to the reconstruction of our society after a period of devastating destruction and division, such as we have lived through. Music therapy in Northern Ireland and other divided societies could well provide an opportunity for creatively exploring our divisions and contribute to our capacity to understand and transform those divisions into harmonious rather than dissonant diversities.

Notes

1. Terry Carlin (1979) Speech at the launch of the NICTU 'Better Life for All' campaign, Belfast.

2. See B. Robson *et al.* (1994) *Relative Deprivation in Northern Ireland*, PPRU, The Department of Finance and Personnel, Belfast.

3. Visual Kinaesthetic Dissociation (VK/D) is a technique which uses a mixture of hypnosis and neuro-linguistic programming to reduce or extinguish symptoms of anxiety associated with traumatic events.

References

Barker, P. (1991) *Regeneration*. London: Penguin.

Bloomfield, K. (1998) *We Will Remember Them: Report of the Northern Ireland Victims Commissioner, Sir Kenneth Bloomfield*. Belfast: The Stationery Office.

Fay, M.T., Morrissey, M. and Smyth, M. (1999) *Northern Ireland's Troubles: The Human Costs*. London: Pluto.

Garbarino, J. and Kostelny, K. (1997) 'What children can tell us from living in a war zone.' In J.D. Osofsky (ed) *Children in a Violent Society*. New York: Guilford Press.

Jensen, J.A. (1994) 'An investigation of eye movement desensitisation and reprocessing (EMDR) as a treatment for post traumatic stress disorder (PTSD) symptoms of Vietnam veterans.' *Behavior Therapy 25*, 311–325.

Malchiodi, C. (ed) (1999) *Medical Art Therapy with Children.* London: Jessica Kingsley Publishers.

Murray, N. (2000) 'The therapeutic use of music with children affected by the Troubles in Northern Ireland and the challenges faced by the therapist.' In M. Smyth and K. Thomson *Working with Children and Young People in Violently Divided Societies: Papers from South Africa and Northern Ireland.* Derry, Londonderry: INCORE/United Nations University/University of Ulster.

Pavlicevic, M. (2000) 'Beyond listening: therapy with children in a violent society.' In M. Smyth and K. Thomson *Working with Children and Young People in Violently Divided Societies: Papers from South Africa and Northern Ireland.* Derry, Londonderry: INCORE/United Nations University/ University of Ulster.

Plummer, D. (1999) *Using Interactive Imagework with Children.* London: Jessica Kingsley Publishers.

Putnam, F.W. (1992) 'Using hypnosis for therapeutic abreactions.' *Psychiatric Medicine 10,* 1, 51–65.

Rackstraw, A. (2000) 'Have basket, will travel: art therapy in informal settlements in South Africa.' In M. Smyth and K. Thomson *Working with Children and Young People in Violently Divided Societies: Papers from South Africa and Northern Ireland.* Derry, Londonderry: INCORE/United Nations University/ University of Ulster.

Smyth, M. (1998a) 'Remembering in Northern Ireland: victims, perpetrators and hierarchies of pain and responsibility.' In B. Hamber (ed) *Past Imperfect: Dealing With The Past in Northern Ireland and Societies in Transition.* Derry, Londonderry: INCORE.

Smyth, M. (1998b) *Half the Battle: Understanding the Impact of the Troubles Conflict on Children and Young People in Northern Ireland.* Derry, Londonderry: INCORE/United Nations University/University of Ulster.

Smyth, M. (2000a) 'The "discovery" and treatment of trauma in Northern Ireland.' In *Future Policies for the Past.* Belfast: Democratic Dialogue.

Smyth, M. (2000b) 'The role of victims in the Northern Ireland Peace Process.' In A. Guelke and M. Cox (2000) *A Farewell to Arms: From War to Peace in Northern Ireland.* Manchester: Manchester University Press.

Smyth, M. (2000c) 'Burying the past? Victims and community relations in Northern Ireland since the cease-fires.' In N. Biggar (ed) *Burying the Past: Making Peace and Doing Justice after Civil Conflict.* Washington DC: Georgetown University Press.

Smyth, M. (2000d) 'Working with the aftermath of violent political division.' In H. Kelmshall and J. Pritchard *Good Practice in Working with Violence.* London: Jessica Kingsley Publishers.

Sparr, L.F., Moffitt, M.C. and Ward, M.F. (1993) 'Missed psychiatric appointments: who returns and who stays away.' *American Journal of Psychiatry 150*, 5, 801–805.

Straker, G. and the Sanctuaries Team (1987) 'The continuous traumatic stress syndrome: the single therpaeutic interview.' *Psychology in Society 8*, 48–79.

Turner, S.W., McFarlane, A.C. and van Der Kolk, B.A. (1996) 'The therapeutic environment and new explorations in the treatment of post traumatic stress disorder.' In B. A. Van Der Kolk, A. C. McFarlane and L. Weisaeth (eds) *Traumatic Stress: The Effects of Overwhelming Experience on Mind, Body and Society.* New York: Guilford Press.

CHAPTER 4

Musical Perspectives
The Politics of Silence: The Northern Ireland Composer and the Troubles

Hilary Bracefield

This chapter explores the impact of the Northern Ireland problem, known as the Troubles, on the composers of serious music, seeking to review how far their work has been affected by living through such a traumatic period. It forms an interesting study in the politics of music.

In what the world perceives to be a 30-year conflict, one might think that the serious composers of Northern Ireland, like many of the poets, playwrights, novelists, visual artists, film-makers and popular musicians, would by now have produced works which related to that conflict. One cannot, however, point to any significant musical compositions which have addressed the troubles. Artists from other forms, on the other hand, have received national and international success through their engagement with the political and social problems of the last 30 years. Composers from other countries might envy the Northern Ireland musician for living through a period which offers the possibility of ready-made material. The stance of composers from the province, however, suggests a blanking out of the conflict, as in common with many of their fellow citizens. Only now, after a kind of peace which seems to be holding, are they beginning to think of acknowledging it.

As one of the composers, Kevin O'Connell, said in an interview in the magazine *Music Ireland* in 1986: 'It rather interests me that the present generation of Ulster poets, however obliquely, are tackling political questions. Irish composers, Ulster composers, seem wary of doing it; I know I've been wary, perhaps I've never properly thought about it' (Byers 1986)

Philip Flood said much the same to me in discussion in August 1995: 'I've never thought about it…I've just got away from all that.' In an important article on the subject, Lydia Goehr quotes the hugely important early twentieth century composer Arnold Schoenberg: 'We, who live in *music,* have no place in politics and must regard it as foreign to our being. We are a-political, at best able to aspire to remain silently in the background' (Goehr 1994, p.107).

This appears to be the attitude of the Northern Ireland composer, an attitude which I had already addressed in an article before reading Lydia Goehr's article (Bracefield 1996). The last 30 years have seen a burgeoning of the arts in the province, partially helped by the wish to rise above the troubles, and the work of the Arts Council of Northern Ireland has helped to foster both the practitioners and the performance of the arts. A considerable number of young composers have had opportunities for study, commissions and performances. Some of the most successful have been interviewed for this chapter. All are now in their thirties or forties and have had national and international success, and most are making their livings largely by composition. Those being studied include Elaine Agnew, Bill Campbell, Michael Alcorn, Stephen Gardner, Deirdre Gribben, Philip Flood, Kevin O'Connell and Ian Wilson. All have had Irish-wide performances; international success has been enjoyed by Deirdre Gribben and Ian Wilson.

Now, of course, the situation in which a Northern Ireland composer lives is not what can be considered a war, nor is it a case of an oppressive state whose dictates one either supports or opposes. Most of the problems in Northern Ireland arise from differing views of the relationship of the province to Great Britain and to the Republic of Ireland; with its inhabitants being characterised in a kind of shorthand as Catholic or Protestant, no matter what their actual religious views may be. The 30-year Troubles have largely been enacted within small areas of the country with the verbal battle enacted by politicians. The middle classes can live virtually untouched by the problems, as nearly all the composers studied showed by their lifestyle.

All the composers grew up with the Troubles, which commenced around 1968. Some lived in neighbourhoods where the other side was barely encountered. Some only encountered the other side through parental friendships. Others lived in middle-class, mixed areas where differences were accepted without much curiosity. All had a passion for music, which to some extent distanced them from other children and other pursuits. Some have direct memories of particular incidents of bombings or destruction of houses, but none felt that their early life was greatly affected by the conflict in their country. In fact, their interest in music often drew them into mixed evening and Saturday music-making which transcended separate schooling and day-to-day living. All pursued their musical careers by attending university: either one of the two in Northern Ireland or Trinity College, Dublin. As I have discussed elsewhere (Bracefield 1996), all were taught composition by Englishmen, whatever university they went to, and through the music of the western classical musical canon. It seems that in their formative compositional years the composers were completely absorbed in deciding their own style in the usual way, by imitation and experimentation.

There was no incentive from their teachers to study the music of Irish composers; relating knowledge of political music from, for example, eastern European composers to their own situation was also not considered. 'Music was one part of my life, and the Troubles another and that's that', as one said. This was very different from the experience of those studying literature, with a rich tradition of Irish political poetry, plays and novels.

The composers first really confronted their nationality when they moved from the province for further study or for performances. They all discovered that the outsider's view of their situation was quite unexpected. The main thing they encountered, to their surprise, was that people outside the province assumed, quite naturally, that anyone from the province was in fact Irish. For those whose upbringing had instilled in them their Britishness, this was a shock, for others from the Protestant tradition who had thought of themselves as from Northern Ireland there was still a need to reposition themselves. Even those from the Catholic tradition found themselves displaced. In the south, as one said to me, they are seen as northerners, and in the north as Catholic, in England, they are Irish. In a way, all composers found a curious dislocation in their position, with which they had to come to terms. Travel outside the province thus made the maturing composer more aware of a physical and cultural relationship to Ireland, but at the same time often reinforced their belief in their own musical language. While it may have made them discuss and question the politics of the place they came from, perhaps for the first time, it did not necessarily inspire them to want to write music about the conflict.

There are, however, several ways in which composers can exploit their Irishness without using the Troubles. I will cite four of these. The first is to write a work as an evocation of the Irish landscape, north or south. This can be manifest to the listener just through the title, but can be reinforced by a programme note. Most of the young composers acknowledge the effect on them of particular Irish landscapes and have written pieces inspired by them. A second is to set poems by Irish poets. Here the composers seem to eschew younger poets and poems about the Troubles. (Joyce is a particular favourite, but not Yeats, the more significantly political.) A third way, and one that might seem to be a particularly fruitful source of material, is to use Irish myths and legends. There are only a few examples so far, which may seem surprising; their reluctance points to the composers' particular attitude of mind. The fourth possibility, much used by composers from the Republic of Ireland, is to harness the language of Irish folk music to the cause. All in Northern Ireland experienced horror at going very far down those paths: no one forgets Brian Boydell's description of 'plastic shamrock' music 'married in a curious mesalliance to a Brahmsian Teutonic textbook harmony' (Acton 1970). But they do recognise the possibilities of using Irish modes and the notes of a particular folk song as a catalyst, and most have done this in at least one piece – sometimes acknowledged publicly, sometimes not.

So are these composers splendidly apolitical, as Schoenberg suggests they should be? Are they missing an opportunity to influence affairs in their own province? One can argue, as do some music philosophers such as Adorno or Attali, that the very abstraction or transcendance of music allows it to represent society by its very freedom *from* it, or, as Goehr (1994) suggests, by its freedom *within*. Many of the composers concentrate on writing technical and abstract pieces, which can be considered as pure music. At least one has turned to the use of biblical themes and passages for inspiration, suggesting a wish to make his music reach a higher plane. It has been easy for the young composer to ignore the Troubles by appearing to transcend them.

Certainly there are very few works written so far in which the composer has admitted, publicly or privately, that there is an agenda relating directly to the situation in which they all live. There are, however, a few. I will give five examples: *From a Beseiged City* by Kevin O'Connell; *Rising* by Philip Flood; *Wanting, Not Wanting* by Stephen Gardner; *Macha's Curse* by Michael Alcorn; *Tribe* by Deirdre Gribbin.

There were two main compositions commissioned to commemorate the 300th anniversary of the siege of Derry in 1689. One was *The Relief of Derry* symphony by Shaun Davey, a Protestant, who seems to be considered a 'popular' composer. It has four movements, huge forces – orchestra, organ, pipe bands, brass bands, three soloists (uilleann pipes, soprano and soprano saxophone) – and quite simply it aims to tell, in music, the story of the siege and its raising. The vocal part, in the third slow movement, depicting the siege wearing on, is a four-verse lament, written by Shaun Davey himself. Otherwise Davey is quite happy to tell the whole story of that 300-year-old event without self-consciousness, as a kind of programmatic musical pageant.

The other commission went to Kevin O'Connell, a 'serious' composer. His work *From the Besieged City* is a cantata for mezzo-soprano and orchestra. O'Connell is a Catholic from Derry working in an unashamedly serial or post-serial idiom. He has never compromised that idiom. How does he cope with what is in Northern Ireland not just an historical event but a piece of barbed current life? I would have to say he does it obliquely, but cleverly. He takes a contemporary poem by the Polish poet Zbigniew Herbert, which is ostensibly about an ancient siege, but of course is written for a modern-day audience. He sets it for declamatory soprano, whose verses are accompanied by and interspersed with orchestral comments and interludes. The siege in the poem is not lifted: the speaker who tells of the event can only look to the future to keep alive

the name of the city – there may be freedom for all or not, there may be
only one survivor (which, at least, he hopes for), there may only be his
document. But it must, the protagonist tells us, be documented. What the
mayor and citizens of Derry thought of this work I do not know, but it is
interesting to note the words that O'Connell has made stand out in his
setting: killing, the enemy, negotiations, cemeteries, mayor, politicians,
defenders, conciliation, death, betrayals. Out of the denseness of the
composition, these words are clearly heard, as is the poem's end: 'Only
our dreams have not been humiliated.' This is as near as O'Connell can
get to commenting on a current situation. Without finding that poem, I
am not sure that he would have completed the commission.

A second example is from the first uneasy peace. A work by Philip
Flood called *Rising* was commissioned by the Ulster Youth Orchestra and
first performed in August 1995 in Belfast, Londonderry, Glasgow and
Edinburgh. Nothing in the programme note says any more than the usual
compositional description of what happens in the music. His previous
orchestral piece of 1993 is named *Kicking Down*, a reference to the
starting of a motor cycle, and the use of the name *Rising* and an upward
four-note motif appeared to be references to the main falling four-note
motif of the earlier work. But in conversation with Philip Flood during
the rehearsal period, he admitted to me that the title was not just about
the main rising motif but had other connotations, because during the
composition he was affected, half-unconsciously, by the fact of the
ceasefire, so that the piece became less questioning than in its original
conception (which had, he said, been *Rising?*, with a question mark), and
more optimistic than it might otherwise have been.

My third example concerns Stephen Gardner, from the Protestant
tradition. He was asked by the BBC to write a piece for a St Patrick's
Night concert performed and broadcast live on 17 March 1992. The
work, for orchestra, is called *Wanting, Not Wanting*. The piece consists of a
long soft section, a brief violent section with much percussion input, and
a short return to the soft, slow material. It ends indeterminately. The piece
sat rather oddly with the traditional nature of much of the rest of the
programme which included 'plastic shamrock' Irish tunes, orchestrated
by Havelock Nelson, among others. The audience was affected by the

piece – uncertain, but drawn into it. However, Gardner's programme note only says:

> The Irish air *Snaidhm an Ghrá (The True Lover's Knot)* provides the source for much of the melodic and harmonic material which I used in *Wanting, Not Wanting.* I found this Co. Cork tune fascinating due to its combination of mixolydian (flattened seventh), pentatonic (five-note and very Irish – probably via Egypt) and whole-tone modes within a veiled major-scale framework. However most of the material is an abstraction. The main tunes are my own – though it's hard to be convinced of an 'original' tune these days. As the work progresses, the 'air' gets sucked in and fresh air materialises, the main body of violins adds the ethereal touch at key points while the other strings supply a meandering framework through which the 'tunes' travel. The piece seems to 'want' something (not least a decent title) and this appears in the form of an *Ulster Processional* which amasses the full orchestra in a comment on our irresolute times. There is an attempt at some form of resolution, though it seems to be left hanging in the gaseous mixture of oxygen and nitrogen.[1]

The harpist Gráinne Yeats played the air just before Gardner's piece was heard and although the notes are definitely there, the audience was puzzled because they were not 'set' as a complete tune as they expected, but interspersed throughout the work. It was obvious as well that the audience responded to the work because they were aware that in some way Gardner was alluding to the Troubles and they recognised the unclarified reference. In May 1995, however, the piece was revived in the Sonorities Festival of twentieth Century Music, during the first uneasy peace, and Gardner wrote a new programme note. After the information on its source material quoted above, Gardner goes on to say:

> At the time of writing in early 1992 there were two utterly senseless acts of mass murder at Teebane and at a bookies' on the Ormeau Road. These tragedies had a profound effect on the mood of music. There is a constant struggle for light to shine through. An *Ulster Processional*, which provides the climax, has a beacon of light in the high trumpet solo, though it is still tinged with sorrow. The work ends reflectively. *Wanting, Not Wanting* is dedicated to those who pointlessly lost their lives in the twenty-five years of conflict.[2]

Only in 1995 did the composer feel that he could reveal there was a political reason for the piece. Incidentally, this quirky composer has recently had a work commissioned in the south of Ireland for southern performances in which he inserts at intervals the notes of *The Sash*, a notorious Protestant political song. I have to say that you do not hear these easily – I have yet actually to find them all even in the score – but it seems to have given the composer a curious satisfaction.

My fourth example is a work begun in 1994 but only completed and performed in 1997. The composer had much trouble working on the composition, and I think part of the problem was his relationship to the Troubles. Originally deliberately ignoring them, he was affected by one small personal incident, but did not know at first how to express it in music. The work is *Macha's Curse* for orchestra by Michael Alcorn – one of only a few pieces using Irish myths. Macha is badly treated by an Ulster king and casts a curse on Ulster for nine times nine generations, and Alcorn wrote in his programme note in 1997:

> The initial ideas for his piece came at the end of 1994 when I was working at Stanford University, California. It was only a matter of weeks after the cease-fires had been declared in Northern Ireland and several months since our local butcher in Crossgar had been murdered. Both these events had been on my mind and for the first time I felt a strong desire to comment in some way on the troubles which have blighted all our lives for so many years. *Macha's Curse* is a personal response to this. It is a work without political, programmatic or symbolic references. Instead it attempts to capture some of the complex emotions which have touched so many lives in the Province.[3]

My final example is a work acknowledged as being about the Troubles and is by Deirdre Gribbin, a composer who has lived and studied in a number of countries, and is one of the two composers living out of Ireland at present: she and Philip Flood both reside in London. Her earlier compositions, if they have an Irish agenda at all, evoke landscape (*North, By Kilbrannon Sound*), Irish myth (*The Isamnion Fragments, Of the Taín, Follow the Horse*) painters (*Jack B, His Eyes*) or, in *Mad Cow Songs*, a setting of a James Joyce text. *Follow the Horse* uses the same myth of Macha as the work by Michael Alcorn and was written in 1996, in the middle of Alcorn's struggles with his composition.

Gribbin left Northern Ireland in 1989 and most of her works have had their first performances in other countries. She feels she has grown beyond the bounds of her native country and has no wish at present to write about the Troubles. Yet *Cease* from 1995 for chamber ensemble uses as part of the source material two political songs, *The Men Behind the Wire* and U2's *Sunday Bloody Sunday*, although the composer says it was the fact that the music was popular rather than the words which led her to use the songs.

There is, however, only one overtly political piece by Deirdre Gribbin, and she intimates that it is the last she wishes to write. She now seems to want to be an international composer. The piece, called *Tribe*, was written in 1997 and given its première in Denmark. The composer does not actually say it is about Northern Ireland, but the piece gives clues: the title, the use of the bass drum, the opposition of groups of instruments, and the composer's directions above the sections. These are 'forceful and aggressive', 'fearful, anxious', 'gradual feeling of unity and solidarity', 'forceful'. The work is in fact a reaction to the annual confrontations surrounding the Orange marches to and from the church at Drumcree every July, but the composer not only fails to address this obviously, but also expresses no wish at present to comment further on the Northern Ireland situation in her music.

She has, however, allowed herself to be drawn into the politics of another art. It is interesting to realise that while composers were only gingerly composing works that might have a political agenda during the peace process, a writer tackles the subject of the artist's reaction to such an agenda with a novel about a Northern Irish woman composer. *Grace Notes*, by Bernard MacLaverty (1997), a Northern Irish writer living in Scotland, appeared in 1997 and is set during the Troubles. As an interview in BBC Music Magazine reported[4], Gribbin realised how closely her life and views paralleled those of MacLaverty's heroine. The novel's climax concerns the performance of a work by the composer, Catherine, using the Lambeg drums, predominant instruments in Orange marches. Gribbin had already written a work in 1994, *Of the Táin*, which also uses the Lambeg drum. She found this parallel intriguing: the novel appeared almost to be about her and she suggested to the interviewer that she might send MacLaverty some of her music.

Since 1998, when that interview was published, Gribbin has indeed been in contact with MacLaverty and has been awarded a Women in Music Commissioning Fund award for a project with MacLaverty. The citation states:

> Her project, *Notes on the Edge*, is a collaboration with fellow Belfast expat Bernard MacLaverty bringing his book about the fictional composer Catherine McKenna to life in an exploration of the creation process. It combines music and spoken word thus having performance possibilities at both music and literature festivals.[5]

It will be interesting to see how Deirdre Gribbin tackles this collaboration without herself writing more deeply about her Northern Ireland roots than she currently wishes.

Perhaps the peculiar nature of the Northern Ireland Troubles has inhibited the Northern Ireland composer from writing directly about them. But this has not been so for other artists. To some extent composers have felt that the time was not right for serious music to confront the problem. The most abstract of all arts perhaps needs time or distance to make its statements. If peace really has come, then the composer can reflect on what the conflict was all about. Those few pieces that suggest this so far have largely appeared after the first ceasefire in 1995. Many of the composers say that only now do they feel that they want to find ways to write about this long drawn out situation: 'The Troubles were one of those unspoken things,' said one, 'but we've put away the darkest moment, perhaps we can say more.' So the young Northern Irish composers may now no longer be silent.

Notes

1. Stephen Gardner, programme note, 17 March 1992.

2. Stephen Gardner, programme note, 2 May 1995.

3. Michael Alcorn, programme note, 2 May 1997.

4. Interview with Deirdre Gribbin, *BBC Music Magazine*, July 1998, 18.

5. *Women in Music Now*, April/May 2001, 3.

References

Acton, C. (1970) 'Interview with Brian Boydell.' *Éire-Ireland 4*, 97–111.

Bracefield, H. (1996) 'The Northern composer: Irish or European?' *Irish Musical Studies 4*, 255–262.

Byers, D. 'Living up to Expectations.' *Music Ireland 1*, 8, 11–12.

Goehr, L. (1994) 'Political Music and the Politics of Music.' *The Journal of Aesthetics and Art Criticism 52/1*.

MacLaverty, B. (1997) *Grace Notes*. London: Jonathon Cape.

Part 3

International Clinical Perspectives

CHAPTER 5

South Africa

Fragile Rhythms and Uncertain Listenings: Perspectives from Music Therapy with South African Children

Mercédès Pavlicevic

This is a revision of 'Beyond listening: music therapy with children in a violent society.' In M. Smyth and K. Thomson (eds) *Working with Children and Young People in Violently Divided Societies: Papers from South Africa and Northern Ireland.* Belfast: Community Conflict Impact on Children.

Imagine this scenario: Mpumi (not her real name) is 11 years old and her tuberculosis is resistant to every drug tried so far. She is frail, moves like an old person, and talks with an ancient voice that has seen, heard, felt and known it all. She is in a ward in a large hospital on the outskirts of Pretoria in Gauteng, South Africa. Her family cannot afford to visit her – they live some five hours' drive away in the Northern Province. In any case, her father is in prison and her mother died when she was 7 years old. Mpumi lives alone – with her illness.

The music therapy room, in the hospital's orphanage and hospice for children with HIV/AIDS, doubles as a locker room for nurses' uniforms and personal belongings. Mpumi, in her hospital gown and fluffy scruffy slippers, is at her weekly individual music therapy session. She sits next to the music therapist at the keyboard and sings a Xhosa song, which the music therapist accompanies at the keyboard, humming and harmonising with Mpumi. The child's voice is old and ill; a voice that has touched death, loneliness and sorrow. The music therapist feels overwhelmed with sadness during the song barely able to contain her tears, even though she does not know the song, and does not speak Xhosa. Tswana is the language of the local people, so Mpumi's family possibly originates from the Eastern Cape, some 1000 miles south of the hospital. In the middle of the song, the door opens and a nurse rushes in – she needs to change into her uniform. Mpumi and the therapist continue their song: interruptions are frequent and not unusual. 'Oh!' exclaims the nurse. 'This is a Xhosa song from the Transkei!' Mpumi and the therapist stop singing. 'This song is about the father who is in prison, and the children are hungry: they sing to their father, crying, saying, Daddy please come home, we need you, we are hungry, we are alone and afraid, please Daddy come home, come home, we are alone! I know this song, I remember it from when I was a child.' The nurse begins to sing the song while changing into her uniform, and Mpumi and the music therapist join in. The song becomes fuller. Mpumi sings with a new energy and strength, the nurse harmonises in a rich dark voice, and the song fills the room with beauty and vigour. There is an immediate community and kinship between the three women.

At the end of the song the nurse rushes out of the room, mumbling about being late for work. Mpumi smiles and the therapist feels the vitality that the shared singing has drawn from this child: her body seems stronger, her face less drained, her eyes younger. For some moments, through the song, the child, the nurse and the music therapist have touched magic, infinity and wholeness. At the end of the session, Mpumi and the music therapist walk slowly to her hospital bed.

Let us unravel this scenario and think more deeply about the fragility of children's lives in a violent society – their needs, our needs as music therapists – and explore the role of music therapy. In this chapter, I begin by exploring the nature of individual and collective violence in South Africa. I draw from psychological explanations of the origins of violence in childhood, and conclude with a discussion on trauma in an attempt to provide a context for music therapy practice in a society in transition.

The nature of violence – individual and collective

Susan Maiello (2000) distinguishes between acts of violence that have an 'object' or specific person (or group) 'in mind', and violence that appears to have no meaning or motive. In other words, Maiello separates what we might see as a directed hostility that expresses feelings of confusion, frustration or rage from violence that is random, bleak, cold, not always directed at specific groups or individuals, but rather at whatever happens to be in the way at that moment. The former suggests the capacity to hold another in mind, and to imagine (at least) some kind of relationship between the self-and-other, whereas the latter, Maiello suggests, is to do with the breakdown of a sense of relationship between 'the self' and 'other' in the external world. Here, acts may not even be 'hostile' in the aggressive sense of seeking relief through acting violently, but seem to be ongoing reflexive acts, without specific focus, and with a vague underlying emotional numbness and confusion. Where the 'other' cannot be imagined or related to, then unthinkable acts of violence are possible.

Maiello's distinction forms the backdrop for these reflections on the nature of violence and trauma, both collective and individual, in South Africa. To live in South Africa is to live in a violent society. I would suggest that violence, here, is not a single phenomenon, but complex and multi-faceted, impacting on all who live there. This violence is not always explicit or sudden with bullets, knives, pangas, and need not result in overt injury, death, or disappearance of family or friends. As a collective, institutionalised phenomenon, there is a violence that is low key, highly institutionalised, 'acceptable' and deadly. This may manifest as slow eroding of 'life': a paucity of material well-being, the absence of a sense of security, the absence of a supportive social network, and fragile life relationships (Stavrou 1997). It is socially sanctioned, either through state bureaucracy (as during the apartheid years), or less overtly (as in the current transition). This invisible and undramatic violence may be understood as a collective manifestation of Maiello's 'bleak' and 'cold' violence that does not have the capacity to relate to an 'other' that is too distant or different, since, historically, there has been little collective opportunity to get to know the 'other'. More extremely, perhaps, and under severe circumstances, this bleakness is acted upon to annihilate the collective 'other'. This phenomenon, incidentally, is not exclusive to South Africa, nor to living memory – as witnessed by other chapters in this book.

This collective bleakness explains the violence of Mpumi's life; borne slowly and softly, over centuries of poverty and invisibility. Her life includes the economic violence that ensures that it will remain materially poor for the foreseeable future; the socio-political-medical violence that prevents her from having access to the most powerful treatment for tuber-culosis – or the most hygienic and caring hospital environment; the edu-cational violence that keeps her mind somewhat dulled and small; and the social violence that imprisons her father, preventing him from caring for his children who are farmed out to relatives in various parts of the Northern Province. None of this violence is dramatic or especially touching: easy to ignore, Mpumi does not impinge too uncomfortably on my life or yours. She is a well-behaved, polite child, quiet and unassum-ing, a 'good' child living out her remaining hospital life and coming to music therapy once a week. Mpumi is a victim of slow, cold, ongoing institutionalised violence.

However, South Africa also experiences another kind of violence: hot focused violence that is not necessarily destructive in intent (although its consequences may be). (Adolf Guggenbuhl-Craig distinguishes between violence that is linked to *eros*, and that linked with *thanatos* – and of the seductiveness created by the thin membrane between the two.) This violence may be seen as an expression of rage directed at one who repre-sents 'otherness' in the mind of the attacker. This is a violence that lives within us all and may also be a response to being attacked. I have come to know it well within myself. For example, in the two instances when I have been the target of 'random' violence, because of representing an affluent group to my attackers, I lost my temper and assaulted them with a demonic power that apparently I possess when I need it. This was a quick, hot, focused violence: what we might understand as 'natural' or primitive retaliation, rather like the violence of giving birth or of two elephants fighting for dominance. This is the violence of some kind of 'survival' mechanism and is finite: once my violent physical act was completed, there was a sense of relief from the intensity that prompted me to act. After acting, I returned to an apparently 'non-violent' state, somewhat shaken, furious at having been targeted, but also pleased at having managed to escape more or less unscathed. Being a victim of violence instantly turned me into an violent survivor (and survivor of violence), and, critically, elicited momentary denial that I was attacking a living being with whom I might, in my work as a music therapist, have an empathic, intersubjective relationship.

Let us take this event a little further. Afterwards I might have decided that I needed a gun in self-defence, because this attack could happen to me again, at any time. A weapon would make me feel 'safe' – whilst also creating the (moral?) dilemma of 'destroying' in order to 'preserve' life. By carrying a weapon, I would be partaking in a spiral of sustained hostility towards some unspecific aggressor, whom I would be ready to 'destroy'. I might feel 'safer', but since the nature of my relationships is generally empathic and reciprocal, this 'safety' would carry some mental cost: I would need to sustain an imagined relationship with a potential attacker who does not exist, but might one day; constantly re-'minding' myself of my fragile existence and my potential to destroy another. Since the immediate energy generated by the act of being attacked would recede with time, I would need continuously to refuel that mental relational energy (which is not difficult given the levels of aggression and violence by drivers on South African roads), and constantly keep this 'other' as different to, and distant from, me as possible.

Here, I suggest, is an inner violence that originates 'innocently' – as a survival mechanism – and needs to become habitual and constantly refreshed so as not to lose a state of 'high alert'. This individual scenario may be seen as reflecting a collective, simmering violence in South African society. This state of 'high alert' is both exhausting and energising, seductive and repelling. 'High alert' can be understood as a psychological defence against feelings of helplessness, loss of control and threat of annihilation. This passive-aggressive violence may be seen as (symbolically) protecting a system that is threatened at a physical and psychic level. Possessing a weapon gives the illusion of control which helps to allay the anxiety that we might not be able to survive, or escape from, a violent confrontation.

These mental strategies (often acted upon physically with devastating consequences) draw from both kinds of violence (as explained by Maiello 2000), and may be understood as a complicated mix of her two categories (of 'relational' violence, and 'objectless' violence). A collective passive violence needs to sustain hostility towards an imagined aggressor who is both present and absent. The aggressor needs to be unknown and 'faceless' in the collective mind, whilst also sufficiently known and present to sustain a sense of distance and difference, emotionally and mentally. In apartheid South Africa, the systematic caricaturing and stereotyping of 'otherness' has achieved this distance and difference superbly. The 'other' becomes a faceless, dangerous, psychically distant and unfathomable, although never too far away. However, the mixture of this 'other' who needs to be both present and absent, needs collective mental energy to be sustained, and is psychically numbing and exhausting to children, adults, and anyone engaged in therapeutic work.

Having reflected on the nature of individual and collective violence, I now explore literature that explains the nature and origins of violence within the individual which has helped to inform my clinical work with traumatised children.

The origins of violence in childhood: a psychological perspective

Attachment and separation

Felicity de Zuluetta (1995) explains individual violence in terms of 'attachment gone wrong'. John Bowlby (1969) understood young children to need constant proximity (physical as well as emotional) to a primary attachment figure (usually the mother), not only for the child's protection and survival needs, but also for the child to develop the capacity to 'monitor' another. Not only does the child need the mother for protection, but also needs her to develop a sense of self-in-relation-to-other. Thus, implicit in 'attachment' are the roots of empathy and relationship. Studies explain that separation from this primary attachment figure can result in severe emotional distress: de Zuluetta reminds us of the work of Mary Ainsworth in the 1970s, which showed how children deal with separation, and how the nature of their distress is directly linked to the quality of their relationship with their mother (or primary caregiver). Since de Zuluetta alerts us to the link between the nature of young children's responses to separation and violent behaviour in later life, these are presented here in some detail.

Ainsworth categorised one-year-olds into three 'groups', which she called 'insecure-avoidant' (Group A), 'securely attached' (Group B), and 'insecure-ambivalent' (Group C). Group A (insecure-avoidant) showed no distress when separated from their mothers and 'ignored or 'avoided' them on return – though their rapid heartbeats belied their apparent indifference to her reappearance. Critically, Ainsworth found that these infants tended to have been emotionally deprived or rejected by their mothers.

Infants in Group B (securely attached) happily explored a room full of toys, using their mothers as a secure base. They were able to move away from her but constantly tracked her position and movements – and occasionally returned to her. Infants in this group were less likely to be distressed when mother left, and promptly sought her out on her return. They were also able to go to their mothers and receive comfort from her when distressed.

Unlike Group A, infants in Group C (insecure-ambivalent) instead of avoiding contact with their mother, seemed to need more of it – and were especially angry when their mother attempted to get them to play apart from her. The infants oscillated between seeking contact and avoiding contact with their mother, with some being actively angry and others more passive.

De Zuluetta (1995) reports on a later study that added a fourth group: 'disorganised-disorientated' (Group D). This group demonstrated ambivalent awareness of and connection to their mother or primary carer. Another study shifted the focus from the children to the mothers' own mechanisms for coping with separation, and how these impacted on the infants (Crowell and Feldman 1991). This alerts us to the links between mothers' own needs and emotional impoverishment and their reduced capacities to meet children's needs adequately – as we shall see later with 'Adam'.

These studies remind us of the risks to children who do not have a warm, empathic primary attachment of developing a limited (and possibly distorted) sense of themselves as being valued, and as having value to others. Group A infants were found to be more prone to angry behaviour than either Group B or C – though, critically, these infants' anger was rarely directed towards their mothers, but more usually towards some physical object. Since the mother–infant pairs studied were from 'non-clinical' households, de Zulueta (1995) comments that the link between Group A (insecure-avoidant) and human destructiveness suggests that apparently 'normal' children and adults can commit acts of destructiveness – as a consequence of not being able to tolerate the unexpected, the unusual – and that which is 'different'. At this point we might ask why and how, at such an early age, we already see signs of relationships at risk – with such devastating consequences.

One explanation is to be found in the developmental psychology literature in the 1980s that enriched our understandings of infants' acute sensitivities to the quality of relationship with their primary attachment figures – backed by psychoanalytic literature on infant observation (Miller *et al.* 1989). Since this literature base is well known, I visit it briefly.

Absence and presence

It seems that when mothers are absent 'mentally', even when remaining physically present with their babies (e.g. by assuming 'blank-face' conditions), babies as young as six weeks become distressed, attempt to elicit in their mothers some response towards them, and eventually give up and become withdrawn and emotionally distant (Murray 1992; Murray and Trevarthen 1985; Sinclair and Murray 1998; Trevarthen and Aitken 2001). Here, demonstrated empirically, are astonishingly early sensitivities to the quality and meaning of relationship and the effects of its absence. James Robertson, in the 1950s, showed that older children who experienced prolonged separation from families when hospitalised (Bower 1995) became emotionally detached and withdrawn, apparently repressing their feelings of need for their parents and developing indiscriminate, superficial contact with whatever adult was available: a familiar scenario to anyone who has visited an orphanage (and incidentally a locked adult psychiatric ward).

To explain these precocious sensitivities, and their links with acts of violence, we need to reflect on the inner conflicts created by emotional absence and its impacts on children's lives.

The conflicts of absence

It would seem that children placed in an intolerable situation (that is, of their mother disappearing, whether physically or mentally), are faced with difficult and conflicting emotions. Attachment theory tells us that in any situation of (emotional or physical) threat, infants will seek proximity and comfort from their main caregiver, no matter how ineffectual or abusive. However, where the mother (or primary attachment figure) is herself a source of anxiety, frustration or rage for the baby (which may be through her incapacity to manage the baby's emotional life) or, more extremely, forbids close physical contact, then infants need to deny their feelings of fear or anger in relation to their mother in order to remain as close as possible to her. This they do through the mechanisms of 'splitting' and 'projection'. In order to 'preserve' a good feeling about their mother, they need to 'split' off their 'good' feelings – making 'mum' wholly 'good' and themselves 'bad' (Maiello 2000).

Here we have an act of violence within the self. These internal acts ensure that the infant will experience one-sided and incomplete emotional states within the self and in relation to 'other'; and risk experiencing 'otherness' as threatening and intolerable, needing to be attacked or destroyed in order to avoid having to face it.

There is a common thread in these examples. At the very least, we see that infants have no choice about needing their mother (or primary caregiver). They need to ensure that she remains close to them, at whatever emotional cost to the child. We see, also, that even very young infants are acutely sensitive to the quality of nurturing and relationship that they receive – and even in a matter of seconds, experience rejection, emotional withdrawal and 'numbing' as they feel the 'loss' of their mother. Thus, a child used to being unloved, who has never known a loving, nurturing 'attachment' able to manage both loving and difficult feelings, finds it difficult – if not impossible – to develop a sense of self in relation to other that can tolerate both positive and negative feelings about both the self and the other. Children whose parents show little empathy and love towards them develop a poor sense of self-esteem, and a poor sense of empathy towards others. They are generally unable to imagine how it might be that the other feels, never having had their own difficult feelings managed for them on their behalf. They have also never been seen or 'known' as whole – both good and bad – by their caregivers. In contrast, then, to a securely attached child, such a child (child A) may find another's pain intolerable on several counts. The emotional pain of any child may trigger A's own split-off, painful feelings, never reconciled within A. A is unable to comfort the distressed child, since A is unable to acknowledge both his or her own and the other's feelings of pain. Moreover, A has no sense of having been comforted with his or her own difficult feelings, and needs to constantly split these off, in order to maintain a fragile sense of 'self'. Such a child may hit another child who cries (or bully a child who appears weaker or feeble), in an effort to make weakness disappear.

Here are some aspects to do with acts of violence as rooted within a child who cannot endure the disturbing feelings rekindled by seeing a helpless or frightened 'other'. So intolerable is this 'difference' between the child and the 'other' that the child needs to attack or destroy this 'difference' (in fact, this 'difference' is false: rather, it is the 'sameness' of the terror and helplessness that provokes a reaction within A). In other words, children cannot 'help' being violent or destructive – and this compulsive and repetitive quality can be seen in how children play, literally, and in how they 'are' in music therapy. More of this later. In contrast to child A, a 'securely attached' child, who has known nurturing and containment by its mother, is more able to empathise with and comfort another child in distress. Not frightened of the anxiety or confusion that the crying child might portray, having had these difficult feelings managed by its mother, this child manages to sustain the emotional links with an 'other' who might be in a very 'different' emotional state.

Adam

At this point I would like to think of Adam (not his real name). He is seven and attends a primary school in downtown Johannesburg. His mother is a domestic worker (cleaning lady) who has had a series of live-in boy-friends throughout Adam's life. She leaves home early in the morning and returns in the early evening. Adam and his mother live in a block of flats in an inner city slum area. Adam has no father and apparently roams the city after school, waiting for his mother to get home from work. We know little of his early life, but can begin to speculate about it, drawing from de Zuluetta's insights. It is probable that the quality of nurturing which he received from his young, single mother was somewhat deficient. We can imagine that she might herself have needed nurturing and care, and attempted to receive this from her various boyfriends. Adam's teachers describe him as cold, distant, unable to relate to other children. The teachers at school do not understand him: he seems impervious to any attempts at care or relationship and his schoolwork is extremely poor. The school has arranged for an educational psychologist to assess Adam, and the report states that his cognitive functioning is below average for his age.

Individual weekly music therapy sessions are provided at the school, and I notice his dirty clothes and unclean smells. He is a slight, pale child with a bland reserve and a courteous, rather 'flat' manner. Each week in music therapy we 'go through the motions' of making music together: we play a greeting song on the guitar and he strums and sings; we play together freely on the drums, cymbals and other percussion instruments; and when we do a turn-taking game on the xylophone, with each of us cross-legged on the floor with the xylophone between us, Adam plays repetitively, barely changing what he does. A listener untrained in clinical music-making would hear our music as coherent, if somewhat repetitive. However, in addition to my clinical-musical alertness, I note my mind-numbing paralysis in sessions: nothing I do (or do not do) in my contribution to our joint music-making appears relevant to who he is and what he does. I feel cut off, non-existent and have no sense of agency or purpose in our sessions. I do not look forward to Adam each week.

Let us now try and make sense of what happens in the sessions. Here is a child whose early life has been one of ongoing violence to the 'self'. He is not an 'abused' child in the usual sense of the word: his mother probably did the best she could for him – although we know nothing about his father or any of the boyfriends who have passed through the household. This child is emotionally 'shut down'. None of us, at the school, have a sense of him; neither does he seem to have a sense of himself or of himself-in-relation-to-other. Here is a bleak interior emotional void – apparently impossible to reach in our music therapy sessions; not even present enough to be aggressive towards other children in the school playground. His manner towards me is courteous and intangible. I have no sense of who this child really is and in his presence I experience a numb alienation from myself. I have no 'warmth' towards him – and neither 'dislike' nor 'like' him. There doesn't seem to be someone 'there' either to like or dislike – this child is vacant and I experience myself as non-existent when I am with him.

After some months Adam vanishes. He has not been at school for the past three days and the staff cannot find out what has happened to him. He has disappeared out of my life. I cannot honestly say that I 'mourn' his disappearance. He was never 'there' in order to 'disappear' in the first place. I cannot say that music therapy 'did' anything for him – I am not sure. It is as though he never existed, never lived, in my mind.

Some months later, I watch a video of one of our sessions together. I notice that in one of our improvisations (Adam on horns and me at the piano) there is a quality – barely present – that suggests a hint of something different. In the video, he watches me closely as I play, he is intent and focused on what we are doing, there is almost – dare I think it – a flicker of interest and warmth in what he does.

And now I see, with some shame, that this child numbed me so much that I missed something, much as Adam himself probably misses much of what goes on around him. Had we been able continue our work, Adam might gradually have been able to begin trusting our being together, and he might have begun 'playing' in the creative, fluid and relational sense of co-creating his life. Our work together was only just beginning – but I may be imagining it. I remain unsure, puzzled, uneasy about our work together.

Making sense of violence in childhood

To recap, we can see how children who have not experienced fluid, reciprocal, intersubjective emotional relationships have a decreased capacity to develop a sense of valuing themselves or others. They may be unable to develop or sustain fluid, intersubjective emotional relationships with other human beings. If we return to Maiello's distinctions about violence (2000), we can begin to understand that a child (like Adam) whose sense of self has been destroyed through continuous lack of relationship, is at risk of becoming the adolescent and adult whose lack of empathy or connection with others can result in numbing, unthinkable acts of violence (Gilligan 2000) – violence that has no remorse or understanding about inflicting pain onto others since 'others' do not 'exist' or are too unknown to exist meaningfully. This random, cold violence is devoid of emotion; it is an isolated, unrelating, unaggressive violence.

In contrast, a child who has known nurturing and relationship is more likely to act violently with a specific 'object' in mind; is more likely to act out of a 'hot' emotional state – and despite brutal, hostile and aggressive acts (of which all human beings are capable), such a child will still retain the potential for relationship and ultimately for repairing the human links that violence risks severing. This is the paradox of a child like Mpumi: victim of slow, systematic institutionalised violence, but at the same time, loved and cared for by her own parents, she retains a sense of relationship in mind and has the capacity to feel lonely and isolated in hospital. In music therapy she expresses feelings to do with missing her family and of remembering emotional warmth and intimacy, recreated in the sessions. Adam, in contrast, has little concept of emotional warmth and relationship. I doubt that Adam feels 'lonely' at school: I suspect that he is too numbed emotionally for this, and it is this numbness that our music-making recreates within me.

If we return briefly to my own act of violence as an adult described earlier, we can see that my 'psychic' survival of these incidents suggests an emotional resilience: the result of having grown up with an adequately caring and psychologically 'coping' mother, able to provide a psychologically, physically and emotionally 'safe' environment. My 'psychological buffer zone' protected my world from crumbling, even though my very existence was threatened. After each incident, I was able to ask for – and receive – emotional support from family and friends. However, I still today feel not the slightest remorse for the physical – or mental – pain I might have inflicted on those who tried to turn me into a victim: and here is the nub. This apparent lack of 'care' about inflicting pain on another (from one generally empathic and capable of warmth) can be understood as psychological denial of the fact that 'someone' inflicted harm on me. This does not fit with my experience of emotional resonance with the 'other', and so I need to distance the 'other' sufficiently in my mind to be able not to 'care' about what I did (or might have done) to them. This 'coping' mechanism enables me to continue living in South Africa – watchfully but not unduly traumatised. However, had I been less emotionally resilient, lacking in a supportive community and (like Adam) unable to want, need and cultivate emotional relationships, then such an act might have resulted in a further 'shut-down' towards 'otherness' and a prolonged fragmenting of my sense of self and my sense of self-and-other.

The above reflections help to clarify that violence within the self, towards the self and towards others, can be seen as linked to 'acts' that have to do with 'separation'. The act of separation is in itself violent, while it may lead to violence within and towards the self, and towards others. Thus, violence separates us from ourselves (resulting in a split within us between 'good' and 'bad', and resulting in our needing to be 'wholly bad', in order to live in a 'good' emotional environment). Violence may separate us from others (literally, when our primary caregiver is absent, physically or emotionally, or when our daily environment is brutally removed or destroyed); and it can separate us from 'society' (as in Mpumi's life which remains small and limited, excluded from educational and medical possibilities).

I believe that an understanding of these internal psychological mechanisms of violent behaviour is critical if we are to begin working with the impact of violence in South African society on those who inflict it, and those who receive it. After all, the two exist in relation to one another.

Trauma and music therapy

One understanding of trauma is that it is the emotional and psychological impact of acts that impinge on the self (i.e. the effects of a violent act or of living in a violent environment). Vivi Stavrou (1997) alerts us to the casual use of the word trauma in South Africa, where violence is pervasive, to describe confusion, anxiety or distress, and what she calls 'losses of living'; whether these are material losses, loss of feelings of safety or power, loss of community or of relationships. This 'psycho-social' trauma she sees as the cumulative build-up of stress.

Minor trauma results from illness, a 'natural' death, or a one-off act of violence. It may result in a temporary fragmenting of a sense of self that is secure, ongoing and coherent. In contrast, major trauma results from acts of war, the ongoing absence of stability and unpredictable, sustained violent acts against the self. Here the impacts may include a more severe emotional fragmenting resulting in a sense of inner annihilation, in emotional flatness and a sense of inner 'deadness' – not unlike Adam. Of course these are rather simple divisions and the effects of any of these acts are tempered by our emotional and psychological state prior to the event. In addition, we need to distinguish between acts of violence that are 'natural' (e.g. natural disasters) and acts of violence that carry human aggression, underpinned by hostility and intentional destructiveness. Here further distinction can be made between being personally targeted (e.g. in an assassination attempt), and being targeted for what we might represent (e.g. a car hijack victim targeted for driving that particular car). The Tavistock model (Garland 1998) presents two axes: an *event axis* ranging from accidents to intentional acts, and an *individual axis* that ranges from acts which are sought out (as in high risk sports) and those not sought out (as in being in the wrong place at the wrong time).

Many children in South Africa lack basic nurturing, thanks to fragmented families (like Mpumi's), or poorly resourced community structures that undermine their parents' capacities to be present emotionally. Many continue to live in abusive and violent situations, with no relief from the lack of nurturing and no prospect of a violence-free environment. What are the long-term effects on children? *DSM IV* (American Psychiatric Association 1994) identifies the symptoms of post traumatic stress disorder as including hyper-arousal (irritability, insomnia, inability to concentrate, nightmares) and emotional numbing (a decreased ability to attend to the environment). However, the persistence of violence means that many children have little hope of returning to a 'trauma-free' environment. They feel out of control in their lives and lose confidence in their (uncaring and unpredictable) environment. At school they exhibit 'bad behaviour'; they are aggressive and disruptive in the classroom and aggressive towards other children in the playground (Pavlicevic 1994; Ross 1996). Here is the potential for another cycle of violence.

What can music therapy offer children who live with and in violence? Improvisational music therapy (Bruscia 1987) offers an opportunity for 'playing' – literally, playing music – by making spontaneous sounds on available instruments or on available sound objects (e.g. tables, glasses, the floor, various parts of the body). This act of music-making is not a solitary one, but happens with the music therapist who joins in with the child's spontaneous music-making. Therapist and child together create a relationship through spontaneous music sounds, which potentially engage, stimulate and evoke the child's imagination, offering an opportunity to 'recreate' and 're-image' life. This musical relationship, which often needs no words, can enable the child to revisit painful events and transform them into a more manageable reality. Everything in 'play' needs to remain open to possibilities, because it is only in this way that children can gain mastery over their world and their lives (Levine 1998; McKeown 2001).

One helpful concept in thinking about music therapy with traumatised children – which I believe applies to any therapeutic work – is the respect for and focus on the whole child. Nordoff and Robbins (1977) write of *The Music Child* – which they describe as that part inside each one of us that is alive, healthy, creative. Their concept grew from their work with deeply handicapped children who, despite profound disabilities, were able to 'play', to live creatively and to engage fully in a dynamic, playful, utterly committed musical-therapeutic event with the therapists (Aigen 1998).

This concept of the *Music Child* has another connotation regarding work with traumatised children. Here I would like to suggest that by focusing our therapeutic work exclusively on children's trauma we risk fitting a multidimensional, complex child into a 'small' space – called 'the traumatised child'. In her provocative and, I believe, 'truthful' paper, Stephanie Grenadier (1995) questions professionals' apparent need to elicit trauma, often encouraging patients to remember and uncover traumatic incidents. This, she suggests, encourages patients to remain 'victims' or 'survivors' of violence and abuse. The *Music Child* concept integrates all aspects of the child in music therapy. Whilst not denying the crisis that children may be experiencing, making music spontaneously with a music therapist offers the opportunity to be heard and known as a 'whole' – managing and evoking the difficult, frightening, playful and creative feelings and tapping into the child's own potential for healing.

I conclude with a last vignette. Some years ago, I worked as part of a multidisciplinary team in a clinic for traumatised children in a Gauteng township. (Townships are distinct from towns in South Africa. The former were developed by the apartheid state as part of the policy of 'separate development', to be inhabited by black people, and generally lacked basic infrastructures such as electricity, tarred roads and sanitation.) I would arrive on Tuesday mornings and find the waiting room full of young children accompanied by mothers or – more usually – grandmothers. Many had been there for hours, awaiting to be seen by 'the multidisciplinary team'. The waiting room always had an air of anxiety and expectation. The team of 'experts' was invested with hope by the adults, and with trepidation by the children. Some weeks after beginning to work there, I saw that (in the middle of medical, psychological and assessments) the most valuable thing that I could offer the children was an opportunity for us to play together. Playing seemed to me the most obvious way to be together, during this difficult day for both the children and their parents. In music therapy they – and often their mothers or grandmas – would come and we would play, sing and dance music together, despite the lack of common language between these children, and between them and me. Their mothers or grandmothers would watch us with pleasure – and chat among themselves (often competing with us for the available decibels in the room). They would see their 'traumatised' children – the victims of abuse, the clinic 'patients' – participating, at times shyly, reluctantly, at times with gusto, leadership, initiative and pleasure in music 'play'. I would see on the mothers' faces a dawning recollection that their child was also creative, playful, able to initiate and respond, to take leadership roles and to support the initiatives of others in our group sessions. During the sessions, the children shifted from being only 'traumatised children' in their mothers' minds.

However, some children, week after week, remained unable to 'play', unable to be a part of the group; unable to experience and co-create relationship. Here I experienced trauma dominating a child's way of being. In my experience, such a child often makes music in a repetitive, less flexible and less transformative way, and is less able to relate to other children in the group. As therapist I need to remain with the child where the child is at that time, in the child's endless repetition and emotional 'stuckness';

'accompanying' the child through his or her own discovery of life in both its fragmented stuckness and in its potential for fluid, creative living (Levine 1998). Anne Alvarez (1992) reminds us that therapeutic work with children who are emotionally 'shattered' (in contrast to children whose lives are temporarily out of balance) needs the understanding that various fragments cannot be 'stitched together', so to speak, but need to 'grow together'. This growing is enabled by the therapist tolerating the child's fragmentation and exploring, together with the child, each of those fragments: a long, protracted task that may feel abusive, draining and very painful to the therapist. Alvarez also reminds us that the very notion of trauma assumes some previous, trauma-free development, and a non-abusive environment that helps children to gain a sense of selfhood. Many South African children lack a violence-free life; many are trauma-tised as a result of experiencing violence in an ongoing, undramatic way.

I have learnt (somewhat slowly) that even a fragmented, deeply stuck child can resuscitate a sense of self that – somewhere or other – remains creative and growthful. It is immensely important, clinically, to hold the *Music Child* in my mind, rather than being preoccupied only with the part of the child that is traumatised (Grenadier 1995). This 'non-traumatised' part of the child – which I parallel to the *Music Child* – has the potential to activate the child's own healing process. It is this latent 'wholeness' within children that I attempt to address and 'grow' in the music therapy sessions, enabling the children to access and become familiar with (and reminded of) their own healing and emotional resources.

The weekly music therapy sessions at the clinic in Gauteng offered the children such an opportunity: whatever and however a child played, sang or danced was not 'pathologised', but rather, was received as an expression of 'self' by the child. And responded to accordingly in music. An interesting sideline here is that the music therapy briefing in the multidisciplinary meetings at the end of each afternoon often reminded the staff of the parts in themselves that were not shattered, exhausted and numbed by the day's stories and events. Here we need to be reminded of how difficult and painful it is for us as adults to see suffering in children. Shirley Hoxter (1983) draws our attention to the dilemma of maintaining our sensitivity towards the child without ourselves becoming numbed by overwhelming and unbearable feelings. In other words, as music therapists we need to ensure that our intentions of offering a relationship do not become impaired and diminished through our own need to distance ourselves from the child's pain and loss. This is what happened to me in my work with Adam.

To conclude

Each of the children described in this chapter was offered a relationship which received whatever the child did as an act of emotional creativity. A child banging loudly and inflexibly on a drum and effectively shutting out everyone else in the room is not only expressing rage, expelling frustration or wanting to shut out the world, as I might experience in the countertransference. This child is also displaying enormous energy, and the quality of this energy has the potential to be transformed into creativity by a therapist who is not disturbed by the 'noise', who can tolerate the child's frustration, who does not need to tell the child to 'play softly', and who can meet the child's chaos through her own music making and, together with the child, allow the vibrancy and potency of the 'noise' to grow a relationship through music – that is, if the child has the capacity to acknowledge another person. In other words, 'transformation' does not deny, ignore, or render meaningless the rage, frustration and fragmentation – but allows the 'duality' of musical energy to emerge. In this way, the musical act can also be one of creativity, relationship and ultimately self-healing.

For Mpumi, able to extend towards and receive human relationship, music therapy offered an opportunity to express and share with the therapist her feelings of longing for her family, of loneliness in the hospital, of sadness at her small life. Her weekly session and the warm intimacy that grew between the therapist and her were a great relief to Mpumi, giving her a sense that someone understood how she felt. For Adam, apparently unable to have a sense of self-and-other, weekly music therapy was a time when I as therapist was there to accompany him and share with him – as far as he allowed me to – his isolated bleak life. Much of the time, however, I was kept on the periphery of his existence, paralysed and with no capacity to act beyond 'reacting' (rather than responding) to what he did in music. For the group of young children, at the Gauteng clinic, group music therapy was an emotional and physical space in which they could recover themselves through the various roles that children naturally assume, with great flexibility when playing together.

Finally, it would be fanciful to suggest that music therapy can reverse the devastating effects of ongoing violence in South African society. Indeed, there is an argument that questions the validity of addressing the effects of violence when clients return, daily, to that environment, rendered more vulnerable by their therapeutic experiences. However, I hope to have clarified that violence in South Africa is enormously complex, and complicated further at this time of sociological, political and economic transition – all of which impact on the music therapy situation. However, despite the adverse environments that many children experience daily and despite their limited experience of nurturing and reciprocal attachment, the act of shared music-making in music therapy offers the opportunity and confidence to rebuild relationships with themselves, with one another and ultimately, hopefully, within their communities.

References

Aigen, K. (1998) *Paths of Development in Nordoff-Robbins Music Therapy.* Barcelona: Gilsum.

Ainsworth, M.D.S., Bleher, M.C., Waters, E. and Wall, S. (1978) *Patterns of Attachment: Assessed in Strange Situations and at Home.* Hillsdale, NJ: Erlbaum.

Alvarez, A. (1992) *Live Company: Psychoanalytic Psychotherapy with Autistic, Borderline, Deprived and Abused Children.* London: Tavistock/Routledge.

American Psychiatric Association (1994) *Diagnostic and Statistical Manual of Mental Disorders Ed 4.* Washington DC, American Psychiatric Association.

Bower, M. (1995) 'Children and institutions.' In J. Trowell and M. Bower *The Emotional Needs of Young Children.* London: Routledge, pp.22–32.

Bowlby, J. (1969) *Attachment and Loss.* London: Penguin.

Bruscia, K. (1987) *Improvisational Modes of Music Therapy.* Springfield IL: Charles C Thomas.

Bunt, L. (1994) *Music Therapy: An Art Beyond Words.* London: Routledge.

Crowell, J. and Feldman, S. (1991) 'Mothers' working models of attachment relationships and mother and child behavior during separation and reunion.' *Developmental Psychology 27,* 4, 597–605.

De Zuluetta, F. (1995) 'Children and violence.' In J. Trowell and M. Bower *The Emotional Needs of Young Children*. London: Routledge, pp.264–271.

Garland, C. (1998) *Understanding Trauma*. London: Duckworth.

Gilligan, J. (2000) *Violence: Reflections on Our Deadliest Epidemic*. London: Jessica Kingsley Publishers.

Grenadier, S. (1995) 'The place wherein truth lies: an expressive therapy perspective on trauma, innocence and human nature.' *The Arts in Psychotherapy 22*, 5, 393–402.

Guggenbuhl-Craig, A. (1995) *From the Wrong Side: A Paradoxical Approach to Psychology*. Woodstock, CT: Spring Publications.

Hoxter, S. (1983) 'Some feelings aroused in working with severely deprived children.' In M. Boston and R. Szur (eds) *Psychotherapy with Severely Deprived Children*. London: Maresfield Library, pp.125–132.

Levine, E.G. (1998) 'On the play ground.' In S.K. Levine and E.G. Levine (eds) *Foundations of Expressive Arts Therapies: Theoretical and Clinical Perspectives*. London: Jessica Kingsley Publishers, pp.257– 273.

McKeown, A. (2001) 'The impact of conflict on children's play in Northern Ireland: play deprivation – causes and effects.' In M. Smyth and K. Thomson (eds) *Working with Children and Young People in Violently Divided Societies: papers from South Africa and Northern Ireland*. Belfast: Community Conflict Impact on Children, pp.231–242.

Maiello, S. (2000) 'Broken links: attack or breakdown?' *Journal of Child Psychotherapy 26*, 1, pp.5–24.

Miller, L., Rustin, M. and Shuttleworth, J. (eds.) *Closely Observed Infants*. London: Routledge, pp.264–271.

Murray, L. (1992) 'The impact of postnatal depression on infant development.' *Journal of Child Psychology and Psychiatry 33*, 543–561.

Murray, L. and Trevarthen, C. (1985) 'Emotional regulation of interactions between two-month-olds and their mothers.' In T. Field and N. Fox (eds) *Social Perception in Infants*. Norwood NJ: Ablex, pp.177–197.

Nordoff, P. and Robbins, C. (1977) *Creative Music Therapy*. New York: John Day.

Pavlicevic, M. (1994) 'Between chaos and creativity: music therapy with traumatised children in South Africa.' *Journal of British Music Therapy 4*, 2, 5–9.

Ross, C. (1996) 'Conflict at school: the use of an art therapy approach to support children who are bullied.' In M. Liebmann (ed) *Arts Approaches to Conflict*. London: Jessica Kingsley Publishers, pp.131–151.

Sinclair, D. and Murray, L. (1998) 'The effects of postnatal depression on children's adjustment to school.' *British Journal of Psychiatry 172*, 58–63.

Stavrou, V. (1997) 'A case of severe word abuse?' *Recovery April*, 3–6.

Trevarthen, C. and Aitken, K. (2001) 'Infant intersubjectivity: research, theory, and clinical applications.' *Journal of Child Psychology and Psychiatry 42*, 1, 3–48.

CHAPTER 6

UK
Music and Human Rights

Matthew Dixon

This chapter is based on three years of work as a music therapist at the Medical Foundation for the Care of Victims of Torture in London. This work gives me a particular interest in the theme of this book, music and trauma, from a particular perspective: music used as therapy for trauma resulting from political violence.

The chapter begins by outlining the work of the Medical Foundation, and introduces some questions raised by working as a music therapist there, in particular questions about the relationship between music and violence. These questions are addressed by referring to a case study of music therapy work. The chapter ends with some conclusions about music therapy as a treatment for trauma, with some implications from music therapy practice for a concept of human rights.

The Medical Foundation

The Medical Foundation is a charitable organisation helping people who have experienced political violence. Political violence is defined as organised physical and emotional violence committed by one group (political, ethnic, or religious) against members of another group. This definition is important in practical terms because it determines access to an organisation whose resources are increasingly stretched. The Medical

Foundation offers a wide range of services: primarily medical, therapeutic, legal, social work and interpreting. On the basis of its work with individual victims, it also campaigns for human rights worldwide.

Work at the Medical Foundation brings up a wide range of issues, some of which are beyond the scope of this chapter. The overwhelming majority of the Medical Foundation's clients are asylum seekers or refugees who have fled oppressive regimes abroad. As well as the traumatic consequences of their experience of political violence, refugees have lost people, home, culture and every familiar aspect of their former lives. Often with very limited English and little assistance, they have to negotiate labyrinthine asylum and benefit systems, with harsh consequences if they put a foot wrong. Frequently they find themselves the subject of aggressive prejudice, particularly since the question of asylum in Britain has become a political football, kicked around with increasing abandon during the 2001 parliamentary election campaign.

It is important to bear in mind the dislocation, losses and uncertainty that are part of becoming a refugee. However, these issues will not be addressed in this chapter, which focuses specifically on the direct traumatic consequences of experiencing political violence. First, I will outline the central concerns of the chapter by discussing the relationship between music and violence.

Music and violence

When Congreve (1697) says that 'music hath charms to soothe a savage breast', he is describing music as a kind of antidote to violence. This line is so often quoted that it must reflect some kind of truth for many people. Music is often talked about as if it had a special link with love, kindness, tenderness and human warmth, and there is some support for this in scientific research. Detailed analysis of interactions between mothers and babies reveals that their exchanges of sounds and gestures are essentially musical. (see Stern (1977), particularly the chapter 'Structure and Timing' (pp. 87–105) and Stern (1985), particularly the chapter 'Affect Attunement' (pp.138–161)). Often he draws specific parallels between mother–infant interaction and music; at other times he implies parallels by using musical terminology in his descriptions. These exchanges develop the baby's primary and formative relationship and so form the basis for their sense of identity, communication and relationship. Naturally, music therapists get very excited about this research, but where does violence fit into this picture? Is music limited to the expression and development of warmth and tenderness? If so, how can it adequately express and contain traumatic experiences of political violence?

Of course, there is another side to music. I gave a talk to psychology of music students at a university and beforehand the students were asked to declare their chosen topics for a project. A strikingly large number had chosen to look at violence in rap music. Music has a long association with violence. Throughout history it has been used in battle, for rousing, rallying and marching. Opposing factions often adopt songs, which are sung to express cohesion within the faction and hostility to other groups. Songs have acquired particularly strong resonances during the Troubles in Northern Ireland, but you can see the process in action on any football terrace.

At first sight, there may not seem to be a contradiction here. Music has many uses and a wide variety of possible meanings, and I have merely illustrated two of them. However, for a music therapist working with victims of political violence, these two facets of music raise an important question: what is the nature of music? Is it able equally to express all sides of human nature, or does it have a particular association with love, as opposed to violence? Is music a neutral medium through which the therapist works, or does it have intrinsic qualities which play a part in the therapeutic process? I shall address these questions by considering an example from my work at the Medical Foundation, and by drawing a distinction between what music *represents*, what it *expresses* and what the act of making music *is*.

Shireen (1)

Shireen is not her real name and I have avoided giving details which might identify her.

Shireen arrived in Britain with her sister as a refugee at the age of 15. Members of her family had been killed and she herself had suffered terrible experiences in prison. When I started working with her she was inseparable from her sister, following her so closely that she seemed like her shadow. Shireen had not spoken since she arrived in Britain. She was clearly terrified and seemed to be trying to hide, even to deny her own existence.

In our first three sessions she was very withdrawn, but with sustained encouragement and help she would reach out and pluck the strings of a guitar, briefly and tentatively interacting with my singing before she withdrew again. As the sessions progressed her playing became more extended and varied, and little by little she seemed to be emerging from her silence.

This gradual progress was interrupted dramatically in the fourth session, when I gave her a side drum and drumstick. After initial silence she played quietly and sparsely, as she had done before, interacting closely with my melody as I played the oboe. However, this lasted for a few seconds only before her playing suddenly changed to a very loud regular beat. The violence of her playing was shocking, both in itself and as a contrast to her previous quiet music. She hit the drum seemingly as hard as she could, and I was forcibly struck by a sense of both anger and determination in her beating. Her playing was reckless, so that sometimes she hit the rim of the drum rather than the skin, and sometimes she caught a cymbal that was nearby. At the end of the session I found that the drumstick was badly chipped and dented.

She hit the drum with such force that I could hardly hear myself as I played with her. Her beating was a steady pulse at a constant tempo, with no rhythmic variation. When I very slightly accelerated the tempo of my playing, offering the opportunity for a mutual change in the music, her response was to play even louder at her established tempo, drowning me out. Her beating was so loud and inflexible that she was effectively blocking out my participation in the music. She was now emphatically asserting her presence, in complete contrast to her previous silence and withdrawal. However, the interaction we had developed through her previous, tentative playing had been lost. Her drum playing was so rigid and forceful that I had no place in it, and as I played with her I felt that it was now my existence which was being denied.

What music represents

A while after I had finished working with Shireen (by which time she had started speaking again), she told me that when she had played the drum so forcefully, she had imagined that she was taking revenge on the 'fat men' who had beaten her in prison. I did not know this at the time and she could not have told me. I could hear the strength of her playing and feel the way it excluded me, but the music did not convey to me the specific scene that she was imagining. This is because music, unlike language or pictures, is not a representational medium. It is not in the nature of music to symbolise or refer to anything else.

During some periods in the history of western music, composers have developed an interest in 'programme music', or music which 'tells a story'. However, the music cannot really 'tell' the story. Once the listener has been told the programme, they can appreciate the way that the music illustrates the narrative, but the listener could never deduce the story from the music alone. In the same way, factional songs are associated with a particular cause through their lyrics, or by conventional association, rather than through any intrinsic quality in the music itself. When the psychology of music students declared their interest in violence in rap music, I wondered where they would find that violence. They would have no trouble finding representations of violence in the words, but would they find violence in the music itself? Where would they even start looking for it – in the act of making the music, in its effects, or somewhere else? I felt that if they were going to discuss music, rather than words, they were taking on quite a subtle and difficult project.

In a number of therapies, particularly those which ultimately derive from psychoanalysis, the naming, analysis and exploration of current difficulties and their origins form an important part of the therapeutic process, bringing conflicts to a conscious level where they can be resolved. Clearly, music cannot be therapeutic in this way, because the processes of naming and analysis are not available. Some music therapists place great emphasis on talking about the music that is made in sessions, and conceive of the therapeutic process as being an analytic one taking place within this talking. Others (and I would include myself in this second group) conceive of the therapy as taking place within the music itself, where the process must clearly be of some other kind. Bruscia

(1987) gives a detailed description of a number of different theoretical strands in music therapy. For a discussion of the nature of therapeutic process in music therapy from different perspectives, see Streeter (1999), writing in the *British Journal of Music Therapy*, and the replies to her article in the next issue: Aigen (1999), Ansdell (1999) Brown (1999) and Pavlicevic (1999). Because Shireen was not talking when we started working together, there was a particular need for this 'other kind' of therapeutic process.

What music expresses

Most of the connections between music and violence which I mentioned earlier are symbolic connections, by conventional association rather than through any intrinsic violence in the music itself; most, but not all, because some of the connections are expressive rather than representational. Music has a particular capacity to animate us, physically and emotionally, and it is this quality that is brought into use whenever music is used for rousing, rallying or marching in battle. It is not a specifically violent quality – the same animating function of music, even some of the very same music, might be used for dancing, for instance – but it is an intrinsic quality of music that can serve as an incitement to violence.

The expressive qualities of musical performance can be altered for particular purposes. When songs get adapted as football chants, the melody remains the same, but it will be sung in a particular way (usually loud, the voice held in the back of the throat and each note emphatically accented) that makes it come across as provocative and combative. The students who examined violence in rap music may well have found some of the same expressive qualities, particularly rhythmic accentuation.

People express themselves through music, and the range of expression includes qualities such as loud volume, forceful accentuation and rough tone, which can be associated with violence, even if not exclusively violent. All of these qualities characterised Shireen's drum playing, and in this sense the violence and anger in her playing were unmistakable. Previously, when she had been silent and withdrawn, I had nevertheless experienced her as a strong presence in the room, her silence very intense. This unexpressed intensity found a voice in her drum playing and this was clearly an important advance in the therapeutic process, moving her from near silence to assertive expression.

This brings us to another common idea of therapeutic process. People's difficulties can be seen as being caused by unmanageable feelings which they hold inside themselves. If they can express these feelings, they achieve a catharsis which resolves the difficulties. Shireen's drum playing illustrates this process well. It was apparent from the intensity of her silence that she was holding something in. In expressing this 'something' through her drum playing, she stepped out of her shadowy, silent existence and back into the world. I would like to expand the explanation a little, to say that music making is a physical and cognitive act as well as an emotional one, and that what Shireen was expressing (and what we all express when we make music) was a more comprehensive picture of herself – perhaps 'state of being' rather than just feelings.

This expanded idea of catharsis gives a pretty good description of the therapeutic process I have described, but it also leaves many things unexplained and unresolved. For instance, the clearest, most direct and unmistakable expression of violence and anger in Shireen's drum playing was the way she damaged the drumstick. But of all the aspects of her playing, this was the most purely physical and the least musical. This suggests that there were other elements in her playing, apart from pure expression, which were essential to its nature as music. If we view her playing just as a cathartic outpouring, we ignore important musical components which define and clarify our relationship. The most crucial of these was the element of organisation, apparent in her steady pulse. This pulse acted as a link between us, allowing us to play together – I could join her at the same tempo. It also acted as a barrier, limiting the development of our playing together – she emphatically refused to change tempo with me, blocking the possibility of interactive flexibility between us.

Shireen (2)

Another shortcoming in the idea of music therapy as a cathartic process emerges when I continue the story of Shireen's music therapy beyond the fourth session. So far, I have described just the very beginning of the process, in which she progressed from near silence to powerful expression. I have described this as her stepping out from her shadowy, silent existence and emerging into the world. However, the inflexibility of her playing severely limited interaction between us and meant that she was still essentially isolated. Though *in* the world she was not yet *engaged with* the world.

Her powerful, rigid drum playing became a constant feature of our sessions over the next ten weeks, to the point where she seemed rather stuck with it. The act of expressing through music had produced important developments for her, but seemed to take her only so far and no further. The main limiting factor was the rigidity of her music, and the important question for me was how I could help her to develop beyond this rigidity. As I played music with her, I tried to build on the small glimpses of variety I caught in her beating, to draw her into more flexible music or to suggest different ways of playing. Gradually she developed a little rhythmic flexibility, particularly syncopations, which added an incongruous, light-hearted touch to her music.

After a break of four weeks, her music once again changed dramatically, so that now her playing was chaotic and discontinuous rather than rigid. As before, the effect was to limit interaction between us severely. As I played with her I found that the lack of structure gave me nothing to hold on to, and her music felt like sand which slipped through my fingers.

I shall not go into this period of the therapy in detail, but instead will move on to the turning point in the process, which happened during the nineteenth session. Shireen was playing constantly shifting, unpredictable music on a piano, as she had done for many weeks. Playing a second piano, I slowly alternated two chords, introducing a strong contrasting element of structure. In order to cut through her thick textures, I made the chords as simple and clear as possible (each consisted of just two notes). Her initial reaction was to play louder, drowning me out, as she had done before with her rigid drum playing. However, she gradually began to respond to the structure, following my harmonic changes. Suddenly, she got up from the piano, went over to a set of bells and played a series of clear and simple melodies based around scale patterns.

Having previously felt excluded by her chaotic playing, I now found myself not only able to accompany her, but also compelled to do so. The clarity of direction in her phrasing was drawing the music out of me. My two alternating chords soon became inadequate and I expanded the range of my harmonies as her melody developed. Each note seemed to have significance, to have an essential place in the whole. The music seemed to have a life of its own, drawing us into playing together with an intimacy we had never achieved before.

From this point onwards Shireen's music changed completely, becoming both structured and flexible, and as a result interactive. She would initiate sections based on pulse, which we would vary together, interspersing them with sections of rhythmically freer music. Each change from section to section was a point of connection between us, something we made together. Development within each section maintained this contact at a more subtle level.

Her development of interaction in the music therapy sessions was paralleled by a developing engagement with the world, leading her to conceive clear ambitions for her life and start pursuing them by going to university. We cannot know the precise connection between her progress in the music therapy sessions and her progress in life, though they mirror each other closely. However, a comment she made a while after we had finished working together gives an indication of the value she placed on the experience: 'Music is the best thing that was ever invented in all the world.'

But what was it about the music we made together that engaged her so powerfully? What it represented and what it expressed both played a part, but, as we have seen, representation and expression do not adequately explain the therapeutic process. For a better understanding of this, we must look at the nature of music itself and at what people actually do when they make music together.

The act of making music

The primary agent of change within the sessions was not a process of analysis or catharsis, but rather one of creative interaction. Throughout the time when Shireen's music was solitary and exclusive, I offered a series of possibilities for interaction, which gradually drew her into a more intimate engagement. This led eventually to music which, though created by the two of us, seemed also to have an independent existence, taking us beyond our individual capacities. I earlier described my experience of this as feeling compelled to accompany Shireen, and having the music drawn out of me. The effect on her was apparent in the transformation of her music from isolated expression to intimately engaged partnership. In my experience as a music therapist (and in that of many other music therapists more experienced than myself), this is the most powerful therapeutic process that music has to offer. Music created through a process of interaction between people can take on a life of its own, and in turn transform those who create it. The transformation is temporary, but the experience of having been transformed, and the discovery of new possibilities, are more permanent.

The act of making music (particularly improvised music) is a process of creative interaction, a particularly intimate form of engagement between people. In this sense music does indeed have a close relationship with love, tenderness and warmth, and stands in stark contrast to violence. Even factional music or music made in battle, though it may express or represent violence, is created through this process of intimate interpersonal engagement. The fine attunement between rapper and DJ, or among a group of singing football fans, subtly undercuts the aggression of their words. Even if a piece of music represents or expresses violence (or disorder, or disengagement) it has been made through a process of fine interpersonal attunement, based on a delicate interplay of structure and flexibility. This is what makes it music. Think of British punk music of the late 1970s and you tend to think of anarchy and alienation, but listen carefully to recordings and you will hear human co-operation at its most intricate and subtle.

We can now sum up the relationship between music, music therapy and violence. Music expresses the whole range of human feelings and relationships, including those that are violent. Expression plays an important part in music therapy, as it did in Shireen's therapy. As far as possible, the therapist must ensure that the music proceeds from the expressive needs of the client, and never loses touch with those needs. However, the primary agent of change in music therapy is a process of creative interaction, inherent in the act of making music, whose nature is the polar opposite of violence. Thus music can encompass a range of violent feelings, urges and instincts, but as a process it will naturally tend towards intimate and creative interpersonal engagement. This explains its particular relevance and usefulness as a treatment for the traumatic effects of political violence, and also suggests its limitations.

Treating the traumatic effects of political violence

It is very important to remember that experience of political violence is not in itself a condition requiring treatment. Some people who experience political violence will be very lucky and suffer no long term effects which significantly hamper them in carrying on their lives. Some may be traumatised, but recover naturally or through their own personal resources, or through their support networks (although for a refugee these networks may be severely limited). It is only those who suffer long term traumatic effects, which prevent them leading a normal or fulfilled life, who need treatment. This seems obvious, but it is surprising how frequently treatment is offered automatically and inappropriately when it becomes known that someone has experienced political violence.

Experience of political violence can have a variety of traumatic effects, and the choice of treatment should depend on the particular symptoms a person is suffering. One common symptom is terrifying flashbacks or dreams. These are best dealt with in a symbolic medium and psychotherapy or art therapy are obvious choices. Other common symptoms are physical, either pain or chronic illness. Medical treatment or some form of physical therapy are most suitable here. In practice, a variety of symptoms are often connected and appear together, and a range of treatments may be needed, or treatment of one symptom may alleviate others.

Because music therapy operates through the development of creative interaction, it is an appropriate treatment when a person's ability to interact is limited by trauma. This is a symptom commonly experienced by Medical Foundation clients, who are often withdrawn or disengaged. Its genesis is explained by Melinda Ashley Meyer (1999, pp.241–2) as fleeing the body when assault makes inhabiting it unbearable; or by Julie Sutton (2000, pp.58–9) as an organic change in the brain's limbic system (which processes emotional experience) to block unmanageable experiences.

Our interactions not only conduct our social relations and our engagement with the world, but also help us to define and maintain our sense of self. When they are limited by trauma, severe consequences can follow. Shireen's difficulties with interaction led to her almost disappearing and ceasing to exist as a person, and turned her into the shadowy figure who first came to the Medical Foundation. Through musical interaction she explicitly developed and explored a new and profound sense of self, and of myself in relation to her. This sense of self, other and relationship is a central part of musical engagement and has important implications for a more general notion of human rights.

Music and human rights

Denying and destroying a person's humanity is a primary aim of torture, often more devastating in its effect than immediate physical pain. An important feature of the definition of political violence I gave at the beginning of this chapter is that the perpetrator and victim are identified not as individuals but as members of opposing groups. A concept of human rights depends on a recognition of the humanity of each individual person, and a breach of human rights, such as political violence, requires a denial or destruction of an individual's humanity.

Music therapy, in contrast, has a history of reaching and drawing out the essential humanity of people who were otherwise unreachable. Striking examples are Dagmar Gustorff's work with comatose hospital patients (see 'Herr G.' in Ansdell 1999, pp.59–64), and Paul Nordoff and Clive Robbins' pioneering work (1977) with children with severe learning difficulties. In both cases, people who were so disabled that they apparently had no means of interacting, found intricate and intense human contact through music-making.

When I first met Shireen, she was so withdrawn that she seemed unreachable. Connecting with the core of her humanity was a long process, but even at the beginning of the first session, her tentative musical interactions gave the first indication of a whole person behind the traumatised exterior. This concept of an undamaged self behind apparent disability became so important in Nordoff and Robbins' (1997) work with disabled children that they gave it a special name, the 'music child'. The concept is equally applicable to adults. An interpreter at the Medical Foundation expressed a similar idea when she said of the beautiful, extended melodies of a very withdrawn and volatile client, 'When he plays music, you see his soul.'

The way that music-making reaches and draws out the essential humanity of the most unreachable people places it in direct opposition to political violence, which denies the humanity and individuality of its victims. Musical interaction draws attention to the uniqueness of each individual, and at the same time reveals the connections between us – our common humanity. In this sense, music-making is a touchstone for human rights, a constant reminder of the value of each person and of humanity as a whole. It is surely no coincidence that the Taliban (the repressive regime of Afghanistan) tried to silence this potential indictment of its attitude to human rights by banning most forms of music-making.

References

Aigen, K. (1999) 'The true nature of music-centred music therapy theory.' *British Journal of Music Therapy 13*, 2.

Ansdell, G. (1995) *Music for Life*. London: Jessica Kingsley Publishers.

Ansdell, G. (1999) 'Challenging premises.' *British Journal of Music Therapy 13*, 2.

Brown, S. (1999) 'Some thoughts on music, therapy, and music therapy.' *British Journal of Music Therapy 13*, 2.

Bruscia, K. (1987) *Improvisational Models of Music Therapy*. Springfield IL: Charles C. Thomas.

William Congreve, *The Mourning Bride* (1697).

Meyer, M.A. (1999) 'In exile from the body: creating a "play room" in the "waiting room".' In E.G. and S.K. Levine (eds) *Foundations of Expressive Arts Therapy: Theoretical and Clinical Perspectives*. London: Jessica Kingsley Publishers.

Nordoff, P. and Robbins, C. (1977) *Creative Music Therapy*. New York: John Day.

Pavlicevic, M. (1997) *Music Therapy in Context. Music, Meaning and Relationship*. London: Jessica Kingsley Publishers.

Pavlicevic, M. (1999) 'Thoughts, words and deeds: harmonies and counterpoints in music therapy theory.' *British Journal of Music Therapy 13*, 2.

Stern, D. (1977) *The First Relationship: Infant and Mother.* London: Fontana/Open Books.

Stern, D. (1985) *The Interpersonal World of the Infant.* New York: Basic Books.

Streeter, E. (1999) 'Finding a balance between psychological thinking and musical awareness in music therapy theory – a psychoanalytic perspective.' *British Journal of Music Therapy 13*, 1.

Sutton, J. (2000) 'Aspects of music therapy with children in areas of conflict: some thoughts about an integrated approach.' In D. Doktor (ed) *Exile: Refugees and the Arts Therapies.* Hertford: University of Hertfordshire, Faculty of Art and Design Press.

CHAPTER 7

Ireland

See me, Hear me, Play with me: Working with the Trauma of Early Abandonment and Deprivation in Psychodynamic Music Therapy

Ruth Walsh Stewart and David Stewart

Prologue

The first author was the clinician in this study and writes about the case in the first person. In collaboration with her, the second author provides a wider theoretical overview, which is presented in the form of short commentaries.

Barbara was referred to music therapy by her mother; she wrote:

Barbara is my adopted Romanian-born daughter. She was abandoned at birth in the maternity hospital where she was born and subsequently stayed in an institution in Romania until she was 1 year and 9 months. She now attends a special school where she is classified as moderately mentally handicapped. Her language skills are poor and she has obviously been deeply affected by her early experiences, even though she has also made great progress. I feel music therapy would be good for her [at this point in time] as she seems to be stuck in a place at the moment where she is frustrated by her lack of speech.

When I read this I was struck by the blatant awfulness and the honesty of the referral. I wondered what lay in store. I arranged an assessment appointment and then continued to see Barbara for a further 30 sessions on a weekly basis.

Theoretical background
Psychodynamic music therapy

The clinical work described in this chapter makes use of a psychodynamic framework. Research has shown that the two strongest trends in current UK music therapy practice are the application of psychodynamic ideas along with those from the field of mother–infant interaction (Stewart 2000). Both elements are key to a training in psychodynamic music therapy (Sobey and Woodcock 1999). This training includes a live mother–infant observation alongside a study of infant developmental research, particularly the work of Daniel Stern (1977, 1985). Key concepts from 'object-relations' theory – Klein, Bion and Winnicott – also make a significant contribution in this approach. Together, these interrelated areas inform both the nature of the patient–therapist interaction and the therapist's role and stance.

Psychodynamic music therapy considers the application of psychodynamic thinking appropriate to the full range of patient groups, both verbal and non-verbal (Sobey and Woodcock 1999). That this model is deemed applicable to work with non-verbal patients is of particular relevance to the case under discussion. It also marks a departure from previous literature on psychoanalytic approaches to music therapy within the UK (e.g. Priestley 1975, 1994), which has emphasised work with verbal patients.

As with other psychodynamic therapies, clear boundaries provide the essential frame for the work (Stewart 1996b).

1. *Consistency of time*: in this case weekly sessions of 30 minutes duration. If any breaks are anticipated they are prepared for, thereby giving the patient an opportunity to communicate something about *missing*, as well as having, sessions.

2.   *Consistency of setting*: providing a range of robust, durable
      musical instruments in the same room each week.

3.   *Consistency of attitude*: a commitment to being with the patient
      with no pre-set agenda other than to receive his
      communications – conscious and unconscious – and to
      respond and give meaning to them.

These boundaries provide environmental and psychic containment for
the patient. They communicate that the room can 'cope' with the
patient's communications and that the therapist can, in Winnicott's terms
(1965), 'hold' on to the patient's mental and emotional experiences. This
holding or containing function of the therapist is similar to that provided
by a mother or father for a young baby.

Psychoanalyst Wilfred Bion has written much on the importance of
the mother as a psychic container for her infant's experience. Commenting on the usefulness of this concept within music therapy Jos de
Backer (1993, p.33) describes the process thus:

> The container (the parents) absorbs the various stimuli and feelings
> spilling over from the baby, hangs on to these experiences, thinks
> about them, makes sense of them, and reacts accordingly. Because of
> this, the child does not feel lonely and experiences the feeling that
> the good object (the mother) is not overawed by these feelings but is
> able to give a form or shape to the chaotic, frightening experiences
> of the child. The frightening and confusing mental feelings can be
> dealt with. (de Backer 1993, p.33)

In addition, the therapist must also feel contained in order to provide a
consistent, containing environment. Hence, therapist supervision is a
further important factor within psychodynamic music therapy. As music
therapist and child psychotherapist Pamela Bartram (1991b) states:
'When her [the therapist's] anxieties and resistances can be explored in a
containing environment they are less likely to impede the communicative
steps of her patients' (Bartram 1991b, p.4). In terms of this particular case,
supervision, both with peers and an external supervisor, was important in
providing a containing network to help the therapist think about the
sometimes extreme communications which Barbara brought to sessions.

In psychodynamic music therapy the developing therapeutic relationship is of primary importance. Play is the medium of this relating and may take various forms. While improvised music-making is central to the work, sometimes other forms of play are appropriate, like making pictures, telling stories, using props. What is important is that the patient is playing and therefore communicating something about him- or herself. It is the responsibility of the psychodynamic music therapist to adapt her play to suit the patient's needs (Bartram 1991a), within personal and professional limits.

There are times, however, when it may be difficult or impossible for the patient to play. This may be the result of an experience of early deprivation, the resurfacing of a trauma, or insufficient ego-strength. An ability to play can be seen as indicative of essentially good emotional health; conversely, not being able to play can point to areas of poor well-being (Winnicott 1971). Winnicott (1964) advocates that we 'put a lot of store on a child's capacity to play'. Here he highlights a belief in the fundamental link between play and well-being. His proposal is that, where there are emotional difficulties, the child's capacity for play is indicative of an ability to make a solution. The psychodynamic music therapist attends to both these aspects of the patient – the playing and non-playing – and is observant of the conditions that allow for a more playful aspect to emerge. She is mindful of Winnicott who says: 'Where playing is not possible then the work done by the therapist is directed towards bringing the patient from a state of not being able to play into a state of being able to play' (Winnicott 1971, p.38). But where does this capacity to play come from and why is it crucial to healthy development?

Four stages in Winnicott's theory of play

In his groundbreaking book, *Playing and Reality*, Donald Winnicott (1971) outlines the aetiology of a capacity to play in the early mother–infant relationship. He particularly notes its critical function in establishing and maintaining a sense of 'self'. With authority he states: 'It is in playing and only in playing that the individual child or adult is able to be creative and to use the whole personality, and it is only in being creative that the individual discovers the self' (1971, p.54).

Stage 1: mother as environment

In the very early weeks of life the infant relies on mother totally for survival. Through her repertoire of caring, adapting behaviours and empathic mirroring, mother attends to baby's physical and emotional needs. At this stage the mother *is* the infant's environment and his or her predominant experience is one of merger and union with her.

For Winnicott, this early environment was crucial to the infant developing a fundamental sense of 'self', the 'true self' (1971). In his model, the self is a product of the relationship between the infant's inherited tendencies and the 'facilitating' or 'holding environment' (1965). The mother's role is central in providing the two cornerstones of this environment, *boundary* and *space*. She acts as a protecting frame or boundary, keeping the impingements of the outside world at bay. This boundary function provides an experience of reliability for the baby, within which a space can then be created for him or her. Space is achieved through the mother's relaxed receptivity to baby's experience and her active adaption to his or her needs.

Together, these various aspects of the mother's care and presence provide the infant with a basic continuity of existence, a sense of 'going-on-being' as Winnicott so aptly puts it (1956). As the infant gradually internalises this experience a more coherent sense of self begins to emerge. This rudimentary sense of 'me' is the bedrock from which a capacity to play can grow and develop.

Stage 2: separation and the discovery of transitional play

These earliest experiences are characterised mostly by psychic fusion and 'at-oneness'. Developmental research has shown that infants have a capacity for some experience of separateness from the start of life (Stern 1985). The next stage sees the infant coming to terms with the concept of the mother as 'object', as separate from him or her. Mother begins gradually to fit the infant into the wider world beyond. While she is not there totally on his or her behalf, she is nonetheless reliable and adaptable to her baby's needs. During this process of separating out, a space opens up between mother and baby which Winnicott terms an 'intermediate' or 'transitional space' (1971). Here is the infant's first playground in which he or she can begin to explore the relationship between what is 'me' and 'not-me'. In this space, play becomes 'a way of being yourself and knowing yourself; it is also about discovering your part in the wider world, a way of discovering the 'otherness' of the world and the limits it presents you with' (Stewart 1996a, p.12).

In his or her play the infant makes use of what Winnicott termed 'transitional objects' (1971, p.2) – the corner of a blanket, a teddy-bear or imaginary friend – as a way of bridging the gap between his or her internal reality and external world. Crucially, these objects are experienced by the infant as both his or her own possession and as part of external reality. They serve as soothing substitutes for the mother's presence and allow for a world of illusion in which the infant's capacity for imaginative play can develop to assist him or her in coming to terms with shared reality.

Stage 3: alone in the presence of another

The third stage Winnicott terms 'being alone in the presence of someone' (1971, p.47). In order to achieve this position there has to be a history of sufficient trust between mother and infant. The baby has to possess a belief in the availability of the mother, a memory of her reliable presence. In this phase it is possible to play alone because, as Josephine Klein (1987) states, 'there is another person looking after you, but you do not experience this other, except through knowing that it is safe to forget about yourself and about any dangers that threaten' (p.247).

Stage 4: the playing relationship

The final phase in Winnicott's (1971) model is where the child is able to 'allow and enjoy an overlap of two play areas' (p.48). Having made her play fit in with that of her infant, the mother now introduces ideas of her own into their playing. There exists a potential for 'playing together in a relationship' (p.48). The internal and external worlds of both parties can now meet. Assimilating this interplay of inner and outer reality can be seen as a lifelong process, played out in the adult's participation in cultural life (Winnicott 1951).

The impact of early trauma on a capacity for play

What repercussions ensue when a mother is not sufficiently available to her baby's needs from the start of life, when the much needed continuity of care is, at best, unpredictable? What happens when there is not a facilitating environment? According to Winnicott, any interferences in the earliest stage of caregiving are experienced by the infant as a dangerous interruption of his or her sense of going-on-being. He or she is left with a 'threat of annihilation' (1956) and fears of falling apart. The infant has no one to help him or her with these primitive ontological anxieties. As Jos de Backer says:

> When children have not experienced this [containment] because their mother has, for various reasons, been unable to assimilate and consolidate these feelings, the feelings remain unbearable and terrifying. They are too much for the child, who cuts off all contact. (De Backer 1993, p.33)

The infant's capacity for play and relating is seriously blunted and creativity is sometimes eroded altogether.

Barbara's earliest experiences in the institution blocked the natural developmental path of play. Her's was not a facilitating environment providing continuity of care. As her adoptive parents reported, it was one where there were grossly insufficient facilities: inadequate one-to-one attention, poor nutrition, no hot water, no nappies. It was a place of privation. It was certainly nowhere to establish the trusting relationship essential to getting to know yourself or to develop a capacity for play. Her adoptive parents told me about how she first related to them. She continuously explored her mother's body, as if to make sure she was really there. It was like the beginning of a relationship with a *real* mother for the first time. It was reported also that, although 21 months old, Barbara was unable to walk. However, as she grew more confident, as well as nourished, based on her mother and father's presence and reliability, she began to walk and to explore her wider environment. Barbara enjoyed physical play such as horseplay and being pushed on swings. However, she seemed to have had an impaired sense of symbolic play and her parents reported that mostly she did not play with toys or dolls.

The loving and insightful parenting that Barbara received from her adoptive parents undoubtedly helped her grow and develop. When referred to music therapy she had apparently reached a developmental plateau, a point of 'stuckness'. Barbara was able to use the music therapy to revisit formative developmental stages. She was able further to redefine her relationship to 'self' and 'other', to work through some of her difficulties about feeling accepted and wanted.

Case Study

Encountering a facilitating environment

> *See me:* I am 8 years old; I am small, blonde and pretty; I flit around the room; I spit, I kick, I pull hair.
>
> *Hear me:* I like the ocean drum; I love to wallow in its sound; but sometimes I hit it and drop it …
>
> *Play with me:* My name's Barbara; I don't know how to play with you.

In the early sessions Barbara mostly played the ocean drum, kneeling or lying on it, dropping it onto the floor, watching the ball-bearings fly in all directions, hitting it, dribbling on it. She was engrossed and enveloped by its sound. When I approached to play with her she turned her back on me. Sometimes she tolerated my accompaniment of her sounds with my voice or on the piano, but mostly it felt like there was no room for an experience of 'two-ness' in the music. Essentially, she seemed to use the ocean drum to evoke a sensuous experience of merging, what Freud termed an 'oceanic experience' (1930). In these early days of music therapy, Barbara wanted to preserve this 'at one' state from intrusion. She had a need to 'return to basics', to return to an essential early experience of connectedness. It was a necessary starting point for her.

Barbara reacted to any perceived intrusion from me – including attempts to protect instruments she had knocked down – by hitting out, pulling hair, kicking and spitting. Zerbe (1990) argues that when there is no symbolic expression to contain mental distress, it is projected through 'action-discharge' and 'concrete communication'. This was the level Barbara was at. On the one hand she was wallowing in a warm experience. On the other she was being destructive, unable to contain for herself, or even allow me to contain her experience of interrupted at-oneness. Whilst Barbara acted aggressively towards me, I felt she also had 'unconscious hope' (Casement 1990) for the work we could do together. On her way to early sessions she would say my name and use her arms and voice to make the shape and sound of the ocean drum. It was as if she was holding me and the music in mind. This, and her continued return and investment in the music therapy, also underscored *my* sense of hope for the work.

Gradually Barbara needed less of the sensuous ocean drum experience and increasingly explored the room, the musical instruments and me. She bounced the beater on the drum, ran her fingers through the chimes, struck the gong loudly and then dampened the sound. She continued to hit out unexpectedly at me when I tried to play with her, but not every time I played. I began to feel unsure about playing with her, yet if I was silent I felt non-existent. It was hard to contain her and to sustain a sense of connection.

I consulted a colleague who had worked in Romania and I procured a Romanian song. This was introduced in session four. Barbara had come to sit on my lap while I was at the piano and she took my hands. I began to sing the song and she immediately clapped my hands together fitting with the phrases of the music. The play extended to inserting clusters of notes on the piano into certain points of the song. It was fun, there was smiling and laughter – we were sharing good feelings together. Suddenly she tugged at my hair, then resumed her play. I was taken aback by her switch in behaviour, but felt I had to hold the feelings behind the attack and continue to sustain interaction. She was able to feel emotionally close in the interaction but part of her wanted to destroy this closeness. It seemed to mirror a situation which psychotherapist Patrick Casement (1990) describes as the 'pain of contrast':

> A negative response to experience that might appear to be 'good' seems to be an unconscious attempt by the patient to preserve childhood memories from comparison, particularly when there is a risk of exposing the depths of early deprivation or the true nature of damaging experience in childhood. (Casement 1990, p.106).

The relation of this to Barbara's experience in the orphanage is, I think, clear. Gradually her ability to include me in her play and to sustain inter-action developed: in session six she played the gong. It felt appropriate to use my voice to resonate with the gong, and to join Barbara's music without her experiencing me as being too close. She smiled and continued to play. Shortly after she went behind the desk, which is in the room but outside the bounds of the music therapy space. I reminded her of this boundary. She seemed to find the intrusion of this limit on her exploration difficult. She attacked me, pulling at my hair, kicking and scratching. I wanted both to defend myself *and* hold on to her distress. I held her hands, saying 'No', but also tried to be still physically and emo-tionally, to contain her anxiety. She stopped attacking me and ran over to a guitar, pulling and sounding the strings as if nothing untoward had happened beforehand.

I felt I had to be active, not retaliating, but being an alive, surviving presence for Barbara. I felt being active would also help me stay in the room. I set up a regular pulse on the conga drum, hoping the rhythmic structure would bring a sense of containment to the room, to Barbara and to me. She stopped playing the guitar and changed to exploring the cabasa. Then she went to the gong and tapped out part of the rhythm I was playing. This was unexpected but significant. I felt she was taking in some of the containing rhythmic element I was offering on the drum. This became more apparent when she came over to the conga and played it a little with me. She took a breather from this mutual play, but later returned to play some more with me. Offering a containing musical structure, instead of retaliating for Barbara's attack, was vital to the devel-oping relationship. In her eyes I could, perhaps, survive her attacks and become a reliable and adaptable mother figure.

This session had really challenged me as I was unsure of how to respond to such situations. I wanted to understand *why* Barbara was behaving this way and not just attempt to change her behaviour. It was time to seek supervision. The outcome of this was, primarily, to address Barbara's unacceptable, aggressive behaviour. It was decided that she would be brought outside for a 'breather' if she attacked either the musical instruments or me. I explained this to her parents who agreed to wait outside to be with her if necessary. This support from the parents was essential to the work. I was no longer going to tolerate physically destructive impulses, even though the environment and I would survive destructive feelings. Importantly, this action was also in keeping with the home and school management of her behaviour.

Commentary

Barbara has brought her earliest experience into the therapy environment. She seems unconsciously to have recognised it as a place to re-experience and, more importantly, re-evaluate her formative encounters with the world. As for the newborn infant, the fundamental quality of the surrounding environment is all important to Barbara's survival and development. Her project this time round is to hold this newly encountered environment up to rigorous scrutiny. Will it be a protecting, nourishing and nurturing place, or will it be a place that is subject to damaging impingements that threaten your very sense of existence?

Barbara's explorations led her to experiences of extreme closeness in play with the ocean drum. This affords her a most primitive form of connectedness, such as the 'primary love' Balint (1968) describes. These explorations also led to a re-enactment of her initially traumatised experience of primary love and its attendant 'unbearable agony' (Winnicott 1974). Hitting out at the therapist-mother is a hitting out at the original source of failure. It is also a form of insistent enquiry. Barbara is asking if *this* mother-environment will survive as reliable and adaptable, breaking the 'pattern of reacting to the unpredictable and for ever starting again' (Winnicott 1971, p.141). Barbara's enquiry then represents her hope that the little good experience she had before can be recaptured and reclaimed. Here, the fact that the therapist *does* survive Barbara's active, concrete questioning is of key importance. It ushers in a tenuous capacity for play, where the differentiation of 'I', 'you' and 'us' can begin to develop.

A transformative experience and the beginnings of play

See me: I am small and vulnerable. Am I separate?

Hear me: This is me – what does it mean? When I get close, sometimes too close, I hit out.

Play with me: I am me and you are you: let's play together.

Asking Barbara to leave the room helped curb her aggressive behaviour. This happened two or three times in four sessions. Paradoxically, it helped focus our time together *in* the room, increasing the number of occasions when we were able to make music together. In session 11 Barbara hit me hard and unexpectedly with a large gong beater and was promptly asked to leave. Once outside, I felt I had to do something. I had reached my tolerance limit. Out of the despair of this situation came an unexpected and intuitive response. I created a circle on the floor out of beanbags and the instruments Barbara had played the most to date – the gong, drum, cymbal, xylophone, metallophone, organ and ocean drum. I laid a yellow blanket on the floor in the middle of the circle. This demar- cated a smaller music playground in the room.

When I fetched Barbara back in and led her into the circle she took off her socks and shoes – it was as if she had come home! I wanted to find a way of welcoming her and keeping her in the circle and so I took the lead. I played a single quiet note on three instruments in succession, the xylophone, metallophone and gong. Barbara imitated me. I then repeated my opening motif to which she made the same response. This was the first time I had actively taken a lead and Barbara had followed. My activity was borne of a drive to 'make things work' between us, to move beyond destruction to greater play and creativity. Next Barbara moved to the organ and I began playing the xylophone. She played and paused; I played in her pause; she played again and waited in anticipation of my reply. Turn-taking was now possible: two separate, creative people making an exchange.

In the following session Barbara did not need to leave the room. She introduced a peek-a-boo game, hiding her eyes behind her hands: 'I'm here, not here'. In later sessions this peek-a-boo transferred to her arrival for sessions, playing either side of the door. She would play when she came into the room too, hiding and peeking out from behind a beanbag.

It seemed this was her way of communicating her experience of me: 'now *you're* here; now you're not'. Her capacity to avail of the 'now you're here' aspect of this experience gradually expanded, with periods of increased music-making reflecting the developing relationship. In session 13 we played a duet. Lasting a record eight minutes, Barbara played the gong while I played the metallophone. I felt it was the circle that had provided the right form of containment for Barbara's internal world. It had enabled her to make a new relationship with the external world through our shared music-making. The music therapy space had become a facilitating environment, a potential playground.

After a couple of sessions within the circle it seemed safe and appropriate to bring in new instruments and progressively to extend the circle to almost fill the room. This was because Barbara seemed more able to contain herself. She could control her inner conflict without needing the external container so much. In session 18 Barbara sat on the floor beside a low table of small musical instruments. One by one she began to put them inside her cardigan: mouth organ, claves, finger cymbals, whistles, cowbell, woodblock, agogo, triangle, guiro shaker, kazoo, African recorder, handbells, beaters; she also tried to pack in a square bamboo shaker and a tambourine! Nearly 20 instruments! It was comical to watch her, but I also thought about how she was putting some of the music 'food' into herself, the ingredients of play and creativity. It seemed Barbara felt she had a container inside her that she could put things into. Not only did she feel contained, but she could also contain. She had internalised some of the containment offered in the therapy space.

Around this time Barbara introduced a new form of play with me and this became a reliable point of connection in subsequent sessions. Bringing a small mouth organ over to me, she would give instructions as to how to play it by moving her hands in front of her mouth rapidly and repeatedly from left to right. Developing this shared music-making further, she would hand me the guitar to play while she played the mouth organ; we would then swap instruments at her request. She had initiated and engineered the interaction. We could play together.

Commentary

In creating a circle of instruments around the blanket, the therapist performs an essential mothering function for Barbara. She transforms her unbearable experience of falling apart. Common to the ancient folk art of many cultures, the circle is a potent emblem of wholeness. Here it provides Barbara with a concrete, visual symbol of containment which she is able to internalise as a containing experience. The circle as symbol of the first container, the womb, evokes a powerful unconscious resonance which is shared by both therapist and patient in this key mutative moment. Similarly, its gradual opening out to fill the entire room strongly echoes Barbara's process of emotional and psychological birth during her time in music therapy.

Following in the line of Winnicott, Christopher Bollas (1987) has written about the importance of the mother's role as a process of 'cumulative internal and external transformations' (p.14). He locates this transformational process particularly in the early part of the infant's life, equating it with a merged-in form of relating. Thus, the transformational process precedes the formation of the transitional space, where a sense of separation is required. Bollas maintains that we seek out 'transformational objects' in later life. At times we have a need to evoke experiences in which something from the external environment holds out the possibility of internal transformation. In Barbara's case, the therapist's act of transformation strikes a powerful chord in her internal world of chaos and collapse. The circle helps put the pieces back together again. This act represents the therapist's determined effort to bring Barbara from her state of not being able to play to one of playfulness. It enables a further part of the developmental jigsaw to fall into place, not as a definitive stage but as a point of reference which may require many returns.

Playing alone in the presence of someone

See me. Hear me. Play with me: I know you're there; I'm thinking about other people in my life and how I fit in; watch me, listen to me, share with me.

Throughout the therapy Barbara's mother had been expecting a baby. The immediate impact of this was not always evident in the therapy other than my observation that Barbara was exploring her relationship with me as if it was a first relationship. In retrospect, it is interesting to consider that Barbara was first referred to music therapy when her mother became pregnant. Perhaps this was an unconscious gesture on the mother's behalf to seek out a containing environment for Barbara in order to enable her better to prepare for her new arrival. She seemed to be trying to find out what sort of baby she was and what mother would do with her. Would she retaliate or would she contain and adapt? This could have been connected to her past or to the imminent arrival of someone who would take mother's special attention, or both.

When the new baby was born Barbara's participation in the therapy and her level of play changed. She was a baby one minute and a mother the next, acting out her experience of exclusion from the new mother–baby pairing in her home. She 'gooed' at me, stroked my hair, held her hand behind my head like a mother would support a baby's head and neck. Suddenly this affection would turn into an aggressive attack and she would bang her forehead against mine. The experience of closeness was instantly shattered. It was as if I was her young sibling whom she was being nice to and then wanted to hurt. She was being a loving mother and a rejecting mother and letting me know what it felt like.

Further play included her lying underneath the blanket and making me crouch beside her with my head on the floor. She reached out her hand to play the nearby keyboard and I played with her. She then stroked my hair and placed my hand across her back. I felt she wanted to have special mothering in a place that was her own, like her new sibling's close relationship with mother. I reflected verbally to her that this was nice for her, she felt close and maybe there was a 'baby Barbara in the room' as well as a 'little girl Barbara'. Here she was putting me into the mothering role to give her the special feeling of closeness she desired. Through my comments I let her know that I understood her actions.

In session 28 Barbara pulled down a large soft toy rabbit from a cupboard. She pulled at his mouth, then jigged him up and down on her lap, before dropping him onto the floor. She was showing me how she felt with the new arrival-rival on the scene. Maybe she felt she had been dropped in favour of the new infant. One by one she took down the remaining soft toys, pulling at their noses and then stroking them. Perhaps she was relating to them in the same ambivalent way she had been to me. She then placed them all in a row and stood looking at them. The number made up her family, excluding her. This was very painful to witness, all her siblings with their natural parents and Barbara excluded, absent.

This symbolic play using the toys as people in her real life continued into the last two sessions. Barbara got under the blanket with the two big teddies. She chatted and giggled and moved around with them. She was playing out what was on her mind about two people 'getting it together', maybe making babies. I wondered if her play was about her adoptive mother and father. Or, perhaps, Barbara was thinking about her natural parents creating her, the baby that would be abandoned. I wondered aloud to Barbara if it was 'nice' or 'awful' under the blanket. She lifted her head and spat at me. She was telling me that things were far from nice. I sat back and observed her play. After a few minutes I said, 'You're showing me what's going on in your mind. There are two people under the blanket and Barbara wants to be part of it.'

Barbara paused in her play and lay silent for a few minutes. I wondered what was going to happen. Barbara stood up. Cloaked in the blanket she came and sat in front of me, assuming a worried expression and then screwing her face into a frown. I felt she was asking me what kind of a 'baby' she was – acceptable, unacceptable? Then she lay down at the keyboard, played a few notes, mouthed some of the keys and finally pulled at one of them, trying to break it off. I said a firm 'No'; she vocalised angrily in return. Then she lay down under the blanket again and indicated for me to lie down too. There she pulled at my hair and then jumped up and out of the room. I fetched her back and she translated her strong feelings into music, playing the drum, tambours and gong. It sounded like angry music. Afterwards she lay down on a beanbag and stayed there until it was time to leave.

Obviously Barbara was experiencing conflicting, persecutory feelings, and especially at this time when her mother had to attend to a newcomer to the family. She was acting out her feelings, but also demon-strating her ability to put them more creatively into music. Playing angrily on the drums afforded her a more appropriate way of managing and surviving her difficult feelings. Through symbolic play she was trying to sort out things in her mind to do with her relationship to other people – to me, her parents – and her earliest experiences.

At this point, the therapy ended unexpectedly: Barbara became unavailable to continue attending. I was disappointed at this premature ending and felt powerless that it was out of my control. However, I felt we had achieved a significant amount in our time together.

Commentary

In this final stage of the therapy Barbara's growing confidence in the holding environment enables her to explore painful aspects of her current situation and their resonance with her past. With the inclusion of the transitional teddybears, the focus of play shifts from form to content. The details are now 'out in the open' and centre on Barbara's primal fears about her own origins. Where has she come from and why? What and who has she come to now?

In *The Beast in the Nursery*, psychoanalyst Adam Phillips (1998) graphically portrays the developing child's curiosity as he engages in 'sexual researches' and 'theory-making' about his own body and those of his parents. In theorising about how bodies work and how different bodies – mother's, father's, his – fit together, the child is searching for a story to satisfy his curiosity about how he arrived into his family and how important he is to his parents. Phillips notes Freud's observation that the arrival of a sibling often stimulates the child's researches, which are 'in a real sense, about how he came to be there, and in what sense he was still there after the birth of a sibling' (1930, p.19).

Barbara's symbolic play may be considered her form of sexual research, an attempt to establish her part in the new order of things in her family. As in other aspects of the therapy process, the spectre of abandonment and loss looms large in Barbara's play. The abrupt ending of the therapy stands as a further poignant reminder of Barbara's history of interrupted caregiving. It can only be hoped that each new experience of gain for her will impact in a cumulative way, making the process of 'starting over again' a little easier. Gain, as well as loss, might now be a possibility.

Conclusion

Arguably, the total provision of the music therapy environment offered Barbara an experience akin to early caregiving. This enabled her to move between the different phases of play development as outlined by Winnicott. It was not a linear process, but one that shifted back and forth. First, she began with the ocean drum, wallowing in its 'at one' experience. This level of play returned in later sessions when, for instance, Barbara wrapped herself up in a blanket and I sang quietly to her. Second, she made music with me. Sometimes she could barely tolerate my contributions; at others she would initiate playful interaction. She could allow an overlap of our two play areas. Third, she used the soft toys for symbolic play, wanting me to witness and try to understand her attempts to accommodate the new position in her family. In using the therapy to develop a capacity for play, Barbara was embarking on the essential process of 'self' and 'other' definition. This is a prerequisite for all creative living (Winnicott 1971).

Introducing both a zero tolerance for aggressive behaviour and the 'transformational circle' proved turning points in Barbara's play development. Together they provided a holding structure for her fundamental anxieties about being a wantable, lovable child. They helped contain her fear of intimacy, of getting close but, at a certain point, not being able to bear that closeness. These structures facilitated more focused play and interaction for Barbara. As Josephine Klein says: 'When there is a frame that gives space and protection, all the resonances and echoes and reverberations of an infant's experiences have time to work themselves out' (1987, p.361).

My capacity to survive Barbara's attacks without retaliation, along with the robustness of the musical instruments, similarly helped contain Barbara. She was able gradually to internalise some of this containing element. Eventually this enabled her to play on her own, to begin to sort out the relationship between her inner world and external reality. Again, I think Klein describes this process well when she says: 'As anyone knows who has glued things, the things to be stuck together need to be held firmly in a kind of frame until the glue holds. Then the frame is no longer needed' (1987, p.361).

Thus a facilitating environment has clear boundaries, offers consistency and reliability, and responds adaptively to the needs of the patient. As we have seen, the therapist's task within this environment involves a complex, moment-by-moment attuning of responses to the patient's developmental level. In this way, the patient can develop a capacity to play and relate to other people.

The Romanian institution in which Barbara spent almost the first two years of her life could not provide these facilitating conditions. In the home of her adoptive parents she learned how to play and how to interact with others. At critical moments however, these early traumatic experiences inevitably resurfaced and needed to be worked through. It is not surprising therefore that the birth of a sibling would trigger Barbara's primitive fears about the reliability of the outside world. We think the music therapy afforded her the opportunity at least to begin to explore these fears. It allowed her to test external reality and, hopefully, to find it a more reliable place than her worst fears would have her believe.

Acknowledgements

Sincere thanks go to Barbara's parents for allowing us to write about the music therapy with Barbara. Their love and concern for Barbara, and their supportive links during the work, helped make the whole process possible.

References

Balint, M. (1968) *The Basic Fault.* London: Hogarth Press.

Bartram, P. (1991a) 'Improvisation and play in the therapeutic engagement of a five-year-old boy with physical and interpersonal problems.' In K. Bruscia (ed) *Case Studies in Music Therapy.* Phoenixville PA: Barcelona.

Bartram, P. (1991b) 'Aspects of the theory and practice of psychodynamic music therapy.' In Scottish Music Therapy Council, *Music Therapy and the Individual.* Edinburgh: Scottish Music Therapy Council.

Bollas, C. (1987) *The Shadow of the Object: Psychoanalysis of the Unthought Known.* London: Free Association Books.

Casement, P. (1990) *Further Learning from the Patient.* London: Routledge.

de Backer, J. (1993) 'Containment in music therapy.' In T. Wigram and M. Heal (eds) *Music Therapy in Health and Education*. London: Jessica Kingsley Publishers.

Freud, S. (1930) 'Civilization and its discontents.' In *Standard Edition, Vol. 21*. London: Hogarth Press (1961).

Klein, J. (1987) *Our Need for Others and its Roots in Infancy*. London: Tavistock.

Phillips, A. (1998) *The Beast in the Nursery*. London: Faber and Faber.

Priestley, M. (1975) *Music Therapy in Action*. New York: St. Martin's Press.

Priestley, M. (1994) *Essays on Analytical Music Therapy*. New York: Barcelona.

Sobey, K. and Woodcock, J. (1999) 'Psychodynamic music therapy: considerations in training.' In A. Cattanach (ed) *Process in the Arts Therapies*. London: Jessica Kingsley Publishers.

Stern, D. (1977) *The First Relationship: Infant and Mother*. New York: Open Books.

Stern, D. (1985) *The Interpersonal World of the Infant*. New York: Basic Books.

Stewart, D. (1996a) 'Keeping things safe – essential aspects of psychodynamic music therapy in relation to Donald Winnicott.' Paper presented at Introduction to Music Therapy Course, Queen's University of Belfast.

Stewart, D. (1996b) 'Chaos, noise and a wall of silence: working with primitive affects in psychodynamic group music therapy.' *British Journal of Music Therapy 10*, 2, 21–33.

Stewart, D. (2000) 'The state of the UK music therapy profession: personal qualities, working models, support networks and job satisfaction.' *British Journal of Music Therapy 14*, 1, 13–31.

Winnicott, D.W. (1951) 'Transitional objects and transitional phenomena.' In D. Winnicott *Collected Papers: Through Paediatrics to Psycho-Analysis*. London: Tavistock (1958).

Winnicott, D.W. (1956) 'Primary maternal preoccupation.' In D.W. Winnicott *Collected Papers: Through Paediatrics to Psycho-Analysis*. London: Tavistock (1958).

Winnicott, D. (1964) *The Child, the Family and the Outside World*. Harmondsworth: Penguin, p.130.

Winnicott, D. (1965) *The Maturational Processes and the Facilitating Environment*. London: Hogarth Press and The Institute of Psycho-Analysis.

Winnicott, D. (1971) *Playing and Reality*. London: Tavistock/Routledge.

Winnicott, D. (1974) 'The fear of breakdown.' *International Review of Psychoanalysis 1*, 1.

Zerbe, D. (1990) 'The therapist at play and the patient who begins to play.' *Clinical Social Work Journal 18*, 1.

CHAPTER 8

Bosnia-Herzegovina
A Music Therapy Service in a Post-war Environment

Louise Lang and Úna Mcinerney

This chapter is a personal account of our combined experiences of work at the Pavarotti Music Centre in Mostar, Bosnia-Herzegovina (B-H) between 1998 and 2001. During that time the authors worked as part of a larger team, to whom thanks are extended.

Our time at the Pavarotti Music Centre (PMC) began after the war (1991 to 1996). The impact this had on the people of B-H was central to our work, and because of this we include some of the history of Mostar, with a description of the PMC where the music therapy department is based. Examples are given of work undertaken by the music therapy team during the post-war years. These are put into context with a look at some specific aspects of working in this post-war environment.

To begin, it is useful to take a brief look at the recent history of the former Yugoslavia, which was a fairly liberal communist state under Tito until he died in 1980. Following Tito's death there were the beginnings of political unrest leading up to Milošević gaining power in Serbia in 1989 and later taking control of the Yugoslavian National Army. The previously good social and economic conditions disappeared at the onset of the war in 1991, when the Serbian army attacked cities and towns in Croatia and later in B-H. The tolerant multi-ethnic society (with many mixed marriages between Serbs, Croats and Muslims) was broken apart by what was later to be known as ethnic cleansing. Having had the second highest number of mixed marriages in Bosnia-Herzegovina, Mostar gives us an example of this previous tolerance. However, during the war, the town was torn apart by the ruthless and devastating ethnic cleansing.

In Mostar there were essentially two wars. In 1992 the town was attacked by the Serbs, and after the Serbs had withdrawn further fighting broke out in 1993, which was led by the Croats. This resulted in a war between the Croats and Muslims, in contrast to the earlier situation, where Croat and Muslim had fought together. The consequence of this second war was that Mostar was divided in two, with the majority of Croats on the west side and most of the Muslims in the east. Only a minority of Serbs remained in the city.

During our time in Mostar, day-to-day life was beginning to return to normal and much reconstruction had been done. However, many people were still living in very poor conditions. Whole families were based in one room or in buildings that were still full of shell holes or without proper roofs. There was little sign of the economy improving and not much long-term sustainable industry. Cafés and small family-run enterprises formed many new businesses, with these surviving from one day to the next. Later, shops gradually stocked a much greater range of produce, although many people in east Mostar were still finding it difficult to cross the town to the larger supermarkets in the west. In response to the situation there were a number of international charities involved in B-H both during and after the war. One of these was War Child.

War Child and the Pavarotti Music Centre

The charity War Child was first formed in 1992 and originally based in London. One of the first projects was a mobile bakery which made and delivered bread in several areas across B-H during the war, including Mostar. Later, the concept of a centre as a place where people could gather to hear and play music together was born and in 1995 Luciano Pavarotti put on his first fundraising concert in Modena, Italy in aid of War Child's Mostar project. In 1996 the official contract was signed with the municipality for a site for the centre and work began to clear the ruined primary school to make way for the Pavarotti Music Centre.

The Pavarotti Music Centre was opened in east Mostar during December 1997 to promote reconciliation through music. It is a place where children and adults of any ethnic background are welcome to gather to make music together or to attend a variety of pop concerts. Many different projects and workshops have been and continue to be offered, including African drumming, national folk dancing, ballet classes, DJ workshops and a rock school. All projects, workshops and concerts are free of charge. The centre is home to the Middle Music School, where children come for their instrumental lessons, and also provides a base for the Schools' Music Programme team who deliver the national music curriculum in the local schools. In addition, there are two professional recording studios which are used by bands from all over the former Yugoslavia as well as many international groups. Finally, there is the music therapy department which is currently funded by War Child Netherlands. The philosophy of War Child is as follows:

> War Child invests in the peaceful future of children who have been affected by war. War Child strives for the psychosocial well-being and empowerment of children, irrespective of their religious, ethnical or political backgrounds. War Child aims to reach its goals through: psychosocial programmes, applying the power of the creative arts and sports to strengthen the children's mental and social development; creative and sports programmes, that reunite groups of children, separated by war, to build a peaceful society; raising awareness on the plight of children in war zones. (from personal correspondance with Willemijn Verloop, War Child Netherlands, 5 June 2001)

The Music Therapy Department

The Music Therapy Department (the first in B-H) was opened in April 1998. It was staffed by three international therapists and three local music therapy assistants who transport children to and from the centre as well as translating both during sessions and for the necessary documents and paperwork. A service is provided for children and young people from all over the Mostar area, as well as outreach work.

The team works with clients who have a range of trauma-related difficulties and with those who have a variety of disabilities, such as cerebral palsy, autism, hearing and visual impairments. Referrals are taken from the local special school, the children's home and from other professionals and parents who have heard about the service. Outreach work has included a special class in a mainstream school, a children's therapy unit of a hospital, a refugee camp for internally displaced people, a centre for mental health and a centre for children with special needs. Often these institutions have been in politically sensitive areas. Sessions take place either on a one-to-one basis or in small groups. During the summer (when the clinical timetable is reduced due to the school holidays) special projects are set up, and in the past these have included workshops with Kosovan refugees living in Mostar. On occasion, after a series of music therapy sessions, clients have joined other PMC projects where they have the opportunity to generalise what they have experienced in individual therapy sessions. This can be a stepping stone towards integration back into the community.

Other music therapy department work has included acting as a support and advice centre. Teachers and carers can obtain information about music therapy, trauma and special needs from the collection of books and articles and from consultation with the therapists. The department also occasionally provides short-term placements for music therapy students and those interested in training.

Music therapy practice in Bosnia-Herzegovina

Over time it became clear that there were a number of issues specific to music therapy practice in B-H, including working with assistants, cultural and political factors and issues of gender. These had great impact on our work and required much thought and discussion. We will outline six of the major issues:

- working with a translator
- cultural aspects for translators
- cultural aspects for music therapists
- the profile of the PMC

- the impact of post-war society
- the need for support.

Working with a translator

We worked with local assistants (male and female) who translated for us. There were many aspects to this collaboration. Having a translator present in the sessions was essential in order for any verbal communication from the therapist or client to be immediately and accurately understood. It did, of course, have implications for the therapy, especially in individual work. Having a third person present in what is usually a one-to-one situation can completely change the dynamics. The clients responded to the presence of the assistant in different ways. For example, initially some clients seemed unsure about why the assistant was there. It may have felt strange for clients if the assistants were not involved in the music. In other cases, clients used the assistant as a refuge when contact with the therapist became too intense for them. Others put the assistants into parental roles. Differences were noticed in clients' responses according to whether the assistant was male or female. For example, when timetabling necessitated a change from a female to a male assistant with one client, a number of factors arose during therapy that were believed to be linked with the sudden loss of the client's father and the subsequent relationship with his mother. This client now appeared to be exploring the potential for a relationship with this new adult male figure in his life. Many boundaries were tested, such as his use of abusive and aggressive language towards the assistant, and his physical dominance over him when he was sitting on the floor. At times there was also the client's obvious need to bond with another male. Therefore, working with assistants, in individual work in particular, required careful consideration and planning by the therapist, as well as considerable sensitivity on the part of the assistant.

Cultural aspects for translators

The work of the music therapy department was with people from all backgrounds in B-H. Occasionally clients themselves brought their own music, especially songs, to the sessions, some of which were specific to their culture. This could be uncomfortable for the assistant if he/she was from a different ethnic background, particularly if they were encouraged by the children to join in the session. This type of situation required open communication between the therapist and assistant regarding the assistant's feelings about the material presented. A way forward had to be negotiated by all concerned, ensuring that the client's music was not simply rejected, while also taking care that the assistant was not placed in an awkard position.

Cultural aspects for music therapists

At times it was difficult when we were not allowed to work in settings where we felt there was a need for music therapy. Sometimes we were not accepted for political reasons and sometimes for more personal reasons, such as fear. It seemed that for some people the events of previous years had resulted in an unwillingness to accept people of a different ethnic background into the workplace, perhaps feeling threatened by them. For example, at one institution the staff wanted to know the background of any of our assistants who might go there, and expressed fear that the children in their care would be negatively influenced in some way.

Profile of the Pavarotti Music Centre

The PMC has quite a high profile and because music therapy in the area of trauma is a relatively new area of work, at times it felt that the work of the department was very much in the public eye. We had many enquiries for information from the general public, from funders and from local and international media. While we were very pleased that there was such interest in the work of the Centre and recognised the importance of this, it sometimes led to feelings of expectation that we would produce results. At times it was difficult to balance speaking and answering questions about our work with taking time really to reflect and think about what was happening with our clients.

Impact of post-war society

Another issue for us was not only working but also *living* in a post-war society. One aspect of this was the physical environment. Mostar was a mixture of destruction and rebuilding and there was often the feeling of living in the middle of a building site. There was not always the freedom to walk in certain areas, because of the risk of landmines. Another aspect was living and working with people who had been through the war. Sensitivity and understanding was required. Often their ability to cope was challenged, especially when presented with unexpected situations. As well as this we became aware that we were viewed as internationals, or as outsiders. We might be linked with military forces and peacekeepers rather than seen as therapists.

Need for support

Because of the fact that we lived in B-H and because of the nature of the actual music therapy work that we did, it was essential for us to think about looking after ourselves. This was sometimes difficult to remember and even more difficult to achieve. The work could be exhausting and 'survival' in a setting such as this required support from each other and from friends, external supervision and regular breaks, preferably outside the country.

As well as this range of issues about the work setting, there was also the factor of working with those who had experienced traumatic events. The following section of the chapter takes a closer look at some of the factors considered when applying music therapy in the area of psychological trauma. It is put into context with a consideration of some of the current literature.

Issues specific to music therapy and psychological trauma

An amount of literature is already in existence regarding children's reactions to war. This literature deals with World War II, Vietnam and the Gulf War (Jensen and Shaw 1992), as well as the effects of the war on children in neighbouring Croatia (Zivcic 1993). Among others, authors list the following reactions: loss of interest in school, general anxiety and specific fears and psychosomatic complaints. Also included are reactions that were observed in sessions at the PMC, such as avoidance behaviours, regressive behaviours, depression, grief reactions and problems in communicating with peers.

Similar features are mentioned in literature on children's reactions to trauma in general. Vulnerability to depression, withdrawal, pessimistic world view, anxiety and fearfulness, as well as excesses of aggression and concern about personal responsibility for trauma are cited by Monahon (1993). Carlson (1997) described trauma reactions in both children and adults, listing six possible responses similar to those already mentioned. Five of these seemed particularly relevant to our work in Mostar – depression, aggression, low self-esteem, difficulties in interpersonal relationships and guilt. However, there was only a small amount of literature dealing specifically with music therapy and psychological trauma, including music therapists' work in South Africa (Pavlicevic 1994), Bosnia-Herzegovina and Northern Ireland (Sutton 1998, 2000).

From the time we began looking at our work in Mostar, it was clear that there were many different factors we needed to consider, in order to obtain a full understanding of why our clients presented as they did. There were factors for consideration from before the war, during the war and after the war. Others have written in the past about factors that may influence responses to trauma (Carlson 1997; Jensen and Shaw 1992) and we have also identified four particular themes that were relevant to our situation:

- the nature of the traumatic event
- the developmental level of the client at the time of the war
- the family situation
- other aspects of post-war life.

The nature of the traumatic event

It seemed important to be aware of what our clients may have experienced during the war. Many had endured over a year of being under constant attack, including shelling. They may have witnessed killing and felt that their lives were in danger. Some were part of families who had decided to leave their homes and become refugees; others may have been forcibly removed from their homes. The majority experienced physical deprivation in terms of food, water and shelter. The intensity and extreme nature of these experiences are well outside the bounds of what most of us consider to be normal daily life.

Developmental level of the client at the time of the war

That children's responses to trauma are affected by their stage of development has been recognised by others in the past (Black 1993; Carlson 1997; Monahon 1993). This includes development on cognitive, social and emotional levels. Research seems to show that the younger the developmental level at the time of the trauma, the more severe the reaction (Carlson 1997). Some of our clients were developmentally delayed and had attended the local special school before the war began. Their learning disability may have affected their level of ability to cope, in terms of understanding their experiences and beginning to process them in some way.

The family situation

Before the war, the family unit was very strong and often included the extended family. During the war many families were split up. Some people may have become refugees in other countries and parents may have sent children and young people abroad for their own safety. In other cases, families became divided because members were of different ethnic backgrounds. In yet other cases, family members were killed or disappeared (indeed, at the time of writing, some bodies have still not been found). During all of this, both parents and children had to contend with feelings that must arise when an adult can no longer maintain a safe environment for a child. In the post-war society, families were in many different situations. Economically, many of them were struggling. Some were living in poor conditions, such as a half-constructed house. Some were living in other people's houses with the constant threat of being forced to leave, yet they may also have been unwilling or unable to return to their original home. There were situations where children were no longer living with their families, having been removed by social services because parents were not coping. In some cases parents put their own children in care. There were also situations where children were living within the family unit, where one or both parent may not have been coping very well. The parents themselves may have had a mental illness or have been experiencing relationship difficulties. All these factors added to the stress under which families were placed.

Other aspects of post-war life

For the people of Mostar there were a number of specific, post-war issues:

- Each person was left in the position of having to try to adapt and accept their new life, both in terms of the physical appearance of the town and also the person that they had become as a result of their experiences.

- It was said that a large number of people living in Mostar had not lived there before the war. For the original Mostarians it could be difficult to accept new people in their town. For those not originally from Mostar there were difficulties adapting to living in a new town, where they might feel displaced and in some cases unwelcome.

- After the war, essentially the town was divided into two ethnic areas. This raised many issues, for example, the loss of friends from before the war who were now living on the opposite side of town. There was a feeling of being unable to cross from one side to another because of the fear of recognition or physical violence. There was awareness in some cases that one side was better off then the other. Others felt unwilling to accept that the town was now divided, when it never had been in the past. A symbolic aspect of the divide was seen in the size of significant buildings such as churches and mosques. Church bells and the call to prayer from the mosques were also amplified and their sounds directed towards the other community. The division of the town had a powerful impact upon the residents in these different ways.

Aspects of psychological trauma in music therapy

The following clinical examples illustrate some of the features of psychological trauma as we observed them. We concentrate on four features:

- depression
- regression
- avoidance behaviours
- aggression.

This section begins with a case study looking at the effects of internal displacement on a particular family. As well as work in the PMC, some sessions also took place at a collection centre for internally displaced people (families who had become refugees in their own country). This camp was situated on a piece of dusty, rocky wasteland and consisted of a series of prefabricated huts. The corrugated iron roofs made life very uncomfortable in the summer, when temperatures could reach up to 40°C. The huts were basic, one-roomed dwellings and the 100 or so families who were still living there all shared a communal bathroom. The only place where the children could play were the stony areas between the rows of huts.

Between summer 1998 and winter 2000, music therapy sessions took place at this centre just outside Mostar. Group work was offered to the children of the camp over this two-and-a-half year period. The referrals came from the camp director in discussion with the therapists, with most of the groups made up of children who were having difficulties adjusting to their new post-war lifestyle and environment. Issues in music therapy sessions included hyperactivity, aggression, withdrawal, anxiety and difficulties in peer relationships.

One such group was made up of two brothers aged 9 and 10 years. Their father was a long-distance lorry driver and often away for days at a time. The mother was at home all day and seemed not to have many friends. She was very anxious about who her sons were associating with and believed that most of the other children on the camp were not good enough to be their friends. She was also the disciplinarian of the family and known to strike the children when they did not behave as she wanted. When the boys' music therapy sessions were first set up, the mother was also referred by the camp director. She was only able to attend three sessions. Also present in the sessions was the music therapist, as well as a local music therapy assistant who translated all verbal input and was an active member of the group.

Between November 1999 and October 2000 there were only 13 music therapy sessions. This was due to illness, absence when the family was away starting to rebuild their house, holidays and sessions missed due to football practice. It is believed that the music reflected the inconsistency of the sessions. The improvisations in each session often contained high levels of anxiety, which resulted in difficulties in forming trusting relationships within the group. The mood of anxiety was apparent in the boys' restless body posture, and there were also problems in establishing eye contact with them. During improvisations they would both watch the therapist very carefully, as if wanting to do it right. They would try and copy exactly what she was doing. Anxiety was also apparent whenever they were addressed directly through speech, but gradually the trust formed through the non-judgemental means of musical interaction transferred to the verbal dialogue.

Despite the sporadic nature of the sessions, a sense of connection was maintained throughout the 11 months that also encompassed the missed weeks. During this time the group was able to explore many different ways of being together musically. For example, instead of playing at just one medium dynamic, the boys gradually began to explore making louder and softer sounds. This occurred first as individual exploration, during solo turns or 'in spite of' what the rest of the group were doing. Later it transferred to a group experience, when members were more aware of how the group was functioning, and deriving much pleasure from taking part in a shared experience.

The issue of being able to share experiences was very important to this group. The boys presented with a certain element of 'I have survived so far by being like this, why change now?' This attitude could be quite isolating and these defences had been erected to ensure that one was totally self-sufficient. It is believed that the music was able to offer a way of being with other people, but still for group members to retain their own sense of identity. Through exploring the world of sound, the boys were able find a voice that expressed how they felt at any given time and then to share that experience with the rest of the group.

Another issue for the group was that of tolerating silence and musical pauses. During the early sessions there was either constant sound, or there was talk, when instruments were put to one side. Over the months, these lines of demarcation began to blur and the group was able to keep hold of a whole musical idea, that framed brief periods of silence. This culminated in one of the final sessions in October when an improvisation lasted for 13 minutes – the longest the group had ever played together. The music contained fragments of material from many previous sessions but instead of being isolated segments, all the 'pieces' came together like a jigsaw. There was much variety – sounds were placed randomly, everyone played in the same beat together, there were on and off beats, glissando effects. There were many pauses, with a sense of anticipation when everyone was looking around the group waiting to see who would play first. The unspoken question was whether something more would happen. There was no discomfort in these pauses and no one spoke, yet the music seemed to speak volumes. It expressed how the group members were finally able to relate to each other in a way that was not threatening and did not compromise self-identity. Considering the upheaval they had experienced of losing their homes during the war and the environment and circumstances of their lives at this time, this represented an amazing achievement in terms of the relationships formed and the freedom of musical expression.

Depression

One of the features of trauma mentioned previously in the literature review was that of depression. The following illustration describes how one client presented as experiencing depression linked with grief reactions and shows how this was addressed in music therapy sessions.

In extreme situations, the belief that you have no control over what happens to you can lead to despair, especially when the events that you cannot control are perceived as extreme and negative. This idea is consistent with a 'learned helplessness' model of depression such as that described by Seligman (1975). According to this model, people can become depressed when they find that they are helpless to control or prevent negative events. They learn that their attempts to protect themselves from harm are of no use and so they stop trying to help themselves.

In traumatised people, depression can take the form of inactivity or lethargy, problems concentrating, or feelings of hopelessness or apathy. Carlson (1997) stated that some forms of depression might reflect the perception of a loss of control over one's ability to modulate or control one's own feelings of anxiety or anger. In other forms it might relate to aspects of the trauma situation, such as losing one's home or altering one's ideas about safety and protection from harm. The following example illustrates some of these aspects.

A young man (R) was 14 years old when he began attending music therapy sessions. He had a mild learning disability, with most of his difficulties apparently due to his own perception of his life at this time. Before the war, his family had lived in west Mostar. The mother had a moderate learning disability. The father had been ill and R would take him for his hospital visits and generally look after him. There was an older brother about whom there was no information. During the war, the family was expelled to east Mostar and it was believed that this was the main contributing factor to the father's death shortly after the move. R felt guilty that he did not help his father enough and considered his death a direct consequence of the war. This could therefore be termed a traumatic bereavement, with R's grief and mourning process complicated by the effects of his own traumatic experiences. Dora Black (1993) has noted that in order to grieve satisfactorily for a dead loved one it is necessary to remember and recollect again and again. However, the need to avoid the traumatic images and memories surrounding the death interferes with this process and this may well have been the case for R.

The music therapy sessions were characterised by a seeming inability of R to make choices or decisions and related to this, an inability to change anything in his music. When verbally offered the choice of another activity by the therapist, R would say things like 'you decide' and 'it's all the same to me'. These responses appeared to reflect what Black termed the 'learned helplessness' associated with traumatic events, which can lead to emotional constriction and sensations of numbing (Black 1993).

During the first nine months of music therapy, the sessions consisted of up to 25 minutes of constant playing, either on the drum or the piano. This produced a wall of sound through which it seemed nothing could penetrate, and appeared to be a self-defence mechanism. There was also a sense that R could change neither the music nor his situation. This fits with what Dora Black was referring to when she noted that learned help-lessness can lead to sensations of numbing. R's body posture was also very held in and he looked very tense, despite the almost bored look on his face, suggesting a young man who was trying very hard to hold himself together and safe. This was difficult work and an important aspect of this was how essential it was for the therapist not to be com-pletely drawn into R's perseverative playing. It was vital to retain a sense of separateness in order to be able to offer R something new from time to time. Without new ideas the music was in danger of becoming overly repetitive and 'stuck' in one or two rhythmic patterns. As R seemed unable or unwilling to initiate changes himself, the therapist felt that it would be useful to offer new ideas which could be taken up by R when he felt ready.

After seven months of sessions, R began to show signs of more explorative musical behaviour, as well as more awareness of the therapist and what he and she were creating together. Sometimes R followed the therapist and sometimes he initiated his own new patterns and speeds. He began to leave very slight gaps in his music – moments of silence that were now more comfortable to be in. It was believed that a safe and trusting relationship had built up between himself and the therapist because of the acknowledgement of what he was feeling and the accep-tance of who he was through the music-making in these earlier sessions. This allowed him gradually to explore the impact he could have on another person and on his environment, enabling him to feel brave enough to try to make these musical changes.

During this development phase of the music therapy sessions, it was hoped that as a result R would later be able to generalise the experiences he had in the music room in other areas of his life; for example, being aware of how interaction can take place between two people. At times, his musical interaction with the therapist had occurred in the form of a con-versation, with question and answer patterns, dialogue and pauses. The ability to generalise this 'musical conversation' could greatly enhance his verbal interaction with people, giving him the confidence to participate in a potentially rewarding experience.

Regression

One feature of trauma that has not been so widely written about is that of regressed behaviour. It may be that this was something more particular to the circumstances in B-H. The following example explores the issue of regression and is based on observations of music therapy work at the PMC with a girl, J.

When music therapy sessions first began, J was 11 years old. She had two younger sisters and they all lived in the local children's home. All three children had a varying degree of learning difficulty. The mother and stepfather also had mild learning disabilities, as well as problems with alcohol abuse. The mother had occasional contact with her daughters.

J displayed what could be termed regressed behaviours throughout her two years of music therapy sessions, although the number and length of the episodes did decrease. These behaviours included rolling around on the floor cushions and giggling, initiating games where she put the therapist and the assistant into parental roles, and asking who the disciplinarian figure was in the room. We thought of this behaviour as related to her perception of the father's role in the family unit. We noted that when this reconstruction of the family took place in the music room, J wanted to know who was taking this role. We felt that this was a positive thing, because through this J appeared to be getting in touch with and exploring the little child inside her.

One feasible interpretation of these regressed behaviours could relate to earlier experiences, and we wondered whether or not it had always been safe for J to be a playful or angry child. At the time of the war she would have been around 7 years old and as the eldest child in the family she was prematurely thrust into a role of responsibility. This may have given her limited opportunities to develop her play skills. J's musical improvisations with the therapist would often incorporate 'musical jokes'. For example, the use of fast trills, sudden pauses, a syncopated rhythm. There were also times when the music was able to reflect her sudden changes of mood, with a loud drumroll or heavy chords on the piano acknowledging an angry outburst.

Through the musical games that were initiated and the behaviours she presented during the music therapy sessions, J was able to re-experience and explore these regressed states. She gradually learned how to take appropriate control of her environment, how to have a rewarding, mutually satisfying relationship and how just to enjoy having fun.

Avoidance behaviours

Avoidance is often noted as a feature of trauma (Carlson 1997; van der Kolk, van der Hart and Burbridge 1995). It can take different forms such as avoidance of places, people or feelings. One possible reason for this may be that avoidance becomes a form of self-protection, when a person may feel that what they are avoiding is too difficult to experience. The next clinical example illustrates this.

A 16-year-old boy, T, attended 39 individual music therapy sessions over a period of one and a half years. T had been in Mostar throughout the war, living in the basement of his house for much of that time. Apparently six grenades had hit the house and it was almost completely destroyed. In addition, there had been conflicting stories about the family situation since the war. It was probable that T's mother may have had a mental illness, and in addition that his father could have had a problem with alcohol. It was believed that T was regularly caught up in the conflict between his parents and frequently used by one against the other.

First impressions of T were of a very polite young man who shook hands on meeting and asked how the therapist was. In the music there was a sense of T being quite disconnected from what he was doing. There seemed to be an avoidance of connecting with emotions, and observations of T playing the instruments suggested that he was engaged in something that involved 'doing' rather than 'feeling'. He held his body away from instruments and moved his hands forward in a jerky way in order to make contact with them. It was difficult for the therapist to create or hold on to any connection between T's music and her own. T played continuously throughout each session, jumping up after he had finished one improvisation and then immediately moving on to choose another instrument. He appeared unable to cope with silence or with any period of uncertainty and maintained a fixed smile and an unvaryingly polite and 'interested' tone of voice.

As the sessions progressed, T seemed gradually to become aware of the potential of music-making and that it could offer him a way of connecting with how he felt. While he was occasionally able to accept this experience, many times he was not. There were also moments when he could allow the therapist to connect with him in the music. Sometimes these moments of contact (both with himself and with the therapist) were followed by music that to the therapist clearly indicated panic. Although T tried to maintain a smiling facial expression, it appeared increasingly more strained and forced.

Towards the end of this period of music therapy T seemed ambivalent in terms of wanting yet not wanting to connect. He was nonetheless more 'present' during the sessions and able to create stronger music. During joint music-making, he occasionally picked up elements of the therapist's music and incorporated them into his own playing. His body posture was more relaxed and his facial expression serious. The music therapist was aware that the feeling and emotions being avoided by T were very difficult and frightening to contain and express. At the same time, the form of self-protection he had adopted had affected his general development, including his ability to interact with others. It was essential that any changes would take place slowly and in a way that did not leave T feeling over-exposed and vulnerable.

Music played an essential role in maintaining the necessary 'grounded' environment that T needed. Within a secure musical framework where he could be 'held' safely, there were opportunities for him to take some risks and try out new ways of being. There were possibilities for exploration of difficult feelings at his own pace as well as opportunities to choose to interact with the therapist in the music-making, whenever he felt able to do so.

Aggression

There are different ways to think about why aggression might be a feature of trauma. One possible explanation is that in order to regain a sense of control, the victim of aggression identifies with the aggressor and becomes aggressive himself (Srinath 1998). It may be that the need to relieve anxiety about one's own vulnerability is so great that it causes a complete reversal of roles so that the victimised becomes the victimiser (Carlson 1997). The idea that aggression can be used to mask excessive anxiety has also been mentioned. The following example explores these ideas further.

B was 13 years old when he attended music therapy. He was the oldest of three boys in his family. His parents had separated before the war and along with one of his brothers B lived with a grandfather for a time. During the war, this grandfather was killed, after which a local woman took B and his brother to live with her. Reports suggested that this was an environment of extreme deprivation and abuse. However, because there was severe bombardment of Mostar during this period, the deprivation and abuse were not noticed for some time. The boys were eventually removed by social services and placed in care with a number of other children. When their care placement began it was noted that they were unable to do basic things such as speak or eat independently. They also rejected the presence of anyone physically close to them. B was referred for music therapy and described as having frequent changes in behaviour, difficulties with speech and language and poor concentration. He was known to become afraid of new situations and of being outside his secure environment.

During the early music therapy sessions B presented with destructive play and showed aggression towards the instruments and other objects in the room. He spent one entire session with a toy lion, hitting it, standing on it, cutting off its paw while saying things like 'I'm killing him', 'I'm hurting him', 'He's dead now'. He used the same type of language while hitting and throwing different instruments around the room. Other sessions consisted of playing the xylophone in such a way that made the keys fly off, followed by flicking the keys around the room. On another occasion he brought plastic bricks with him to music therapy and spent a lot of the session crawling on the floor, hammering the bricks with a beater. B was also aggressive towards the two adults in the room (the therapist and the translator-assistant). He showed how difficult it was to listen to the therapist and often shouted 'shut up' or 'shut up, I'm going to kill you' while the translator was translating the therapist's words. He attempted physical aggression and needed very clear boundaries in order to keep the sessions safe for him.

A number of possible reasons for the aggressive behaviour were thought about. At times it appeared to be a form of limit testing, where B was investigating how safe the music therapy environment was, wanting to know where the boundaries were and if they would be enforced. On other occasions the aggression was governed by his need to create a situation where he was powerful and completely in control. It was also felt that it might, at times, be the only way that B could manage to express something of what was going on in his life.

In terms of the music therapy space, what seemed vital during this time was the absolute consistency and reliability of the therapist. Her ability to witness and survive the aggression and destruction while continuing to be present for B week after week was essential. Through her music it was possible to reflect the awfulness of what was being expressed through B's behaviour so that he could feel heard and understood during this difficult time.

Summary

When therapy began with our clients at the PMC, it was first of all important to create a safe and containing environment. This included the boundaries of a regular session time, the reliability of the therapist always being there, a positive and non-judgemental approach, and for many the knowledge that the therapist could survive any overwhelming feelings they were experiencing. For some of our clients, exploring their experiences verbally would have been extremely difficult. Many simply did not have the words to say what was clearly expressed through the non-verbal medium of music. Through music-making they were able to re-experience and explore difficult feelings that had arisen from the traumatic events which they had witnessed. The music provided a support for these feelings, leading to an acknowledgement and acceptance of each person as they were. Over time, clients could begin to retake control over some aspects of their lives. One important part of the music therapy work was addressing the issue of endings – the ending of therapy, or a therapist or assistant leaving. Many clients had experienced the sudden loss of someone close to them and so it was important that this issue be dealt with sensitively and planned for very carefully. This allowed clients actually to engage in the process of saying goodbye and to express feelings that it evoked within the security of the relationship with the therapist.

One of the questions considered in hindsight was the actual timing of a music therapy service being offered to a community such as Mostar, which had been traumatised by the effects of war. It was interesting to hear local people say that in the immediate post-war period what they had most wanted was opportunities for group activities such as attending pop concerts. For them this seemed to contribute to a sense of community, an affirmation and possibly a celebration of having survived the war. The potentially more intense individual and small group therapy may have been better suited to a later time, such as coinciding with the opening of the department in 1998. Even then, setting up such a service in an environment that was not yet completely stable was a highly complex task.

The challenges presented and the impact of these challenges have been discussed earlier in the chapter. However, in spite of these challenges, it is clear that it is not only possible to set up a music therapy service in a post-war environment, but that it also has something unique and valuable to offer. Contact from parents, other professionals and organisations, as well as the number of referrals received and the response to the subsequent clinical work, was proof of both the need and value of the work of the department.

References

Black, D. (1993) *Traumatic Bereavement in Children.* Highlight No. 121. London: National Children's Bureau.

Carlson, E. (1997) *Trauma Assessments: A Clinician's Guide.* New York: Guilford Press.

Jensen, P. and Shaw, J. (1992) 'Children as victims of war: current knowledge and future research needs.' *Journal of the American Academy of Child and Adolescent Psychiatry 32*, 4.

Lanyado, M. and Horne, A. (eds) (1999) *The Handbook of Child and Adolescent Psychotherapy*. London: Routledge.

Monahon, C. (1993) *Children and Trauma – A Parent's Guide To Helping Children Heal*. New York: Lexington Books.

Pavlicevic, M. (1994) 'Between chaos and creativity: music therapy with "traumatised" children in South Africa.' *Journal of British Music Therapy 8*, 2.

Seligman, M.E.P. (1975) *Helplessness: On Depression, Development and Death*. San Francisco: Freeman.

Srinath, S. (1998) 'Identificatory processes in trauma' In C. Garland (ed) (1998) *Understanding Trauma*. London: Gerald Duckworth & Co.Ltd Publishers.

Sutton, J.P. (1998) '"A kind of wound" – aspects of music therapy with children in areas of community conflict: some thoughts about an integrated approach.' Presented at the Exile Conference, University of Hertfordshire, July 1998.

Sutton, J. P. (2000) 'Aspects of music therapy with children in areas of community conflict.' In D. Docter (ed) *Exile. Refugees and the Arts Therapies*. Hertford: University of Hertfordshire, Faculty of Art and Design Press, pp.54–73.

van der Kolk, B., van der Hart, O. and Burbridge, J. (1995) 'Approaches to the treatment of PTSD.' In *Extreme Stress and Communities: Impact and Intervention*. NATO Asi Series, Series D: Behavioural and Social Sciences, Vol. 80. Norwell MA: Kluwer.

Zivcic, I. (1993) 'Emotional reactions of children to war stress in Croatia.' *Journal of the American Academy of Child and Adolescent Psychiatry 32*, 4.

CHAPTER 9

UK

In the Music Prison – the Story of Pablo

Helen M. Tyler

Introduction

> The little boy lowers his pistol in an arc, like the second hand of a
> clock progressing from twelve on its slow way out to three. The one
> eye he keeps open, to get a better shot, has placed the faraway head
> directly behind the sight sticking up from the tip of the barrel of his
> gun. First the head of his own mother, but then, changing his mind,
> of the strange man standing near her. He has the enemy right where
> he wants him. 'I'll kill you, you man', the dialogue runs in Zero's
> mind. 'I'm Zero the Kid. I'm going to shoot you DEAD!' (Senstad
> 2001, pp.45–6)

In this scene from Senstad's novel, *Music for the Third Ear,* we are introduced to 4-year-old Zero, child of war and rape and the pivotal figure in
this exploration of the repercussions of war. Throughout the story he is
inseparable from his toy pistol. It is his weapon, the symbol of masculin-
ity and of the aggression which has ruled his short life, but also his
plaything and his comforter. As his uncomprehending foster father
writes, attempting to justify his inability to care for him:

> He also refuses to relinquish the white-handled cap pistol he was
> carrying the day we received him from you; he threatens my wife

with it, and, ludicrous as it may sound given his size and his age, he actually does frighten her. (Senstad 2001, p.157)

This ability to inspire fear emanated, no doubt, from the depths of hatred, violence and despair in which Zero was conceived. The soft blanket, lock of hair or cuddly toy which usually represents the absent mother's presence to her baby, was replaced by that most stark symbol of conflict, the gun. As an autistic child will often clutch a firm hard object for security, so Zero needed a transitional object with powerful and deadly connotations.

Pablo (as I will call the child who is the central character of this chapter), also had the power to frighten people. The first thing I heard about him from his headteacher was that he was threatening children in the playground, saying that he was going to get a knife, stab them and then kill himself. While this was viewed on one level as 'atten-tion-seeking behaviour', school staff were concerned enough to refer him for music therapy, which was a service available to a limited number of children from the special needs school which he attended.

I had very little information about Pablo before meeting him, and indeed, the school also had few details. The known facts were that he had recently come to England with his parents and two sisters, fleeing from the repressive regime in his home country. His father had been tortured, shot and severely injured, with Pablo being present and witnessing the whole event. The reason for Pablo's placement in a special school was that he was born with various physical disabilities and had only one arm. He was alert and intelligent, and was quickly picking up English. He could have coped academically with mainstream schooling, but physically and emotionally he was vulnerable. The hope was that the sheltered environ-ment of a small special school would help him to adjust to life in a new country and equip him with the social skills he would need to integrate with his peers. His disturbed behaviour, however, and his aggressive attitude to the weaker children was seen as delaying the adjustment process and so therapy was considered appropriate.

Pablo was referred through his school to the music therapy centre in London at which I was based. After talking to his headteacher I decided that it would be ideal for two therapists to work with Pablo, myself and my colleague, Donald Wetherick, whom I shall refer to as DW. From our past experience of music therapy with emotionally disturbed children we felt that Pablo might well benefit from the extra containment that we could provide working together. Using the model pioneered by Nordoff and Robbins and described by them (1977, pp.91–2) I was to be the primary therapist, while DW would take a supportive role as co-therapist. I would take responsibility for the musical direction of the therapy in the moment, working from the piano where appropriate and, afterwards, listening back to the audio recording of the session and writing up the notes. DW would bring Pablo to the music room from the waiting room, and would then be available to be used by Pablo in whatever way he needed. We wondered at this stage whether DW would literally be 'an extra pair of hands'. We also knew that Pablo's father was undergoing psychiatric treatment and that his mother was struggling with the three children so that a model of the parental couple as thera-pists could also be useful to Pablo. As Turry writes: 'Working in a mixed gender team can create the possibility of corrective emotional experi-ences for the client within the traditional model of an intact family unit' (Turry 1998, p.193).

Pablo was eight and a half when he began therapy and over a period of 18 months he attended 38 half-hour sessions during school term times out of a possible total of 60. This reflected not only hospital appoint-ments which conflicted with therapy times, but also an unsettled period in the first year of therapy when the family split up. Pablo had briefly stayed with his father before moving to live with his mother and sisters.

Before looking at the clinical material of Pablo's therapy, I return to Senstad's story of Zero. Eventually, Zero is reunited with his mother, Zheljka, who is now pregnant. This is no 'happy-ever-after' ending, however, and the reader is left, uncomfortable and uncertain, in the bleak post-war landscape. The final paragraph describes the homecoming:

> Zheljka flees into the building and up the stairs with her son running after her.
>
> She locks and bolts the apartment door, then leans her weight against it.
>
> Zheljka, her womb a clenched fist, looks at Zero. Zero, hand jammed in his pocket, clutches his gun. (Senstad 2001, p.255)

Neither did the story of Pablo come to a satisfying conclusion as his therapy terminated abruptly, precipitated by a move to a new school. We the therapists were left with the anxious and disturbing feelings which he had evoked in us, as though we ourselves had been involved in a terrible traumatic event and left to recover in the devastated aftermath. This, however, seemed to be an appropriate response to working with such a damaged and traumatised child. The major work of the therapy was to help Pablo to explore the results of both his physical and emotional trauma and to enable him to contain the pain which was inevitably encountered in the process.

Sifting through the mass of notes and audio tapes which were the product of Pablo's therapy, I have re-experienced the feeling that I often had at the time, that there was far too much material to be contained in a half-hour session or, as now, in one chapter. Similarly in supervision, which was essential to the work, I found it hard to know where to begin, as there were several other equally needy children calling for my attention. This feeling of being overwhelmed, both by the quantity and the emotional quality of the sessions, was a key feature of the therapy for Pablo and for the therapists. The planned holiday breaks in the therapy turned out to be important features of the process, both in terms of con-solidation of the work done and in order for Pablo to experience surviving the separation. I am therefore looking at the sessions in two roughly equal periods, on each side of an eight-week summer break.

First period

From silence to storytelling

In the first period of the therapy Pablo was generally reluctant to leave the waiting room and needed cajoling from the school staff member who had accompanied him to persuade him to go with DW to the music room. Our initial impression was that Pablo was passive, withdrawn and mute, depressed in posture with his head hanging, or slumped awkwardly in a chair. He appeared to need help to access instruments, looking at them as though he wanted to play, yet could not think how. In Pablo's class at school he was the only child who had normal speech development, the others relying on non-verbal means such as eye-pointing or sign language to communicate their needs. It seemed that Pablo was making himself more disabled and helpless than he really was, testing us to see if we could cope with such a damaged boy.

In the first session he remained silent as DW guided him to each instrument in turn, a drum, cymbal, metallophone, piano and set of large bells. Once at the instruments, however, Pablo revealed both dexterity and musical competence at playing, using a stick to beat firmly on the percussion instruments. From the piano I matched his tempo and dynamics and repeated his rhythmic patterns so that he would know I was listening to him. He showed immediate awareness of being reflected in this way and tested me further by making sudden changes or unexpected stops, watching closely to see if I could follow him. This need to be mirrored and matched exactly was an ongoing feature of Pablo's therapy and in the early sessions it had a controlling quality as he would insist, non-verbally, that I imitate him precisely, shaking his head sternly if I was not accurate.

In her case study of music therapy with an autistic boy, David, Sandra Brown suggests that his musical omnipotence 'covered fear of inner and outer chaos' and that this was the root of his need to control the musical interaction. For David, the structure and order inherent in music provided security until he was ready to allow some flexibility and 'the creative possibilities of mutual relationship' (Brown 2002). In Pablo's early sessions too it felt vital to give him a sense of musical control so that he would eventually come to trust the therapeutic relationship with his own inner chaos.

On a purely practical level, Pablo showed resourcefulness and determination in mastering every instrument that was offered to him, using his teeth, feet and right shoulder to supplement his left hand. We had provided him with a bass drum and high-hat cymbal operated by foot pedals, but these were not necessarily his first choice. In the early sessions, before he had begun to speak, he explored the possibilities of all the instruments. He set up complicated instrumental sequences where he would play, for example, piano, drum, tambourine, cymbal, reed horn and piano in quick succession, running from one to another rather like an assault course. On more than one occasion DW and I were directed silently to play the foot pedal instruments, while he conducted us from the piano. We wondered if Pablo was making us experience his feelings of being 'armless' while he took on the role of the powerful adult at the biggest instrument, the grand piano.

An indication that trust was developing came in the fifth session when Pablo spoke his first words. He had been occupied for 20 minutes, putting the instruments in order and then playing each in turn. Eventually he came to the piano and, sitting by me with DW on his other side, put his head down on the keys as though tired, making clicking sounds with his teeth and playing the piano with his chin. The dialogue proceeded as follows:

> HT   [*Helen Tyler*]: [singing teasingly] I heard a little noise. Who's come to music?
>
> [*Pablo makes a squeaking noise.*]
>
> HT: Was it a mouse?
>
> [*Pablo makes a roaring noise.*]
>
> HT: Was it a dinosaur?
>
> Pablo: [*speaking*] It was a tiger! The tiger eat the meat…eat Donald's teeth…hungry for lunch…eat a house…eat the music room … eat the window…eat us all up and Donald escaped to the shop…tiger eats us all up…it can eat everybody, eat all the music room and – school and all the houses.

Pablo spoke in short phrases, at first hesitantly and then gathering momentum. I responded in the pauses, echoing his words and playing suitable 'tiger' music with tremolos in the bass of the piano and chromatic ascending and descending 'roars' in the right hand. Pablo smiled and seemed very pleased with his story and the way it was received. It felt as though he had been testing DW and me to see if we would be damaged by him or whether we would retaliate, but instead we accepted everything he said and listened attentively, while I matched the quality of his words in the music. Perhaps it was this experience which gave him the confidence to bring further stories to the sessions on the theme of physical attacks, which, at an unconscious level, could be seen to relate to fantasies about his disability as well as the memory of the actual attack on his father.

Many other therapists have noted references to wild animals in their client's therapy. Sekeles (1996) describes 7-year-old Alon acting out 'oral-sadistic fantasies' as a vicious man-eating tiger in response to stimulating drumming music. She says:

> The therapeutic space became Alon's jungle (as he saw it) in which he was free to act out the wild beast and to transmit to the therapist his aggressive feelings to his full satisfaction. … Clear awareness of a make-believe situation enabled him to be aggressive with no risk of guilt feelings. (Sekeles 1996, p.133).

Brown refers to the 'Monster' and 'Wild Cat' brought by David into his sessions:

> I became aware of how this use of 'wild cats' to hold aggressive emotions for the child had occurred before in my therapy work, and mused on the connections of this image with Jung's idea of the collective unconscious and archetypal images. (Brown 2002)

While the tiger story in session five had something of the quality of an intimate, shared bedtime story, in session nine Pablo expressed his aggression in a more graphic way and again forced us, the therapists, to share something of his inner world. Pablo was dressed that day (as he often was) in army-type clothes in camouflage colours. He came in scowling and grimacing, blowing out his cheeks and grinding his teeth. I reflected, singing, that today he was 'an animal with sharp teeth'. He snarled and growled in response to this and began to beat the drum vigorously while I accompanied on the piano with intense rhythmic music based on two simple chords, E major and D minor 7. The repetitive nature of the music provided a supportive framework to hold whatever Pablo would bring to it, while the parallel chords and dotted rhythms evoked a Spanish idiom which often emerged in Pablo's sessions, possibly connected to his Spanish-speaking country of origin.

Suddenly, Pablo stopped playing and grabbed the wooden drumstick between his teeth, like an animal snatching its prey. From between his clenched jaws came the words 'Help me, help me', as though his victim, the stick, was calling for help. I continued to play while DW, singing 'someone needs help', approached Pablo as though to 'rescue' the stick. Pablo instantly dropped the stick, and pretended to bite DW's hand. He then grabbed the stick and 'stabbed' DW with it, then did the same to himself, groaning and falling to the floor. Throughout this, I kept a firm pulse going, and reflected Pablo's movements with tense, staccato chords while DW, arming himself with a stick, beat the drum in time with the stabbing motions.

This scene was repeated several times, DW going to rescue the stick, which was calling for help, only to be stabbed himself. Eventually, I too was 'stabbed', becoming aware of a very real sensation of fear as Pablo lunged at me with his stick. At that moment he reminded me of a boy in a horror film I had once seen who was taken over by an evil spirit and became murderous, even to his parents.

At the end of the session Pablo arranged the three of us in a tableau, holding our sticks to our chests as though stabbed. We sang goodbye and he went out, looking satisfied. Although we were left feeling shaken, the music, which had continued throughout, had helped both to contain and stylise the drama. We felt that this containment had enabled Pablo to be aware of the make-believe situation of therapy, although the emotions he expressed were painfully real.

This session was a turning point. From now on, Pablo seemed to have lost his inhibitions about sharing his fantasies with us. He began to use the sessions to tell a series of stories beginning 'Once upon a time', for which DW and I provided the music and sound effects. I would also interject with phrases like 'and then?' or 'what happened next?' An example of this is in the following section of a story from session 11. Pablo was wearing an army shirt with 'Survival' across the front and a commando badge.

> *Pablo*: [*speaking*] Once upon a time there were three children. They heard a noise downstairs. They sang a song 'Twinkle Twinkle little star' [*We all sing it.*]. Then another song about me when my mum was singing a long time ago about me, 'I'm big and strong'. [*We all sing 'big and strong'.*] Then there was lots of monsters and the monster broke the badge off the boy and pretends to stab him with the needle and the boy sang the song again. 'Big and strong'. [*We all sing.*]

Then there was soldiers, helicopters, guns, guard dogs, and the monster came and it was bigger than the sky, bigger than God, bigger than the sun, bigger than everything and the giant guns and power rangers came to help – 'TAKE THAT YOU BIG FAT MONSTER' and the monster died, his life was finished but he had another one, like a ghost.

The next session preceded a two-week Easter break. Pablo, a boy who did not have a pair of hands, came in with a pair of toy handcuffs. He locked and unlocked everything during the session, skilfully manipulating the tiny silver key with his teeth. At the end of the session I too was handcuffed and Pablo triumphantly threw the key across the room as though I would be locked up for ever. As the clasp snapped round my wrist I felt trapped, helpless and panicky, a response that was out of proportion to the actual event, but reflected the intensity of the feelings which Pablo projected.

At the time I felt that this episode had a connection with the break and that Pablo wanted to be sure that we would not lose touch with the enormity of his need over the holiday. On reflection I could see it was also an enactment of incidents at school when he would threaten and victimise other children. Here, in the safety of the therapy room, Pablo could explore these impulses without fear of retaliation or punishment, while we could hold, contain and begin to make sense of his unmanageable feelings, even in his absence. As Garland writes, such containment is hard work and calls on the therapist to survive 'the severe internal buffetings of the counter-transference' (Garland 1998, p.30).

The first period of therapy concluded with two important sessions. First, Pablo told me that he had had a dream about a dog that he stroked. The dog was friendly and didn't bite him and it laid some eggs. This seemed hopeful, as though a potentially fierce object, which could have damaged his surviving hand, was able to become creative. In the final session before the long summer break, Pablo took the role of a television newsreader. Against a rhythmic accompaniment provided by DW and myself, he began to announce the news, chanting in 'rap' style:

Pablo: Ladies and gentlemen, here is the news.

If you see a danger sign you must stop, stop, stop!

If you see a fire you must call 9 – 9– 9!

If you see a skeleton you must stop, stop, stop!

If you see something really horrible you must stop to help,

When you see a chicken that is hungry give it some corn,

If you see a monkey that is hungry give it some bananas,

If you see a horse that is hungry give it some hay,

If you haven't got any dinner go to your friend

Your friend should look after you,

So if you see a fire call 9–9–9!

Ladies and gentlemen, that is the end of the news.

Thank you for listening and goodbye.

I responded, 'Thank you for singing to us.' It was the end of the session and we were all able to sing the goodbye song together. It seemed that DW and I were the 'lady and gentleman' who needed to hear Pablo's news, which now could contain both destructive and reparative elements. For example, the destructive fire is mediated by the reparative 999 call to the fire brigade; hunger is assuaged by the giving of food; and even the horror of death, in the form of a skeleton, can be confronted with the potential for help.

This reverberates with Klein's (1986a) theory of the depressive position in which the baby recognises that the good, idealised mother and the bad, hated mother can coexist. This is a development from the splitting between good and bad that occurs in the earlier para-noid-schizoid position. Klein described these two positions as belonging both to the first months of life and also as part of an ongoing and uncon-scious process of the development of the personality. In therapy, however, these powerful drives are awakened as part of the relationship between client and therapist, and also, in this case, the client and the music. We shall see how at times Pablo experienced the music itself as bad and persecutory or as good and idealised like the baby's experience of the 'good and bad breast'.

Talking to Pablo's teacher at the end of the school year, I was encour-aged to learn that he was more settled in class and, although still having outbursts of difficult behaviour, he was more likely to become upset when reprimanded and want to make amends.

Second period

Tigers and torture

After the long summer break Pablo was eager to come to his sessions and wanted to 'get on with the game' as soon as he came in. Now DW and I were essential characters in the drama, rather than observers or witnesses. The music room became transformed each week into a variety of dramatic settings: a bench became the court-room, a locked cupboard was the prison, inside which were the tigers. There was also a palace, a castle, a jungle and a river. There were cages, searchlights and security cameras, electric wires and bombs, but also magic spells and sleeping potions. The instruments and the room took on new guises as follows:

- windchimes = magical powers
- tambourines = protective shields
- metal beater = screwdriver to connect the electricity
- cupboard = cage full of tigers
- whistle = for taming tigers
- drumsticks = swords
- bass drum = a signal
- high-hat cymbal = crocodile's teeth
- swanee whistle = for shooting arrows or a laser gun
- video camera = security lights or CCTV.

The tortures with which Pablo threatened his prisoners included hungry lions, electric shocks and the eating of limbs by the crocodile. While some of these are familiar themes in children's fiction and fairytales (such as *Red Riding Hood*, Barrie's *Peter Pan* or Sendak's *Where the Wild Things Are*), they also demonstrate the level of his sense of persecution and his premature knowledge of real-life torture. Once again, Pablo's dramatic stories can be seen not only in terms of the psychoanalytic concepts of the oral-sadistic phase and the castration complex (Klein 1986b), but also as a personal expression of his traumatic experiences. The fantasies of aggression and destruction which are a normal part of child development were to him a frightening and horrible reality.

So what had happened to the music? Was this now a form of play therapy, using musical instruments as props in the game, and was the music merely like a film score, highlighting moments of drama? This was a question I pondered both in the sessions and during supervision, particularly as Pablo became more controlling in defining the musical limits of the session. For example, he would tell me that the piano was 'live' so that if I touched it I would get an electric shock unless I knew a magic password to make it safe. One way of thinking about this was that he experienced the music as dangerous and then projected these persecutory feelings onto me. There was also an element of sadistic delight in preventing me from playing the piano, thus making him the torturer and rendering me impotent. Despite his frequents efforts to silence the music, however, I felt that the music had brought us to this point and therefore continued to be a vital ingredient, either in its presence or absence. A connection can be made here with Jean-Paul Sartre's concept of negation, described in *Being and Nothingness*.

> It is evident that non-being always appears within the limits of a human expectation … It would be in vain to deny that negation appears on the original basis of a relation of man to the world. The world does not disclose its non-beings to one who has not first posited them as possibilities. (Sartre 1969, p.7)

It was only because together, DW, Pablo and myself had the experience and the expectation of music in the session that its absence could be significant. Pablo's frequent refusal to allow music, except on his own terms, indicated the power that he attributed to it and his fear of being overwhelmed or annihilated by it. For Pablo to experience a relationship that contained some reciprocity, it was important for him not to become an omnipotent dictator. Therefore I timed my musical interventions carefully, so as not to be either too provocative or too submissive. For instance, there would be regular occasions when a march or fanfare was called for – when the king, guards or soldiers were coming and Pablo would accept this, or magic music for taming the animals. There was also frequently a march to the prison to which DW or I would regularly be sent. One week I improvised a song to the words 'Off to prison, off to prison, we must go'. The music to this was a minor key version of the French song 'Frère Jacques'. It was only after the session that I made the association between this tune and its ironic use in Mahler's First Symphony, where he portrays the animals mockingly carrying the dead hunter to his funeral. Pablo responded to this tune and joined in enthusiastically. I generally found that when the music came from within me, responding in the musical countertransference (Scheiby 1998), it would have an authenticity which Pablo recognised, but when I was struggling to use music out of duty, he would often reject it.

By this time Pablo's behaviour and self-confidence had improved sufficiently at school for him to be beginning the process of integrating into a mainstream school. According to his teacher, Pablo was finding this stressful and claimed to have been bullied in the playground. We were told that once he was offered a permanent place he would leave his special school immediately and would no longer be able to come for music therapy. Pablo knew that these changes were imminent and in sessions became increasing anxious and manic in his play, and in his need to have control of the music. It seemed that, in Kleinian terms, the depressive position had regressed to the paranoid-schizoid position with a splitting into good and bad objects, An extract from session 23 illustrates this. Pablo and I are both speaking, without music, until he gives the command to me to play:

Pablo: I said no music allowed in this room – I'll shoot you! I am the king and you are in prison.

HT: But this is a music room!

Pablo: The King would like some beautiful music but if you do it wrong the King will send you to prison. [*HT plays the piano and DW plays the drum.*]

Pablo: STOP! [in a different voice] Your Highness, did you like that music?

Pablo: [in the King's voice] It was too loud so we have to shoot them.

HT: Can we try again and play some quieter music?

Pablo: Try again!

This scene was repeated with HT trying different kinds of music, which were again rejected. The third time the music was like a lullaby, based on the 'child's tune' (Nordoff and Robbins 1977, p.102).

> Pablo: The King says, 'The music is nice.' Play music for the guards to guard the castle. I'm stealing all the music. Don't worry, I'm the King, I'll get the music back.

In traditional fairy stories there are often three questions to be answered or three tasks to be performed to save the hero's life or to win a reward. In Pablo's story there was never an end to the ordeals. As soon as the music was 'nice' it was stolen, as the story continues:

> Pablo: Come on, we have to get the music back. Use your laser and use your magic drum. [*We all play together – DW and P on swanee whistles, HT the tambourine: this reminded me of the magic flute and bells in Mozart's opera* Die Zauberflote *which guided the lovers through the ordeals of fire and water.*]

> Pablo: I think I'm shot – all the music in the world is broken and it's all your fault.

> HT: Can I give you a magic shield to help you? [*offering the tambourine*]

> Pablo: I'm going to put a prison round you. You failed. You made me get shot, now I'm going to die. I don't need you any more. You go back to your house – I can do it by myself. You can't help me.

The despairing nature of this outburst and the annihilation of both the music and the therapists were, I felt, connected both to past events and to the impending loss of both the music therapy and the haven of the supportive small school. Rustin's thoughts about psychotic children have relevance here:

> Children and adolescents susceptible to psychotic states show a profound helplessness, often hidden by omnipotence. This helplessness corresponds to an inability to comprehend certain experiences of mental pain. Clinical work shows that these experiences reflect earlier situations where the mental pain was not matched by the capacity of the self, often still very immature, for comprehension. (Rustin *et al.* 1997, p.9)

It is not hard to link Pablo's story with Rustin's concept of omnipotence concealing helplessness. His words – 'You failed – you made me get shot' – conjure up the poignant image of a small disabled boy looking on impotently, unable to comprehend the situation. Through his re-enactment of this event by the symbolic destruction of a good, containing object, the music, he could project his feelings of failure and despair onto the therapists. At these moments it was vital that we did not also despair, so I continued to offer Pablo the protection of the magic tambourine. Testing me again, he commanded: 'Tell me the password!' This password, 'Air beneath me', had been used in several previous sessions to call up what Pablo called a 'protection shield', usually at moments of terrible danger in the story. I remembered the password and Pablo accepted that this could save him. He summoned his guards to come to the rescue and we were able to sing the 'goodbye' song together before the end of the session. It was as though the evidence of me keeping him in mind between sessions, by being able to recall the password, served a reparative function that enabled Pablo to allow something to be restored.

It was confirmed that Pablo would be leaving the school and therefore therapy at the end of term, so there were a potential six sessions remaining. Pablo was fully aware of the impending move and reacted by telling his teacher that he did not want to come to music therapy any more, as it made him feel ill. He attended only three of the last six sessions and showed a sense of real desperation in his play. This is an extract from the penultimate session which illustrates him projecting his anger and disappointment onto me:

> Pablo: It' s the end of music. *I'm* the King of music. Guards, take away the music. I'm going to arrest that lady. I'm taking you to the music prison and the lions will eat you for lunch. We hate music and we're going to take all your music stuff and sell it!

In the last session Pablo set up a courtroom scene, in which DW and I were interrogated:

> Pablo: Who was the murderer – was it you? You used to be the King and Queen of music but you was murdered. They shut up the music – the law says they shouldn't do that. I am your friend

but I have to put you in prison. We're going to find out the
truth. Now what is the truth? *Tell me the truth!*

With this question, and the intensity with which it was asked, we seemed
to be put in the position of torture victims being interrogated, knowing
that we would not be able to answer without failing Pablo and letting him
down. He needed us to fail, and so we were sentenced.

> *Pablo*:   Guards! Take them away into the school where they treat
> you very bad and they whack you. They treat you like a baby
> and they don't give you anything to eat. Hurry up, get up. I
> am the teacher!

This last sentence came as a sudden surprise to me. Here, at the very last
moment in the therapy emerges a little boy who is anxious about going to
a new school. Out of his inner world of tigers and torture comes
something that belongs in the 'here and now', as though he was
beginning to make connections between fantasy and reality.

Conclusion

Pablo's therapy finished too soon, and under stressful circumstances with
many issues unresolved. All we could do was to write a report for the new
school which recommended that Pablo should be offered continuing
therapeutic input of some kind, because he had shown a profound need
for therapy and the ability and readiness to use it.

Looking back and reflecting on the work with Pablo, I am aware that
we were often treading dangerous ground in entering into the chaos of
his trauma. The psychotic state never felt very far away, and yet Pablo was
constantly able to allow himself to be grounded by the 'here and now' of
the music and the relationships in the music therapy room.

So why does music therapy have the power to contain the emotions of
a trauma victim like Pablo who would appear to be in a state of disintegra-
tion? There seem to me to be several reasons, all of which are significant.
First, the therapeutic frame within which DW and I worked gave Pablo an
experience of the absolute reliability and attentiveness that a mother
gives her playing child. Our careful timekeeping, observation of boundaries and preparation for breaks provided a secure and containing base
for the therapy. Our stance of accepting everything that was brought to

the session, in music, words or play, as potential working material and our willingness to allow ourselves, the room and the instruments to be used in symbolic play offered Pablo a freedom to be himself in whatever way he needed. Of equal and parallel importance, the music, as the primary medium of the therapy, connected Pablo to a wide range of feeling states, and enabled him to explore a rich creativity which was as much a part of his inner world as chaos and destruction. As Nordoff and Robbins wrote:

> Music is a universal experience in the sense that all can share in it; its fundamental elements of melody, harmony and rhythm appeal to and engage their related psychic functions in each one of us. Music is also universal in that its message, the content of its expression, can encompass all heights and depths of human experience, all shades of feeling. (Nordoff and Robbins 1971, p.15)

As well as the feeling aspects of music, the ever-present elements of motif, repetition, structure and form provided a stability and security when the content became highly emotional and potentially uncontained, as in session five. Finally, Pablo's use of the sessions as a space to play in every sense of the word enabled him to experience a normal and healthy part of child development in a safe setting. As Winnicott has said, children's play is inherently exciting and precarious. He writes of therapy that it contains 'the precariousness of magic itself, the magic that arises in intimacy, in a relationship that is being found to be reliable' (Winnicott 1985, p.55).

For Pablo, music therapy provided all these elements: magic, intimacy, precariousness and reliability, within the experience of a unique relationship with DW, myself and the music. In the introduction to this chapter I quoted passages from the beginning and end of a novel, *Music for the Third Ear*. The story of Zero finished without hope and with the cycle of war, violence and suffering unbroken. Pablo's story is not complete and will continue to unfold throughout the rest of his life. My hope is that in the future others will recognise his needs, and the needs of children like Zero, and rise to the challenge which Pablo himself issued:

If you see a danger sign you must stop, stop, stop!

If you see a fire you should call 9–9–9!

If you see something really horrible you must stop to help.

If you haven't got any dinner go to your friend

Your friend should look after you.

Pablo's words show that out of suffering, aggression and destruction can come the potential for creative transformation. Music therapy is one medium through which this potential can be realised.

References

Brown, S. (2002) 'Hullo object! I destroyed you.' In L. Bunt and S. Hoskyns (eds) *A Handbook of Music Therapy*. London: Routledge.

Garland, C. (ed) (1998) *Understanding Trauma – A Psychoanalytic Approach*. London: Duckworth.

Klein, M. (1986a) 'Notes on some schizoid mechanisms.' In J. Mitchell (ed) *The Selected Melanie Klein*. London: Penguin.

Klein, M. (1986b) 'The psycho-analytic play technique: its history and significance.' In J. Mitchell (ed) *The Selected Melanie Klein*. London: Penguin.

Nordoff, P. and Robbins, C. (1977) *Creative Music Therapy*. New York: John Day.

Rustin, M., Rhode, M., Dubinsky, A., Dubinsky, H. (eds) (1997) *Psychotic States in Children*. London: Duckworth.

Sartre, Jean-Paul (1969) *Being and Nothingness: An Essay on Phenomenological Ontology*. London: Methuen and Co Ltd.

Sekeles, H. (1996) *Music: Motion and Emotion: The Developmental-Integrative Model in Music Therapy*. USA, MMB Music Inc.

Senstad, S.S. (2001) *Music for the Third Ear*. London: Black Swan.

Scheiby, B.B. (1998) 'The role of Musical Countertransference in Analytical Music Therapy.' In K. Bruscia (ed) *The Dynamics of Music Psychotherapy*. Gilsum: Barcelona Publishers.

Turry, A. (1998) 'Transference and Countertransference in Nordoff-Robbins Music Therapy.' In K. Bruscia (ed) *The Dynamics of Music Psychotherapy*. Gilsum: Barcelona Publishers.

Winnicott, D. W. (1985) *Playing and Reality*. London: Pelican.

CHAPTER 10

Israel

Developmental Trauma and its Relation to Sound and Music

Adva Frank-Schwebel

Musical improvisation is fundamental to music therapy. It is offered to patients as the royal road through which communication, self-discovery and change take place. At times, however, other forms of sound and music experiences may become therapeutic. When given freedom of choice, some patients seem to avoid playing music and find other, more primary, ways to experience sound, revealing often a preference for auditory and vocal experiences. In the present discussion, I will attempt to make a connection between this phenomenon and the idea of regression in therapy. In my opinion this link is relevant to patients who have experienced recurring disruptions in the area of early mother–child interaction. This developmental trauma is manifested in adulthood in a variety of symptoms ranging from various psychosomatic phenomena to characterological defensive formations, such as false-self, borderline and narcissistic disorders (Balint 1968; Fairbairn 1954; McDougall 1986; Winnicott 1984a).

Early infancy trauma and the idea of regression as a curative factor

In the last decades of the twentieth century psychoanalysis has directed its attention to disorders related to early disruptions in the relationship between mother and infant. A distinction has been drawn between acute maternal psychopathology such as depression or psychosis and the maternal failures discussed presently, which do not consist of a single, dramatic event, but are found in the mother's subtle misattunements to the infant (Khan 1974). If repeated in frequency and intensity, these maladaptations crystallise in the infant's inner world into a traumatic experience. Khan used the concept of cumulative trauma to describe these breaches in the mother's role as protective shield that accumulate 'silently and invisibly over the course of development ... gradually get embedded in the specific traits of a character structure ... and achieve the value of trauma only cumulatively and in retrospect' (Khan 1974, p.47). Research in the area of infant development has been important in exploring how these breaches are effected (Stern 1985).

Often talented and high achievers, individuals who have experienced this type of trauma develop symptoms in the interpersonal domain, for example, in a difficulty to experience intimacy or to maintain lasting meaningful relationships. Their suffering is also present in their sense of self: they express feelings of emptiness, falseness, low self-esteem, depression and deep loneliness. These phenomena are grouped under well-known clinical diagnoses such as false self and narcissistic personality disorders. Other typical symptoms are of a somatic nature. They are manifest in somatic conditions, such as allergies and eating disorders, or in more diffuse bodily complaints and sensations. The nature of these early maternal failures, which are not representationally remembered and therefore cannot be told verbally, runs through the grapevine of the transference relations and is communicated unconsciously in somatic ways, by acting out or through projective identification processes. Unable to remember and tell their early experiences, patients reconstruct in the therapy setting all the nuances of the infantile scenario (Khan 1974a). The therapist must be able to perceive these non-verbal cues and make them communicable in more symbolic ways.

When this kind of clinical picture is encountered, the treatment is linked to the idea of regression, which in the last decades is viewed as one of the main avenues through which curative changes are achieved. (Balint 1968; Khan 1974; Winnicott 1984b). The therapeutic setting and the therapist's attitude constitute an environment that provides the patient with the emotional conditions which were lacking in early infancy, namely trust and reliability. Given these conditions, the patient may regress to earlier states of being, where the original disruptions occurred. The therapist's attitude consists then in not interfering with or causing unnecessary disturbances in the patient's internal life, thus giving 'recognition of the existence of the patient's internal life and of the patient's own unique individuality' (Balint 1968, p.144). Winnicott emphasised the importance of the therapist's facilitation of an atmosphere where the main message conveyed is that nothing is expected of the patient. The patient is allowed to exist in a state of formlessness and un-organisation. This experience, lived in the presence of the facilitating therapist, enables the patient gradually to let go of his defences and thus release the liveliness and creativity of the true self (Winnicott 1971, pp.62–75; 1984b). Bion's idea of containment refers to similar processes of relating between therapist and patient in the regressive phase (Bion 1962).

Early infancy trauma, regression and sound

It is here that the subjects of sound and music become relevant to the processes described above. Striking evidence has been obtained in the past decades from research and clinical experience in diverse fields about the importance of sound and its enormous impact on emotional development and its role in structuring the sense of self and other (Lecourt 1990, 1991; Maiello 1995; Stern 1985; Trevarthen 1980). Attention is increasingly being paid to the momentous encounter between sound and ear, first between the mother's voice and the foetus's, ear followed by the interplay between mother and baby voices and hearing organs. This interplay is not only the precursor of music but is essential to human contact, the sense of presence and absence, the sense of recognising and being recognised, the sense of communication, validation and agency. It represents and expresses the whole range of human emotion in the context of a relationship. This aspect of human communication – non-verbal sound – does not disappear with the acquisition of verbal language. It remains as a more archaic component of communication that underlies our expression and perception of the other. Rather than conceive of a split between verbal and non-verbal communication, I believe that we experience a continuous interplay between these modes of relating. In working with patients with disorders related to the self, it is my feeling that, especially when in regressive states, their early trauma is made present both in their sounds and in their sound needs.

The ideas I am proposing developed while working with verbal patients, for whom music-making is not self-evident and many times avoided. It might be argued that these patients choose listening to music in order to avoid the threatening experience of playing an instrument, of which they usually have no knowledge. This may be true, but indeed for patients who need to experience regression to dependence it is important that no knowledge or performance will be expected of them. For these patients the important thing is to be able to let go and depend on someone else's knowing (holding), while they are allowed to experience a state of simple 'going-on-being'.

The question is how to integrate what music has to offer in the thera-peutic dialogue without it resulting in 'organised chaos' (Winnicott 1971, p.261), and what may seem sometimes like the promotion of the music therapist's own agenda. When working with patients with false self and narcissistic personalities, there is a danger consciously or uncon-sciously to pressure them into compliant behaviour.

It is only too easy for such a patient subtly to perceive and perform what seems to be expected by the therapist. This replica of past patho-genic situations, which resulted in precisely the characterological symptoms in question, would prove disastrous to the therapeutic process. I therefore try to start a session without preconceptions or preferences for any particular music activity. I let the patients lead the way, allowing music and sound to develop naturally and spontaneously during the session as possible responses that stem from both patient and myself, always in relation to the moment. Music and sound may thus assume many forms and roles in the course of the treatment.

As a result of this approach, my attitude over the years has become increasingly non-interventive and the *listening* aspect of my role more prominent. I became more attentive to that sound aspect of the session that is non-musical (in the conventional sense), and have expanded the margins of music to include sound in all its manifestations, especially the wide range of vocal and body-sound productions that is regularly heard in the therapeutic dialogue. Steven Knoblauch, a psychoanalyst who is also a jazz musician, gives a fascinating account of the ways he experiences patients through his natural sensitivities to sound, timbre and rhythm and his own internalised experiences as a musician (Knoblauch 2000). The therapist's heightened attention to musical components in the patient's vocal and bodily expression existing alongside verbal content proves to facilitate essential clues in understanding the patient's untold drama.

It is evident that patients do 'play' their inner states through body language and sound, even when they are not actually playing an instrument or singing. This has led me to the realisation that my own sounds are also 'at play' and I became increasingly aware of the effects of my voice. Patients will not only opt to listen to played back music but are also deeply attuned to the therapist's voice, being 'played' by it as well as influencing it unconsciously. It seems that at times the patient elicits from us a certain tone of voice, prompts us to a certain way of saying things. I feel almost compelled to speak softly with a certain patient, my sound becoming aqueous or nebulous matter, while with another my words are carried by a solid, well-articulated tune. I believe that these exchanges indicate the re-enactment of very early communicative experiences when sound reigned as a prominent vehicle of communication.

The therapeutic couple's dialogue has many musical aspects, even when it is not explicitly making music. In spoken dialogue we may sense a tonality, a harmony or dissonance, stretto and counterpoint forms, dramatic pauses and changing tempi. The sounds of breathing, sighing and coughing, as they resonate in the session, punctuate and articulate the interaction. Silence in all its facets and colours, as a form of sound or non-sound, silence as absence and more often than not as presence, occurs regularly and has dramatic meaning in the therapeutic dialogue. It is always a question how the patient and I are *played* by our respective sounds. For example, I believe we are all familiar with gastric sounds that resonate in the therapy room. I had a patient whose enormous need of me I began to experience in depth when I heard his hungry sounds in sessions. Yet another patient was so oblivious of my presence that my stomach would proceed to grumble in protest. This she could not bear, because it represented not only my existence but also indicated that I have needs.

The experience of producing and hearing sounds implies the expression of deep, often unconscious, relational meanings. Auditory experiences can be equated in the mind to soothing, holding, even feeding experiences. At other times they can be felt as an intrusion or the registration of an absence. Producing sounds can be a release or an attack of the other. Patients project onto sound and music the qualities and modalities of relating that originate in their experience of the primary object. Their regressive longings are sometimes displaced onto the medium of sound and made present in the sounds they produce, in a wish to hear music, or expressed in a heightened auditory sensitivity to the voice of the therapist (Bollas 1987, p.15).

I am suggesting that, from a psychoanalytic perspective, sound and music may constitute representations of the object and of the subject's relation to it. The ways in which patients use sound inform us about emotional needs, their internal life and the nature of their relationships, including the transference relationship. These ideas have been proposed before by music therapists and psychoanalysts (Bollas 1987; De Backer 1993; De Backer and Van Camp 1999; Knoblauch 2000; Lecourt 1990; Maiello 1995; Odell-Miller 1991; Stern 1985, Streeter 1999). The wish to listen to music can thus be apprehended as a deep longing within the individual to re-experience the primary object, as Bollas suggests in his discussion of the transformational object (Bollas 1987). Singing or playing with the voice may represent the experience of the object at a somewhat later developmental stage, such as in a transitional area of experiencing (Winnicott 1971). The following clinical illustrations will attempt to demonstrate this direction of thinking.

Clinical illustration 1

Within the setting of a hospital centre for eating disorders I conducted a
music therapy group for anorexic women, aged 19 to 40, voluntarily hospitalised for periods of three to six months, mostly inpatient. The centre's
treatment approach is multidisciplinary. It includes behavioral-cognitive
therapy that addresses food and body issues, as well as group and individual psychotherapy via various media, verbal and the arts. Presence in
therapy is compulsory although active participation is not. I will describe
only the first phase of this group, comprised of up to 12 anorexic women
in an ongoing setting that existed for almost two years.

I began with a more or less established idea of group work, which
integrates music and sound experience with psychoanalytic group theory.
This means that the goings-on in the group are understood in terms of the
unconscious and transference relations – and interpreted in good time.
My comfortably established ways were soon challenged by the group
which probably experienced them as preconceptions, or rather as
pre-processed, undigestible food.

Those of us who work with anorexic individuals are familiar with the
difficulties they present in therapy. The psychoanalyst Gianna Williams
(1997) designated the term 'no-entry defence' to portray the anorexic
stance towards the world. Epitomised in the refusal to take in food, the
anorexic dreads outside inputs. These are perceived as poisonous foreign
bodies, or alternatively as tapping unbearably the anorexic's denied star-
vation for physical and emotional nurture. The tone of this defence is one
of resistance, hostility, frank aggression at times, and a general attitude of
'belle indifference'. These intelligent and often gifted patients create a
characteristic countertransference of failure in their caretakers and
engage them in a dynamic that is rich with anger, potential coun-
ter-aggression, guilt and hopelessness. There is much literature on the
question of psychotherapy with anorexic patients, in an attempt to find
alternatives for the engagement of these individuals in an effective
curative process (Davis 1991; Johnson 1991; Robarts 1995; Stern 1991;
Williams 1997).

Expecting the above I was not taken by surprise. Still, the impact of
the 'no-entry' defence displayed by the group in the first weeks was
enormous. It was manifest in the women's open resistance to going into

the room, in their tenacious silence within sessions or complaints like: 'we don't need a music lesson', 'I am tired'. The patients refused to engage in the musical activities offered and many times responded with aggression or anger to my interventions. Their hostility was certainly the cause of a stomach ache I would develop regularly on the eve of the group meeting and in my acute feelings of not wanting to go to work.

At first I tried to engage the group in musical improvisation. The response was lukewarm at best. I then offered the group the opportunity to listen to music and the participants were given the choice to lie down on mattresses or remain seated. The women seemed to enjoy this (my group being the fourth of the day after three verbal ones). From then on they began demanding, even while entering the room, to repeat this activity. 'Mattresses!' they would plead in a whining tone which I find hard to describe. When I acceded they would make individual physical arrangements: some would pile up a few mattresses to provide extra cushioning to their emaciated bodies, lie down and cover themselves over their heads with coats or an occasional blanket, and then withdraw. A number of patients would fall asleep. A few would remain seated, closing their eyes, yet a few stared vacantly into space. One or two would pace the room restlessly – which I allowed. My attempts to elicit verbal response following the music would produce silence, angry looks and bored semblances. I would emerge from these meetings feeling defeated, afraid that I had been manipulated by the group into a situation in which my professional knowledge and experience were being annihilated.

I debated for some time what to make out of this: a group 'resistance'? Was the attempt to evade the group encounter a reaction to the dangerous (because too intimate) stimulus of music or a ploy to gain a free nap? Or perhaps their whining demands could be understood as conveying a true need that could be granted in good faith? I opted for the latter, not easily, but in a conscious decision to trust the participants and respond positively to their wishes, even when not fully understanding the meaning of their need. This entailed a change in my perception of the situation and in the character of my presence and interventions. I veered towards seeing the group's behaviour as a defence, not as a resistance, and learned to respect it. Sensing that many times my words fell like dead weight in the middle of the circle, I had to find other ways than verbal to communicate to the group my understanding of the situation.

For example, in periods of silence, instead of reflecting verbally or eliciting a response as I would normally do, I might say: 'It seems like it's a good time to hear some more music' or 'Maybe it's too difficult to talk now, let's hear some music'. Affirmative nods would usually signal me to go ahead. It was my impression that my own tone of voice became softer. This corresponds to Williams's description of her 'soft tone of voice, and use of pastel, rather than primary color type of words' (1997, p.928) when working with anorexics.

Attentive listening to the whining sounds of the anorexic women informed me of a need that could not be expressed in any other way. The particular pathology of these women, many of whom also suffer from character disorders and depression, did not allow for direct expression, or even contact, with such longings and needs. The demand to lie down, to leave the upright posture, was the expression of a developmental need, not a resistance. When I really *listened* to the whining sound of the plea for 'mattresses', I finally perceived the image of a group of hungry, alienated infants crying out to be held, warmed and soothed. I also saw that for some strange reason, which I did not yet understand, the music-milk would not be rejected.

The expression of the true self is always dependent on the other's interpretations. Acknowledging the group's need changed the situation and allowed for a new experience and the beginning of a therapeutic alliance. The group stopped complaining, as did my anxiety, and as it developed and gained strength, other sound and music experiences took place, including group improvisation, singing, dancing, reading poems, performances of single members and more. Listening to music was something the group reverted to, especially when the depression level rose.

Discussion

The above is an instance of music being used as response to a need in a state of severe regression. Responding to the group in such a concrete way reinforced the cohesion of the group self, and facilitated later 'higher' functioning, like a verbal discussion or an improvisation. In terms of sound-as-object, sound acts here as a concrete provision, as physical holding or milk. It seems that the played back music and the sound of my voice complemented each other and became a substance that 'held' the group. In view of Winnicott's idea of regression (1984b), the group's withdrawal was transformed into a regressive experience.

Bollas's concept of the transformational object (1987) can be usefully related to the above illustration and to the idea of regression in music therapy. According to Bollas, at this time the baby experiences the mother not as a distinct entity or even a part object, but *as a process* that takes place on a temporal continuum. This mother-as-process is responsible for alterations in the baby's self-experience. The transformations which the baby experiences are not phantasised. They are real and physical. The mother *does* things that change and transform the baby's world, perhaps from a state of tension to one of relaxation. This happens many times a day. The mother holds, turns, bathes, lulls the baby to sleep in her own personal style, which Bollas calls her 'maternal aesthetic' (Bollas 1987, p.35), or in our present context, her 'maternal music'. It is indeed a startling realisation to grasp the similar effects of both mother and music as transformational objects.

The transformational experience is the subject's earliest memory of the object. It is a memory of being held, carried and transformed by a process, an aesthetic of being. As adults we long to repeat these sensations by seeking and finding objects such as music in the outside world that will resonate with that primary experience. Bollas designates these as *evocative* objects (1992), not of chance. The aesthetic feeling that arises in the encounter with music evokes self-experiences which originate in early life. It is a memory: existential, non-verbal, non-representational, not specific, although it may be sometimes, but of a psychosomatic sensation of fusion.

Music embraces and carries us in her lap according to her specific aesthetic of being: Bach's aesthetic holds and carries us differently than Bob Dylan's. We merge with the music movements and oscillations and we lose ourselves in it (Bollas 1992, p.17). We know we have been somewhere only when we 'wake' and 'come back'. It is music's specific structure that makes it so closely related to the maternal process. Music derives from voice and hearing and evolves on a temporal dimension. It is articulated in dynamic forms that do not tell us their precise content (Pavlicevic 1990, 1998; Stern 1985). All this is similar to the way in which we once experienced life as babies: as a temporal continuum of oscillations between moving and stillness, tensions and resolutions – and isn't that what music is about? Similarly, the therapist–music environment sustains the patient 'like the earth or the water sustains and carries a man who entrusts his weight on them ... no action is expected from these primary substances ... yet they must be there and must ... consent to be used.' (Balint 1968, p.145). Winnicott also proposed the idea of the therapy environment acting as a medium around the patient, holding him, without being too active or expecting anything from the patient (Winnicott 1984b). It seems that music can be used in a similar way – as environmental medium – in states of regression.

The anorexic patients' demand to lie down and hear music expresses a longing for a transformational experience of a somatic nature. My recognition and acknowledgement of this longing and subsequent facilitation can be paralleled with the maternal act of transforming the baby's world. The group needed to experience this long enough until other, more mature, forms of expression evolved. The group's refusal of a more developmentally advanced form of communication such as an improvisation can be understood as a developmental need as well. Winnicott describes a stage in development where the act of refusal of the potentially satisfying object is the patient's most important experience (Winnicott 1984b). Interestingly, Winnicott notes that the issue of refusal becomes a 'truly formidable problem for the therapist in anorexia nervosa' (p.182).

Clinical illustration 2

Some months after the group was engaged in simple listening (simple 'going on being'), the participants began using this experience in more elaborate ways. Albinoni's Adagio in G minor became a favourite. It was selected by me the first time, and then chosen time and again by the participants. It 'belonged' to the group, and received a name: *The* Adagio. 'Play the adagio!', they would demand, and we all knew what they meant. 'The Adagio' became something intimate that belonged to our mutually constructed experience. Although it was I who had presented it, the group appropriated it and made it its own.

The Beatles' 'Yesterday' featured as another favourite in the group, but it also 'belonged' to a specific woman. She loved the song and repeatedly asked to hear it. The group identified the song with her. Once it was played in her absence, which the group regretted 'because it's *her* song'. When a guitar was available, they would ask me to accompany them while they sang. Once, in the absence of the guitar, they decided that it could be sung nevertheless, which we did, softly.

Discussion

Unlike Bollas, Winnicott did not refer to music in specific ways, but he did mention sound as a transitional phenomenon (Winnicott 1971). The theory of the transitional object relates to the baby's active choice of an object; an act that is experienced by the baby as creative. Winnicott described the baby's relation to the object, and his theory is relevant to the subject's relation to music. Music that is meaningful to the individual is an object that is in the outside world, but is experienced as part of the self ('*her* song'), at times even created by the self. It is experienced as characterised by liveliness and texture, with a capacity to evoke feelings of love and sometimes pain or hate. What is important is that music as the development of a transitional phenomenon does not simply symbolise the mother, but represents a primary relationship and the fact of the simultaneous presence and absence of this relationship. In creating the transitional object, the patient recreates a relationship – from a developmental point of the beginning of separation. Perhaps for this reason music offers consolation and yet at the same time can evoke feelings of pain and longing.

In the group, The Adagio acquired the quality of a transitional object. In a Winnicottian sense, it was created by the group. It had a special meaning and the magical ability to soothe. I would reflect at times on the musical structure of the adagio with its slow, steady beat, its undulating phrases that sound like long, drawn out sighs and its uncanny evocation of a feeling of pain. But what was of paramount importance was the use the group made of it. 'In health, the infant creates what is in fact lying around waiting to be found ... A good object is no good to the infant unless created by the infant' (Winnicott 1984a, p.181) The use of 'Yesterday' in transitional ways was more elaborate than the use of 'The Adagio'. The differing positions of the group in relation to me in the recreation of the song were meaningful. Asking me to accompany their singing was a way of expressing their need of me in facilitating their singing, or in other words recognising their dependence. Yet when the guitar was not available, they discovered that the song was not lost; it could be retrieved by just singing. The ability to sing 'Yesterday' and experience the moment in all its spontaneity was a sign that a reliable object experience had been internalised by the group.

Conclusion

I have attempted to link the phenomenon of patients with early infancy trauma who reveal sensitivities and preferences to certain auditory and vocal experiences, to the idea of regression in therapy. Phenomena encountered in the area of sound and music reflect some of the ways that individuals remember and re-enact early experiences with the object, the vicissitudes of early mother–child interaction as well as the longings for the provision of unattended developmental needs. While musical improvisation has been traditionally regarded as a more primary way of expression than verbal, a point is being made that playing an instrument requires nevertheless a certain level of organisation and maturity such as the the ability to sit upright, relate to a physical object outside the self and so on. This implies that psychologically there has been a development and the self has reached some ability to relate to the outside world. If music therapists are prepared to facilitate regressive states in the process of therapy, they may have to accept and facilitate more primary forms of sound needs and experiences. This requires the capacity of the therapist to be completely open to diverse sound phenomena that are not included in preconceived operational models. In the patient's regression lies hope for a new relational experience. The music therapist's unconditioned and attentive listening will create a safe space for hidden music to find its way.

References

Balint, M. (1968) *The Basic Fault.* London: Tavistock/Routledge.

Bion, W. (1962) 'A theory of thinking.' *International Journal of Psychoanalysis 43*, 306–310.

Bollas, C. (1987) *The Shadow of the Object.* New York: Columbia Univeristy Press.

Bollas, C. (1989) *Forces of Destiny.* London: Free Association Books.

Bollas, C. (1992) *Being a Character.* London: Routledge.

Davis, W.N. (1991) 'Reflections on boundaries in the psychotherapeutic relationship.' In C. Johnson (ed) *Psychodynamic Treatment of Anorexia Nervosa and Bulimia.* New York: Guilford Press, pp.68–86.

De Backer, J. (1993) 'Containment in music therapy.' In M. Heal and T. Wigram (eds) *Music Therapy in Health and Education.* London: Jessica Kingsley Publishers.

De Backer J. and Van Camp, J. (1999) 'Specific aspects of the music therapy relationship to psychiatry.' In T. Wigram and J. De Backer (eds) *Clinical Applications of Music Therapy in Psychiatry.* London: Jessica Kingsley Publishers, pp.11–23.

Fairbairn, W.R.D. (1954) *An Object-Relations Theory of the Personality.* New York: Basic Books.

Johnson, C. (1991) 'Treatment of eating disordered patients with borderline and false-self/narcissistic disorders.' In C. Johnson (ed) *Psychodynamic Treatment of Anorexia Nervosa and Bulimia.* New York: Guilford Press, pp.165–193.

Khan, M.M.R. (1974) 'The concept of cumulative trauma.' In *The Privacy of the Self.* London: Hogarth Press, pp.42–58.

Khan, M.M.R. (1974a) 'Ego distortion, cumulative trauma and the role of reconstruction in the analytic situation.;' In *The Privacy of the Self.* London: Hogarth Press, pp.59–68.

Knoblauch, S.H. (2000) *The Musical Edge of Therapeutic Dialogue.* London: Analytic Press.

Lecourt, E. (1990) 'The musical envelope.' In D.Anzieu (ed) *Psychic Envelopes.* London: Karnac, pp.211–235.

Lecourt, E. (1991) 'Off-beat music therapy: a psychoanalytic approach to autism.' In K.E. Bruscia (ed) *Case Studies in Music Therapy.* New York: Barcelona, pp.73–98.

McDougall, J. (1986) *Theatres of the Mind.* London: Free Association Books.

Maiello, S. (1995) 'The sound-object: a hypothesis about prenatal auditory experience and memory.' *Journal of Child Psychotherapy 21*, 1, 23–41.

Odell-Miller, H. (1991) 'Group improvisation therapy: the experience of one man with schizophrenia.' In K.E. Bruscia (ed) *Case Studies in Music Therapy*. New York: Barcelona, 417–432.

Pavlicevic, M. (1990) 'Dynamic interplay in clinical improvisation.' *Journal of British Music Therapy 4*, 2, 5–9.

Pavlicevic, M. (1998) *Music Therapy in Context*. London: Jessica Kingsley Publishers.

Robarts, J.Z. (1995) 'Towards autonomy and a sense of self.' In D.Dokter (ed) *Art Therapies and Patients with Eating Disorders*. London: Jessica Kingsley Publishers, pp.229–246.

Stern, D.N. (1985) *The Interpersonal World of the Infant*. New York: Basic Books.

Stern, S. (1991) 'Managing opposing currents: an interpersonal psychoanalytic technique for the treatment of eating disorders.' In C. Johnson (ed) *Psychodynamic Treatment of Anorexia Nervosa and Bulimia*. New York: Guilford Press, pp.86–105.

Streeter, E. (1999) 'Definition and use of the musical transference relationship.' In T. Wigram and J. De Backer (eds) *Clinical Applications of Music Therapy in Psychiatry*. London: Jessica Kingsley Publishers, pp.84–101.

Trevarthen, C. (1980) 'The foundations of intersubjectivity: development of interpersonal and cooperative understanding in infants.' In D. Olson (ed) *The Social Foundations of Language and Thought: Essays in Honor of Jerome Bruner*. New York: W.W.Norton.

Williams, G. (1997) 'Reflections on some dynamics of eating disorders: "no entry" defences and foreign bodies.' *International Journal of Psycho-Analysis 78*, 927–941.

Winnicott, D.W. (1984a) 'Ego distortion in terms of true and false self.' In D.W. Winnicott *The Maturational Process and the Facilitating Environment*. London: Karnac.

Winnicott, D.W. (1984b) 'Withdrawal and regression.' In D.W. Winnicott *Through Paediatrics to Psychoanalysis – Collected Papers*. London: Karnac.

Winnicott D.W. (1984c) 'Communicating and not communicating leading to a study of certain opposites.' In D.W. Winnicott *The Maturational Process and the Facilitating Environment*. London: Karnac.

Winnicott, D.W. (1971) *Playing and Reality*. London: Penguin.

Part 4

The Support Perspective

CHAPTER 11

Supervision

Processes in Listening Together – An Experience of Distance Supervision of Work with Traumatised Children

Louise Lang, Una McInerney, Rosemary Monaghan and Julie P. Sutton

This chapter evolved out of a more unusual supervision experience where the supervisees lived in one country and their supervisors in another. While there were a number of face-to-face meetings, a significant amount of ongoing supervision took place via telephone. The challenges of this situation invited us to think about the process of supervision in general and our experience in particular. This in turn has enabled us to acknowledge the vital role that supervision has in clinical practice with those who have experienced traumatic and life-threatening events. The chapter has been written by the two supervisees and two supervisors involved. It covers a total period of three years and was written after the supervision had finished.

In this chapter we use the term *supervision* to indicate a space into which the supervisee brings their thoughts and feelings about particular aspects of their clinical work. The space allows supervisor and supervisee to think together about the client, or about other issues relating to their role as a clinician. The working together that music therapists undertake as supervisees and supervisors is seen as an essential part of taking care of oneself in order to be able to function healthily in the work. It is also a more complex matter than that of work with clients, because usually the supervisor has not seen the client and relies upon the material chosen by the supervisee. Both supervisor and supervisee are also affected by the professional, organisational, personal and social factors that are outside the supervisory space (Hawkins and Shohet 1994, pp.5–6).

Rather like in the therapy room, the supervision process is unique in every situation, with the relationship between the supervisee and supervisor influencing the pacing, intensity and content of the work. Typically the supervisee shares with the supervisor their work with clients, as well as broader issues about their practice. The supervisee reflects on the musical, emotional and psychological content of the session, with an awareness that this may resonate with or parallel personal processes. The supervisor aims to enable the supervisee to observe and think about these processes occurring between themselves and the client. This facilitates the therapy process and the potential for the client to develop within a healthy and contained environment further. As Dileo (2001) has noted, implied in the supervisory relationship are 'therapy-like' and 'parent-like' qualities. The supervisor should be aware of these qualities and be prepared to safeguard and maintain the boundaries between supervision and therapy.

In music therapy supervision the most common approaches involve the use of audio and/or video documentation of the session/s. This material is accompanied by the therapist's descriptive narrative regarding the history of the client and the content of the work to date. It is recognised that the supervisee will need to share work that is difficult for them. Therefore, the objectivity of the supervisor within this process is essential, in order to assist in the supervisee's development and understanding of a therapeutic relationship in which they are often deeply involved. We consider that an awareness of this part of the process is vital, particularly when working with the vulnerable, traumatised client group. It is interesting that discussion of the personal component of the work is rare in the literature, yet the ability to maintain the boundary between supervision and therapy is a central requisite skill in the registration scheme for specialist clinical supervisors in the UK. In this context the scheme relates to supervisors who wish to become registered to work with recently qualified therapists planning to become full members of the Association of Professional Music Therapists in the UK.

The supervisor should also share with the supervisee any concerns they have about their fitness to practise and at times recommend the exploration of personal issues in therapy. In work with traumatised clients, the therapist's personal history can be particularly exposed (Sutton 2000). Making use of the concept of the *wounded healer*, Austin has demonstrated the importance of 'fine tuning' for therapists working in depth with traumatised clients (Austin 2002). Austin recommends clinical supervision and personal therapy in order to safeguard both client and therapist.

During the supervision we describe in this chapter, two clinicians who worked at the Pavarotti Music Centre (PMC) in Mostar, Bosnia-Herzegovina during the immediate post-war period. The supervisors were based in Belfast and London and had previously made several preliminary visits to the PMC between 1996 and 1998, both before and just after the centre was opened. The supervision we describe took place via telephone, email and some face-to-face contact in the UK.

We have thought separately about the experience of distance supervision in this situation. Not meeting before documenting our initial thoughts was both an intuitive decision and a practical consideration, because at this point we were living in different countries. On reflection we realise that this process of writing has echoed the supervision process itself. As such it also enabled our different thoughts and experiences to be heard separately before we began the combined writing. This variety of responses is reflected in the chapter, through the voices of the supervisees' and supervisors' experiences. The chapter is divided into five sections:

1. The beginning

2. Changes in supervision focus

3. Central issues relating to clinical work:

    - working with a translator
    - traumatised clients

4.   Telephone supervision and the long-distance relationship

5.   Final thoughts.

The work we write about took place over a three-year period, a time during which a total of seven therapists worked either as volunteer or salaried staff. We therefore acknowledge our colleagues Alison Acton, Charlotte Dammeyer Fonsbo, Thomas Schepelern, Katrina Bergman and Patricia Braak. While this chapter explores our supervisory relationships, we also wish to recognise the valuable contribution of these therapists to the work as a whole.

The beginning

In preparing this chapter we thought about the role of supervision from the very beginning of the work in Mostar. This was a particularly challenging time for the community and for the therapists joining this community. Over time we have noticed that the initial period of adjustment when beginning the work has been a common experience for other colleagues in Mostar. The space that supervision offered has been an important aspect of this.

The supervisees' experience at the beginning

We have perceived the supervision in different ways, as the situation and our individual needs changed. The initial months of supervision were characterised by discussions about settling into a new culture, implementing a service previously unknown to the community and learning how to work within a system that was initially quite resistant to our efforts. For the first two months no clinical work was undertaken due to a lack of promised instruments. At this stage there were also practical difficulties in maintaining the transport and communication infrastructure.

Supervision time focused on the practical difficulties of equipping the office and liaising with local colleagues. We thought about the relationships with local colleagues, what we could and could not ask of them and the possible reasons for this. Many different emotions were experienced during these early months and even mundane events during the day could affect one deeply. The supervision brought out the realisation of how vulnerable both the whole community and ourselves were. Not only were personal issues being challenged, but also one's feeling of self-worth as a therapist. For instance, at this stage there was a tangible feeling of mistrust towards those from outside Mostar. We were outsiders and in the early days the word 'therapy' implied doctors and drugs and also that a family member was 'mentally retarded'. Clearly there was a stigma attached to attending therapy sessions. Supervision provided a space were one's professional identity could be reclaimed, as well as keeping these issues in context. It was an affirming and strengthening exercise.

It should be noted that for therapists joining the team after the first year of work, the supervision contact was one of a larger number of support networks that were by then set up. These networks were not available at the beginning and at this early stage the supervision was the major component of support for therapists.

The supervisors' experience at the beginning

We had to deal with a highly complex and challenging supervision scenario and one that continued to evolve over time. The unique perspectives of this work were directly related to the post-war situation in Bosnia-Herzegovina. The primary client group was children and young people in Mostar who had wide-ranging special needs. These 'needs' not only related to their disabilities, but also to the direct trauma of the war. There were additional factors of the country being in economic crisis – a community that was still divided and a state where international peace-keeping forces were a constant presence. Finally, we saw that the challenges of the situation also resonated with the training and early work experiences of both supervisees and supervisors.

Our own experience of the Mostar community over time enabled us to understand how powerful the impact of life there could be. We both also had an experience of living in Northern Ireland during periods of stress, tension and violence and this too was a valuable resource in our evolving understanding of the feelings of vulnerability being expressed by our colleagues. These telephone calls were challenging to hear, process and contain initially and were undertaken without the benefit of sitting together in the same room. While the intense nature of the early contact was part of the work at this stage, it also brought up a number of issues about telephone supervision. We will focus on these issues in the fourth section of the chapter.

During these months there was one face-to-face supervision, which took place in Mostar shortly after the first therapists had begun clinical work. This was an intense, powerful experience during which we were sought out for support by many other staff members, both within and outside the therapy service. It became a central, challenging task to establish and maintain sufficiently secure boundaries within which the work with the supervisees could take place. For instance, this applied to keeping to time, the physical setting for meetings and whether or not smoking was allowed. At this time it was usual for meeting to take place in social settings such as the café/bar that was also open to the general public. We have associated the blurring of boundaries of time and place with responses in the community to the post-war environment, as well as to the underlying cultural context. As van der Kolk and others have described, the ongoing process of adaptation after a period of intense, violent acts during war is complex and multi-layered (McFarlane and van der Kolk 1996; van der Kolk1996).

After discussing this visit on our return we made a decision to meet outside Mostar for face-to-face contact. We felt that the physical distancing enabled a sense of increased objectivity, a space for personal reflection and a break from the intensity of the working environment. It also provided a concrete, geographical boundary between the workplace and the supervisory setting. At this time we kept in constant contact with each other. We undertook supervision on this work with an experienced colleague who had also visited Mostar during the post-war period.

At this stage the supervision had a direct role in preventing 'burnout' for our colleagues. As therapists they were working with a challenging client group who expressed needs at many different levels. Their non-therapist colleagues also frequently sought them out for advice and support. We had a great deal of respect for the immense pressure our supervisees were under and it was important to discuss the issue of burnout. Without a space for conscious containment of the overall stress and strain it would have been difficult to undertake the clinical work. As

Wosket (2001, p.201) has noted, supervision can be seen as a process within which such pressure can be released in an open, non-judgemental environment, thus helping to safeguard the mental health of the supervisee.

One of the most important features of this early work was the acknowledgement of the challenges of the situation inside and outside the therapy room. This was achieved through recognising the personal impact upon the therapist, their increased vulnerability and a need consciously to place limits on what could be achieved. Central to our approach was to support our colleagues in this difficult task without taking on a role as therapists. Our colleagues had no access to personal support at this stage, which made it even more important to maintain the supervision–therapy boundary.

Changes in supervision focus

After the period of adjustment, the supervision concentrated on clinical issues. As the supervisory relationships developed there were changes in the focus of the work.

The supervisees' experience of changes in supervision focus

Once clinical work was in progress the supervisor took on a new role, the long-awaited discussion of clients in therapy. Compared to previous clinical work, it was easy to continue to feel somewhat insecure in the challenging new work environment. There was a desire for answers and solutions. Relying on the telephone contact one sometimes felt that the more experienced supervisor should know how to solve all difficulties. These expectations changed as confidence grew in the ability to deal with both living in the stressful environment as well as the issues raised in music therapy sessions. The focus of supervision became the joint exploration of clinical issues. From initially looking to the supervisor for answers, the relationship felt equal and as the therapy work progressed the time was spent discussing clinical material in more depth. This was a very satisfying development, shared by supervisee and supervisor alike.

Supervision was primarily a form of support in every aspect of the job.

The main elements of the regular contact included:

- having a space to share some of the difficult personal feelings and reactions that arose in moving to a different culture, in a town that was physically devastated

- discussing practical issues such as setting up the service, administrative support, documentation and work with translators

- continuing to think about and work with very challenging clients

- maintaining an objective perspective on different issues

- exploring theoretical frameworks in which to place the work.

These elements related to the uniqueness of the setting within which the work was undertaken, as well as supervision issues that are common to all clinical work. There were elements that came up frequently in supervision and while already thinking about ways to deal with them, it was important to be able to share this process with someone else. In doing this one was no longer carrying everything alone.

Finally, there was one underlying feature throughout the supervision at this stage. This was the knowledge that the supervisor was resilient and strong enough to contain the therapist's feelings and thoughts about the work, in order that these became manageable, and that the clinical work could be thought about objectively. It was important to know that the supervisor had their own safety measures for dealing with 'third-hand' trauma, because supervision would often involve relating clients' and friends' harrowing experiences, accompanied by the supervisee's own responses and interpretation. This material could be shocking and chal-lenging. Therefore it was important that the impact upon the supervisors was also considered.

The supervisors' experience of changes in supervision focus

The supervision relationship in this context evolved through various phases, which related directly to the therapists' changing needs. The initial period of intense cultural, social and emotional adjustment brought elements of both a personal and practical nature into focus in the supervision. To a lesser and differing extent this is the case for any therapist establishing themselves in a new environment, workplace and clinical team. As mentioned earlier, there were also resonances with training and early work experiences. At these beginning stages we can become overwhelmed with feelings of helplessness, incompetence and failure. Scheiby and Amir have observed that it is the supervisor's role to listen and provide containment for these feelings (Amir 2001; Scheiby 2001). As supervisors in this initial phase it was essential to ensure a consistent, supportive and validating stance, while showing sensitivity to their often difficult and harrowing experiences. Key issues that emerged at this level were:

- practical details such as accommodation, travel and lack of resources

- difficulty in communicating and feeling understood

- cultural differences – adjusting to living in another country, as well as the organisational infrastructure

- logistics involved in setting up the service, referral procedure and compiling promotional literature

- team dynamics, including adjusting to different personalities and needs – with the lack of outside contact and support team members were dependent on each other

- the danger of becoming the 'therapist' to everyone and the meshing of personal boundaries

- the effect of the widespread 'trauma' in the community and how this began to manifest itself through relationships within and outside the therapy setting.

It was interesting to note how many parallels there were with the therapists' experiences and aspects of the interaction in the supervision relationship. The most prominent of these was safeguarding of boundaries. Frequently the supervision demanded the incorporation of elements of therapeutic containment, initially with very little reference to the actual work with clients. We felt that these basic needs of the therapists had to be met in order to be able to view the pressures of the music therapy situation in a healthy and contained manner. The absence of access to personal therapy for the therapists was an issue that had to be held clearly in mind throughout the supervision process. We therefore undertook this initial work in an attempt to ensure the correct balance between offering personal support and specific clinical supervision.

Following this initial phase the supervision began to focus on clinical music therapy with clients. It is important to note that personal issues were still an important part of the work, but now the focus and thinking was targeted primarily on the clinical situation.

Central issues relating to clinical work

In terms of the clinical work itself, the main themes that emerged were:

- the difficulty of having translators/assistants present in the sessions

- the frustrations of not feeling confident in dealing with clients directly, due to the language/communication barrier

- difficulties in feeling a sustained connection with clients, presenting in some of the following ways: ambivalent responses; very short concentration span; lack of eye contact; fragmented responses; loud, incessant playing; nervous anxiety/embarrassment/avoidance

- when connections became well established with some clients, there could be difficulty in confronting and containing the issues to be dealt with in the therapy, particularly those directly related to the trauma

- feelings of guilt and helplessness when coming to the end of the therapy.

These themes are not uncommon in work with many client groups. However, in this instance they should be seen within the overall perspective of a post-war environment, into which the therapists came as cultural outsiders.

In supervision there was potential to explore in depth the individual clients, their case histories, reasons for referral and progress of their work in music therapy. There were usually two or three clients who needed to be discussed more than others and who illustrated common aspects of the work. The supervision process evolved through an initial focus on the actual events taking place in the room. This incorporated reflections and accurate descriptions from the therapist about the exact nature of the interaction, along with physical descriptions of events and of the nature and quality of the music.

To begin with there was a need for answers, solutions and remedies. Supervisors felt pulled into this sense of urgent desire to solve problems and to make observations which would be based on limited material and resources. Part of this difficulty was related to the fact that telephone supervision made it difficult to grasp an accurate impression of what was needed in terms of intervention. We were all working with the verbal illustrations provided by the therapists, for whom this was the only means of outside support. As the work progressed this became easier, through the regular intensity with which we all held the clients in our thoughts. We were nonetheless aware of the amount of projection taking place in this situation. There was a real danger of over-interpretation in relation to this and it was important to bear in mind just how selective were the impressions with which we were working. Therefore, the face-to-face supervision within this period was essential. Further on in the process, it became possible to relate discussion to the clinical work we had looked at or heard. With the benefit of the regularity of contact by telephone and in person, we could also place the work in the wider context of the setting in which the clients and the therapists were living.

Two main themes emerged from this supervision and were linking features throughout the work. These were working with a translator present in the sessions and specific features of the work with traumatised children.

Working with a translator

This was a new experience but a necessary part of the sessions. We developed the title 'music therapy assistant' to describe the many different ways in which the translator functioned during a session. These included:

- supporting the client physically
- being a group member
- supporting a musical structure developed by the therapist
- being a voice from one side of the room (when translating the client's or therapist's words).

On all occasions the music therapy assistant was responsible primarily for translating any verbal communication from clients and therapists.

During supervision we explored translator issues and how the music therapy assistant's role could be defined and evaluated, as well as putting the therapist's expectations into context. It was important to bear in mind that what was being presented by the client could resonate deeply with the translator coming from the same community (see: McFarlane *et al.* 1996, pp.39–45). We thought of ways of containing this unconscious material, both in the sessions and in discussion with the translators afterwards. Monitoring the stress levels of the music therapy assistants was another containing aspect of this approach to the work. In addition, we expanded and formalised the discussion space in order to offer the translators more information about music therapy techniques and basic theory. Thus the discussion time also had an education and training perspective.

There were features of the sessions where the client enacted aspects of their life experience that placed therapist and translator in symbolic roles (for instance, as parent or invader). Again feedback and discussion with translators outside the sessions was explored during supervision. The work with translators was further extended into the setting up of regular team clinical meetings, during which therapists and music therapy assistants had an equal voice in bringing their experiences of the clients. This too was part of our thinking together in supervision. It related to the necessity of making conscious the main themes of work with traumatised clients and how this impinged on colleagues who could have had similar experiences. There had to be an active consideration of the vulnerability of those who had lived through the war. In working with clients, these adults would be all the more vulnerable to retraumatisation. To make the working environment safe, outside support was offered. In addition changes could be made with regard to responsibility and workload, through discussion and mutual agreement.

Traumatised clients

As the clinical work developed, we noted some of the apparently similar ways in which clients presented in sessions. We came to think about this in supervision as specific to their traumatic experiences, as well as to traumatic experience in general. The clients often presented:

- a 'wall of sound' (i.e. continuous and very loud playing)
- extreme difficulty in tolerating quietness or silence
- difficulty in staying in the room
- dissociation
- acting out the 'invader' or invading army.

When the client presented a 'wall of sound', we acknowledged how difficult it was to hear and stay with this music. We thought about re-enactment of an experience of being constantly under barrage during prolonged mortar attack. Families in Mostar had taken refuge in cellars for days on end, while being outside was a hazardous, dangerous activity. Hearing the constant sound of mortar shells exploding was then compared to what would be an unfamiliar quietness and silence. To experience oneself in a quiet or silent state could result in a flooding from the past, where attacks upon the secure place (home) were linked with loud, violent sounds. For some clients there would also be flashbacks associated with this.

We thought about how difficult it would be for clients to stay in the therapy space when experiencing themselves in these ways. Other clients took refuge in becoming distant or dreamy, in some cases moving suddenly from a state of connectedness to one of being unconnected or disconnected. While physically in the room, they were also absent from it. Some clients took on the symbolic role of the invading army, leaving the therapist and/or therapy assistant in the position of the one being attacked and obliterated. We discussed how these experiences could be thought about and provide us with much useful information about the client's inner world. We remembered in supervision how important it would be to remain a real, alive presence in the room in these cases. The complexity of the therapeutic relationship and the sensory medium with which it took place would have a particularly powerful impact upon the client. Lindy (2000) has recognised this when writing about the ways in which the client's experience of the therapeutic setting could increase their vulnerability to somatic re-enactment, anxiety states and feelings of extreme terror or shame. Paradoxically, there is also potential in the therapy room for the client to recollect and reconnect with safe feelings relating to the original trauma. Both types of response enabled the therapists to observe how past trauma could be brought into the present.

We acknowledged how the behaviour of clients would be on these different levels, both linked to what was taking place in the room, while also immediately and inextricably connected with the traumatic experience itself. The ability to remain both in touch with and also separate from (and able to think about) the intense emotional force of what was presented in the sessions presented a central challenge for the work with these clients.

To further safeguard this work, in supervision we spent time thinking about the ways in which it would be possible to place the work in an overall perspective. This perspective included an overall cultural context, the setting in which the therapy took place (the institution), the home setting (the family home, the refugee centre or the children's home) and the context within which the therapist lived and was supported. We also thought together about the experience of living in another culture, away from friends and family and the professional support network, as well as the impact of being in the therapy room. This thinking was vital in enabling a realistic stance from which to view the work as a whole. As Turner, McFarlane and van der Kolk (2000) have observed, therapists as well as clients experience the impact of traumatic material. Repeated exposure to such experiences can be overwhelming for clinicians, resonating with their own vulnerability and wounds (see Austin 2002; Sutton, in press).

The supervision was seen as a containing space within which this cumulative impact of the work could be searched for and reflected upon.

This is of course important to all clinical work, but it is even more so for work with clients who might not only be experiencing the aftermath of traumatic events, but also re-experiencing these events in the form of flashbacks. Finding theoretical frameworks for redefining traumatic experience and re-experience in context was also an important aspect of supervision. The theoretical framework provides scaffolding within which therapists' – and supervisors' – experiences of clients can be reflected upon. One example that we found helpful was that of Garland, who hypothesised the importance of such a containing theoretical framework with reference to flashback, using the concept of the differentiation between the *I* and the *event* (Garland 1998, p.110). Garland suggested that when experiencing a flashback there is loss of the space within which 'thinking-about-something' can take place. The absence of this space, or container, makes it impossible to be able to think about what one is experiencing, with the result that a memory of an event becomes an actual, overwhelming re-experiencing. During a flashback there is no difference between the *I* and the *event*, as the person is effectively robbed of the containing thinking process. The intrusive memory becomes in itself traumatic.

We are in agreement with Garland's hypothesis and have considered that the supervision presented one place within which therapist and supervisor could engage in 'thinking about' what had taken place in the sessions. It should also be noted that the impact of repeated exposure to traumatised clients was also transmitted to the supervisors. To contain and process this secondary impact, both supervisors maintained regular contact and continued to avail of their own supervision and personal therapy work. This extended network of reflecting, containing spaces was essential.

Telephone supervision and the long-distance relationship

An additional factor that influenced the supervision process was the very practical situation of the supervisees living in one country and the supervisors living in another. This resulted in a significant amount of supervision taking place by telephone, with face-to-face meetings at regular intervals. The physical distance between supervisee and supervisor brought to focus some insights into the supervision process and in the roles and relationships in which supervisees and supervisors can be placed.

The supervisees' experience

The telephone brought certain pressures and made the supervision time very intense. These pressures included taking care not to waste time, trying to convey possible meaning and emotion succinctly and needing to order one's thoughts very carefully. It could be difficult to hold on to concepts at such a physical distance and it was important to have time to document these thoughts and ideas. Silence in particular felt more pressured. At times a silence that could be given over to thought during a face-to-face conversation could feel tense and uncomfortable via telephone. It was also less easy to interrupt silences with thoughts because there was not the added dimension of body language or facial expression. At the beginning in particular, the telephone supervision was an arduous and draining experience.

Previous knowledge of or familiarity with the supervisor made this task somewhat easier, because the person could be easily visualised mentally. This made the task of holding the supervisor in mind somewhat easier and more closely echoed the usual supervision process of building the relationship, becoming more familiar with each other and developing the internal supervisor. However, telephone supervision also required a particular approach, for instance, being very clear about the clients, how one described the music, the room and one's reactions. It was necessary to provide more detail than in face-to-face supervision, so that the supervisor could build a picture of what was happening with the client. This became even more apparent when undertaking the first face-to-face supervision. We realised how important it was that the supervisor could actually see the clients and hear the music we had talked about. In retrospect we probably heard more music in the first face-to-face meeting than on any following occasion. This was most likely due to a combination of this important moment in developing the supervisory relationship further, as well as the impact of this intense first period of clinical work. So much had been happening in the music that the clients made and the music that we played together. It felt so important to share some of this and obtain another's reactions and opinions. There was also a certain element of pride in being able to show video extracts of the work that was taking place in such a challenging environment, as well as a need to feel nurtured and validated.

The supervisors' experience

We also found the early telephone supervision a challenging experience. The unique factor of providing music therapy supervision in a situation where the supervisor and supervisee are physically apart (and may not have even met before) created a complex and somewhat illusive influence upon the evolving relationship. In face-to-face supervision the supervisor has access to see and hear recorded audio and/or video material of sessions, as well as the supervisee themselves. The telephone relationship between therapist and supervisor is veiled in the obscurity of there being no visual reference to the whole world of body language, eye contact and the strong projective cues that occur when two people sit together in the same room. When undertaking telephone supervision, significance is attached to every nuance in the conversation, the tone of voice, its pitch, pacing and intensity. Listening is stripped of all visual factors, with the unseen becoming loaded with fantasy. One example was during a long silence when the supervisor was left wondering if the supervisee were thinking, looking out of a window or becoming distracted by something else in the room – yet in fact they had been carefully making notes. When brought into discussion (and therefore to consciousness) we realised that this was also an experience for the supervisee. We remembered to note aloud when we needed extra time to think or to make notes, or if there was a distraction from outside. In telephone supervision there is therefore the added dimension of needing carefully to hold in mind the unseen therapist as well as the client.

In many ways we were experiencing a parallel process to that of the therapists we supervised. While they were finding skills in their new work, we were developing ways of working as supervisors in this context of distance supervision. Supervision by a combination of telephone and face-to-face contact is a relatively new phenomenon in music therapy in the UK, although it has become a more acceptable method where geographical distance is a factor. In the area of counselling this has been a practice for some time – for instance, the Samaritans organisation is based upon this way of working. Rosenfield (2000) has written about this method for counsellors and supervisors, even noting a range of advantages for both counsellor and client and suggesting that the use of the telphone can help 'equalise' the power in the relationship. This has been our experience, shared with our supervisees. The process of developing skills in telephone supervision has left us with a sense of mutuality.

Final thoughts

Working in the way in which we have described has presented us with many challenges, both in practical terms (distance supervision) and in the nature of the clinical work itself. Exploring this three-year period of supervision has enabled us to make a number of recommendations.

In terms of telephone supervision we can recommend the following:

- awareness of the need to provide clear, detailed descriptions of clients, therapists' responses to them and their music, sequence of events in sessions, etc.

- the setting up of regular face-to-face meetings in conjunction with telephone supervision

- face-to-face meetings to focus on audio/video recordings of the work

- the acknowledgement of silence and its purpose (e.g. 'I need some time to pause and think about that')

- detailed documentation by supervisee and supervisor

- awareness of the supervisor's need to ask questions in order to clarify aspects of the work (and that this may be more necessary than for face-to-face supervision)

- awareness of one's own voice quality

- awareness of the challenge for supervisee and supervisor to keep the clients and each other in mind throughout the course of the telephone call.

In terms of clinical work with traumatised clients we consider regular clinical supervision to be not only strongly recommended, but also essential. While the situation in which the supervision work we have explored in this chapter was by no means ideal, it raised issues that are fundamental to clinical work in this area. Apart from the book by Forinash (2001), little has been documented about the music therapist's process of safeguarding clinical work. Therefore, as well as showing the central importance of supervision in work with those traumatised, this chapter is also a contribution to the growing awareness of the essential role of clinical supervision in ethical professional practice.

References

Amir, D. (2001) 'The journey of two: supervision for the new music therapist working in an educational setting.' In M. Forinash (ed) *Music Therapy Supervision*. Gilsum NH: Barcelona, pp.195–210.

Austin, D. (2002) 'The voice of trauma: a wounded healer's perspective.' In J. P. Sutton (ed) *Music, Music Therapy and Trauma: International Perspectives*. London: Jessica Kingsley Publishers.

Dileo, C. (2001) 'Ethical issues in supervision.' In M. Forinash (ed) *Music Therapy Supervision*. Gilsum NH: Barcelona, pp.19–38.

Forinash, M. (2001) (ed) *Music Therapy Supervision*. Gilsum NH: Barcelona.

Garland, C. (1998) 'Issues in treatment. A case of rape.' In C. Garland (ed) *Understanding Trauma. A Psychoanalytical Approach*. London: Duckworth.

Hawkins, R. and Shohet, R. (1994) '"Good-enough" supervision.' In R. Hawkins and R. Shohet (eds) *Supervision in the Helping Professions*. Buckingham: Open University Press.

Lindy, J. D. (2000) 'Psychoanalytic psychotherapy of posttraumatic stress disorder.' In B. A. van der Kolk, A. C. McFarlane and L. Weisaeth (eds) *Traumatic Stress. The Effects of Overwhelming Experience on Mind, Body, and Society*. New York: Guilford Press, pp.525–526.

McFarlane, A. C. and van der Kolk, B. A. (1996) 'Trauma and its challenge to society.' In B. A. van der Kolk, A. C. McFarlane and L. Weisaeth (eds) *Traumatic Stress. The Effects of Overwhelming Experience on Mind, Body, and Society*. New York: Guilford Press, pp.24–46.

Rosenfield, M. (2000) 'Telephone counselling.' In C. Felthan and I. Horton (eds) *Handbook of Counselling and Psychotherapy*. London: Sage, pp.667–674.

Scheiby, B. B. (2001) 'Forming an identity as a music psychotherapist through analytical music therapy supervision.' In M. Forinash (ed) *Music Therapy Supervision*. Gilsum NH: Barcelona, pp.315–317.

Sutton, J. P. (2000) 'Aspects of music therapy with children in areas of community conflict.' In D. Dockter (ed) *Exile. Refugees and the Arts Therapies*. Hertford: University of Hertfordshire, Faculty of Art and Design Press.

Sutton, J.P. (in press) 'A kind of wound. Aspects of music therapy with children in areas of community conflict: some thoughts about an integrated approach.' In P. Jones and V. Karkon (eds) *Resistance, Destructiveness and Refusal*. London: Jessica Kingsley Publishers.

Turner, S. W., MaFarlane, A. C. and van der Kolk, B. A. (2000) 'The therapeutic environment and new explorations in the treatment of posttraumatic stress disorder.' In B. A. van der Kolk, A. C. McFarlane and L. Weisaeth (eds) *Traumatic Stress. The Effects of Overwhelming Experience on Mind, Body, and Society*. New York: Guilford Press, p.552.

van der Kolk. B. A. (1996) 'The complexity of adaptation to trauma.' In B. A. van der Kolk, A. C. McFarlane and L. Weisaeth (eds) *Traumatic Stress. The Effects of Overwhelming Experience on Mind, Body, and Society*. New York: Guilford Press, pp.182–213.

Wosket, V. (2000) 'Clinical supervision.' In C. Feltham and I. Horton (eds) *Handbook of Counselling and Psychotherapy*. London: Sage.

CHAPTER 12

The Wounded Healer
The Voice of Trauma: A Wounded Healer's Perspective

Diane Austin

How does one lose a self? It can be sacrificed at birth to fill up an empty parent. It can be shattered into fragments from unspeakable terrors like abuse, neglect and emotional and/or physical abandonment. It can become numb, deadened to life as the only way to exist in an unsafe environment. Or essential parts of the self can be hidden away because when they first came forth they were not welcomed, seen, understood and valued, but were judged, shamed and rejected for being too different, too needy, too much. Sometimes, the authentic self retreats into an inner sanctum because it was envied and even hated for the bright light of potentiality it possessed.

Analysts and psychiatrists have various ways of describing this phenomenon. British object-relations theorists like Winnicott (1965) and Miller (1981) speak about the loss of the true self; the young, feeling part of the personality and its replacement by a false compliant self. This psychic split is caused by a chronic lack of empathy and/or erratic, over-stimulating or grossly neglectful behaviour on the part of the primary caretaker. Masterson (1988) describes how the healthy, individuating real self can become impaired early in childhood when threatened with abandonment by the mother. This leads to the creation of a protective false self that suppresses painful feelings and impedes autonomy. In

Jung's (1947) view, the psyche tends toward dissociability and is comprised of complexes or part-personalities. Critical injuries to one's developing sense of self could result in the ego's identification with one complex (for example, the parental complex), to the exclusion of others. In his theory, one part of the psyche is capable of actively attacking and persecuting another part, thus causing it to recede from consciousness.

Different manifestations of 'self-loss' have been given different labels by the psychiatric community over the years. Narcissistic, borderline, schizoid and other personality disorders are the terms that have been used to describe the wide range of symptoms and defences that occur when connection to one's authentic and vital centre of being is broken. Many of my clients, however, describe their plight in more poetic and poignant terms. They speak of being hidden inside a cocoon, trapped behind a glass wall, enclosed inside a bubble or hovering around the edges of life, longing yet afraid to enter. Alice alternately perceives herself as a helpless child or evil incarnate. Sandy thinks she is broken. Mike feels there is nothing inside of him except a black hole, and Beth doesn't know who she is; she just wishes she would stop having such horrible nightmares.

These clients are all in various stages of working through unresolved trauma. The traumatic experience, as well as the meaning attributed to it, critically affected each person's experience of self and his/her capacity to participate in an intimate relationship (Ulman and Brothers 1988). The term 'trauma' is used here to refer to any experience that causes the infant or child unbearable psychic pain and/or anxiety. Since the rupture, breach, shock or shocks occur before a coherent ego and its defences have been adequately formed, the intense effects are too overwhelming to be metabolised and processed normally; thus, the devastating effects on the traumatised person's body, mind and spirit (Herman 1992; Kalsched 1996). Some of these effects can be observed in the way that traumatised clients often alternate between a state of 'overwhelm' and intense re-experiencing of the trauma, and a state of emotional constriction and numbing which can include avoidance of people, places and events that might trigger traumatic associations and bring on intolerable anxiety or panic (Levine 1997; van der Kolk 1987).

Traumatic experiences encompass a wide range of occurrences from the horrors of sexual and physical abuse to the more cumulative traumas of unmet dependency needs, inadequate nurturing and interruptions of the attachment bond. Common to all these experiences is the rupture to the integrity of the self and the feelings of confusion, helplessness and terror this rupture evokes (Kalsched 1996; Terr 1990). The inner world of the traumatised client contains split off, dissociated parts of the self which are often externalised in the client–therapist relationship and can be worked with in the transference–countertransference situation (Davies and Frawley 1994). In music therapy, the relationship field is enlarged to include transference and countertransference to and in the music. Parts of the self can also be projected onto the voice, the music and the musical instruments (Austin 1993).

Clinicians who have studied trauma from different theoretical perspectives have discovered the prominence of one dyadic structure that results from a split in the ego or personality of the client. This dyad consists of a regressed part, usually 'feeling' in nature, and a preciously advanced part usually associated with mental processes (Kalsched 1996). This advanced part persecutes the regressed part in what seems like a misguided effort to protect it from the dangers of connection to the self and others. Getting close to others is perceived as dangerous because the primary caretakers of infancy and/or childhood were undependable, neglectful or abusive. Making connections among the self-parts is threatening because psychological survival once depended upon the ability to disconnect thoughts from feelings and emotionally to distance oneself from experience. I turn to my clients once again for vivid descriptions of the inner persecutor – the witch, the predator, the beast, the rapist; as well as the inner victim – the orphan, the hurt puppy, the broken doll, the homeless man. These images are personal and archetypal in nature and emerge in dreams and in creative expression like vocal and instrumental improvisation (Austin 1991, 1993, 1996, 1998, 1999).

Primitive defences like denial and dissociation protect the self from annihilation, but also affect the integrity of the personality. Severely dissociated clients experience the self as enfeebled, fragmented and/or lacking in continuity. Clients who were unable to form a secure attachment to the primary caretaker and/or lacked an emotionally available and consistent 'good-enough' mother (Winnicott 1971) have an accumulation of unmet dependency needs that pave the way for problems with identity formation and self-esteem regulation. Without a fully developed sense of self as a basis for ego functioning, these clients are compromised in their ability to function as mature adults. 'Adult-children' like Peter describe it this way: 'I wake up every morning feeling anxious and all I want to do is hide under the covers … I know I look like a grown-up and I have an important job and everything, but I feel like a fraud and it's only a matter of time before they find out I'm faking it.'

So how do we help these clients recover from unbearable life experiences so they can have access to more of themselves and feel more authentic and alive? I have found the combination of improvised singing and verbal processing to be one very effective way of working with the unresolved traumas of childhood.

Giving trauma a voice

Children who are raised in an atmosphere of fear, hostility, violence or neglect, and children whose parents are alcoholic, emotionally disturbed, or absent (physically or emotionally), have been silenced. Sometimes this silence takes the form of withdrawing into a private world and choosing not to communicate because it is not safe to do so. Sometimes the silence is selective. Some things are allowed to be talked about, some feelings are allowed expression and others clearly are not. Sometimes the silence is loud: words and feelings come tumbling out but fall on deaf ears or are beaten down and stifled. Needs and feelings remain unmet and the voice becomes inaudible, tight and tense, breathy and undefined, or simply untrue, perhaps lovely to listen to but not connected to the core of the person. In essence, the traumatised person often survives by forfeiting her own voice.

The process of recovering one's true voice involves reinhabiting the body. As previously discussed, the dissociative defences that initially protect the psyche from annihilation sever the connection between the body, mind and spirit. Embodiment requires the courage to remember and experience the sensations and feelings that were overwhelming as a child, intolerable because no one was present to help the child contain, make sense and digest the intense effects.

Singing is restorative for a variety of reasons. On a physiological level, singing facilitates deep breathing. In order to sustain tones one has to take in more air, thus expanding the belly and diaphragm, and then has to fully release the breath in order to continue the process. This kind of deep breathing slows the heart rate and calms the nervous system, stilling the mind and the body. Relaxation is the result – a state that is beneficial to everyone, but is especially helpful to anyone in a state of panic or extreme anxiety who is hyperventilating, or breathing in short, shallow bursts. There is a reciprocity between the physiological and the psychological effects of breathing. By restricting the intake and release of breath, we can control our feelings. This is obvious when I watch clients hold their breath after revealing an emotionally charged issue. When encouraged to exhale fully, they often come in contact with a feeling they have been suppressing. Likewise, the inability to take in nurturing or other kinds of experiences and information is mirrored in restricted inhalation. The way we breathe influences how we feel and what we feel has a direct effect on how we breathe.

Singing is also a neuromuscular activity and muscular patterns are closely linked to psychological patterns and emotional response (Newham 1998). When we sing, we are the instrument, and the vibrations that we produce nurture the body and massage our insides (Keyes 1973). Internally resonating vibrations break up and release blockages of energy, allowing a natural flow of vitality and a state of equilibrium to return to the body. These benefits are particularly relevant to traumatised clients who have frozen, numbed off areas in the body that hold traumatic experience. According to Levine (1997), this residue of unresolved, undischarged energy gets trapped in the nervous system and creates the debilitating symptoms associated with trauma. Singing can enable the traumatised client to reconnect with her essential nature by providing her with access to, and an outlet for, intense feelings. Singing offers a way for the disembodied spirit to incarnate because the way home can be pleasurable and the painful feelings can be put into an aesthetically pleasing form. Lynn explained it this way: 'When I sang just now, I took something ugly that happened to me and made it beautiful.' The structure inherent in songs and present in vocal improvisation can shore up a weak inner structure in the psyche and help contain strong emotions, thus making it safer to express them (Austin 1986).

I have often said that music and the arts saved my life. Being able to express myself through singing and songwriting preserved my personal spirit and helped me through a very difficult childhood and adolescence. Looking back, I feel I needed the secure container provided by a song in order to feel safe enough to express feelings and aspects of myself that were otherwise too threatening.

The act of singing is empowering: sensing the life force flowing through the body; feelings one's strength in the ability to produce strong and prolonged tones; experiencing one's creativity in the process of making something beautiful; having the ability to move oneself and others; and hearing one's own voice mirroring back the undeniable confirmation of existence. Owning one's voice is owning one's authority and ending a cycle of victimisation.

Vocal holding techniques

'Vocal holding techniques' is the name ascribed to a method of vocal improvisation I have developed and codified. It involves the intentional use of two chords in combination with the therapist's voice in order to create a consistent and stable musical environment that facilitates improvised singing within the client–therapist relationship. This method provides a reliable, safe structure for the client who is afraid or unused to improvising. It supports a connection to self and other and promotes a therapeutic regression in which unconscious feelings, sensations, memories and associations can be accessed, processed and integrated. These unconscious experiences are directly related to parts of the self that have been split off and suspended in time due to traumatic occurrences. When contacted and communicated with, these younger parts can be reunited with the ego and the vital energy they contain can be made available to the present day personality. Developmental arrests can be repaired and a more complete sense of self can be attained.

Unlike jazz or other forms of clinical improvisation where shifts in harmonic centres are to be expected, this improvisational structure is usually limited to two chords in order to establish a predictable, secure musical and psychological container that will enable the client to relinquish some of the mind's control, sink down into his or her body and allow his or her spontaneous self to emerge. The chord pattern is played repeatedly as a basis for the client's improvisation. The simplicity of the music and the hypnotic repetition of the two chords, combined with the rocking rhythmic motion and the singing of single syllables (sounds, not words initially), can produce a trance-like altered state and easy access to the world of the unconscious. The steady, consistent harmonic underpinning, the rhythmic grounding and the therapist's singing encourage and support the client's vocalisation. Within this strong yet flexible musical container the client can explore new ways of being, experience the freedom of play and creative self-expression and allow feelings and images to emerge (Austin 1996, 1998, 1999). The client's voice, feelings and emerging aspects of the self are all held within this musical matrix.

This method is especially useful in working through developmental injuries and arrests due to traumatic ruptures in the mother–child relationship and/or empathic failures at crucial developmental junctures. Interpretation and illumination of psychic conflict is of minimal value in working with adults traumatised as children, until the link between self and other is rebuilt and the client's capacity for relationship is restored (Hegeman 1995; Herman 1992). Improvised singing seems ideally suited for this reparative work. The voice is a primary source of connection between a mother and her child. Even in utero, infants begin to recognise the voices of those who will care for them. Babies begin to vocalise at around five weeks of age and the attachment between the infant and its caretaker develops slowly over the baby's first year of life through physical closeness and an ongoing dialogue of cooing, babbling, gazing and smiling. The gaze between mother and infant contributes to the vocal rapport between the two (Bowlby 1969; Winnicott 1971). Vocal interaction in sounds, song and later speech are critical to the child's development (Newham 1998). Tomatis (1991) has even suggested that the mother's voice is just as important to the child as the mother's milk in providing adequate relational bonding. The importance of the voice and vocal holding in building and repairing the connection between self and other has significant implications when working in depth with clients suffering from the consequences of pre-verbal wounds to the self.

It should be noted that vocal holding techniques are not meant to be a prescription or recipe and are not necessarily used in the order that follows. For the sake of clarity, I will describe the process as it appears to complement the developmental stages. As with any therapeutic intervention, however, the client's history, diagnosis, transference reactions and unique personality and needs should determine the approach taken to accomplish therapeutic goals. For example, when improvising, some clients will initially feel safer using words and may experience vocal sounds as more regressive and associated with loss of control. Other clients may feel less exposed in the more open realm of non-verbal singing because words are more specific and definitive. Still others may need even more structure, in which case pre-composed songs may be more appropriate, particularly in the beginning phase of therapy.

In the initial 'vocal holding' phase, the client and the therapist sing in *unison*. Singing together on the same notes can promote the emergence of a symbiosis-like transference and countertransference. This is important for clients who never had a satisfactory experience of merging with an emotionally present, calm, consistent mother. Through a replication of early mother–child relatedness, these clients can eventually internalise a stable sense of self and then gradually renegotiate the stages of separation and individuation. Sometimes sounds and phrases emerge that are reminiscent of the babbling sounds of a three to six month old (Gardner 1994). The next phase of *harmonising* creates the opportunity for the client to experience a sense of being separate yet in relationship. *Mirroring* occurs when a client sings his or her own melodic line and the therapist responds by repeating the client's melody back to him or her. Mirroring is especially useful when a client needs support in finding his or her own voice and/or when new parts of the personality are emerging and need to be heard and accepted. This musical reflection provides encouragement and validation. *Grounding* occurs when the therapist sings the tone or root of the chords and provides a base for the client's vocalisation. The client can then improvise freely and return to 'home base' whenever he or she wants to 'refuel' (Austin 1998, 1999). One client referred to the grounding tones as 'touch tones'.

This musical intervention is reminiscent of a typical pattern of inter-action between the child and the maternal figure that occurs when the child begins to move away from the mother to explore the environment. In the ideal situation, the mother stays in contact with the child and supports and encourages her increased efforts to individuate; otherwise the stages of separation-individuation become associated with object loss. Lack of empathy, attunement and of course abandonment and/or impingement during the earlier developmental phases will negatively impact the child's ability to individuate (Bowlby 1969; Mahler, Pine and Bergman 1975).

Vocal holding techniques are introduced into the music psychother-apy session in various ways. With a client who is especially anxious about improvising but wants to try, I might explain this method in detail. Usually, however, I give a minimal description or simply ask: 'Would you like to try singing about this (person, situation, feeling, etc.)? We could improvise or make it up as we go along.' I then ask the client if he or she wants two or more chords. He or she sometimes chooses the exact chords or gives a general description ('something minor'), but if he or she has little or no knowledge of chord structure or needs help finding the sound he or she wants, I might play examples of different chord combinations (major, minor, suspended, etc.) and ask for his or her preference. Occa-sionally, a client will describe a mood or feeling he or she would like to evoke and together we search for and find the fitting chords (Austin 1999). The client may also suggest a rhythm and a piano setting. (I use a clavinova that has various settings such as organ, strings etc.) Giving choices and working collaboratively empowers the client and helps to create a safe therapeutic environment.

We begin by breathing together. As previously described, deep breathing is critical in focusing, relaxing and grounding the client in his or her body. Breathing together begins the process of vocal attunement that continues as the therapist attempts to match the client's vocal quality, dynamics, tempo and phrasing. Being present to the client as an empathically attuned companion may also involve matching her physical movements (for example, rocking together) and making eye contact. Eye contact can reinforce the intimacy engendered by singing together, but may be too intense an experience for some clients and even distracting for others. The most effective way to meet the client's musical-emotional needs (in terms of singing in unison, mirroring, using words or sounds, etc.) is determined by the therapist's knowledge of the client's history, musical proficiency, general diagnosis, developmental stage, current life issues, transference-countertransference reactions, as well as the musical cues provided in the improvisation. A rudimentary example of the latter, is when Sam, a client who is musically capable of holding his own note, continued to join my tone as I attempted to harmonise with him. I think this musical interaction reflected Sam's need to merge with an idealised object in order to maintain some sense of self-cohesion. Another example is illustrated by Beth, a client who liked to sing but preferred singing alone. As the therapy progressed and Beth found she could express her anger toward me without experiencing abandonment or retaliation, she began to invite me to sing with her. We often harmonised together. My sense was that she now felt she could come closer to me without fear of being engulfed and losing herself.

In addition, the therapist is also informed by the client's body language, facial expression and of course his or her own creative intuition. When the client is aware of his or her own needs and there is sufficient trust in the therapeutic relationship so that he or she is unafraid of expressing his or her preference, much information can be gathered directly in the verbal processing that usually follows the vocal improvisation.

Vocal holding techniques are not the only musical approach I use when working with traumatised clients. It is a method, however, that has proven effective in creating an opportunity for a safe, therapeutic regression in which dissociated and/or unconscious feelings, memories and sensations can gradually be accessed, experienced, understood and integrated. This musical approach often constellates the intense transference and countertransference reactions that are essential in repairing arrests in development. Vocal holding initially tends to promote a positive transference, that of the longed for good mother of early infancy and childhood. This highly empathic musical environment is fertile soil in which trust can grow and feelings can be brought to light. If the therapeutic relationship feels trustworthy enough, the traumatised client will begin to differentiate feelings such as grief, terror and rage. At these moments, the therapist and the music have to be experienced by the client as strong and resilient enough to withstand these intense affects. The therapist might alter the music somewhat to reflect the client's changing emotional intensity. This can mean using alternate chord voicings, extending chords (adding 7ths, 9ths, 11ths, 13ths), adding dissonant notes and employing changes in volume, tempo and rhythmic accents. These musical interventions can be made instrumentally and/or vocally.

However, it is important to stress here that an advanced level of training is necessary to practise this type of in-depth music psychotherapy. In addition to a master's degree, a doctorate and/or institute training, I believe it is essential for a music therapist interested in working psychodynamically to have his or her own personal psychotherapy and supervision.

The wounded healer

Any therapist working in-depth is using him- or herself as well as the music as an 'instrument'. This human instrument needs the continued 'fine tuning' that personal psychotherapy and/or supervision provide in order to achieve the self-knowledge and self-awareness necessary to recognise and work effectively with transference, countertransference and other unconscious dynamics that emerge in a therapeutic relationship.

The intimacy of creating music together is especially challenging because the unconscious contents for both client and therapist are easily accessed through music. Client and therapist can deeply affect each other on a level that goes beyond words. The music therapist needs to be well acquainted with his or her own issues, feelings, strengths and vulnerabilities, not only better to understand and empathise with his or her clients, but also to be able to differentiate the client's feelings from his or her own. This issue is intensified when the therapist is a 'wounded healer'.

Guggenbuhl-Craig (1971) describes the 'wounded healer' as a therapist who has been deeply wounded and has undergone a healing process, yet continues to recognise both his or her own 'wounded' part as well as the 'healer' part: 'Such an analyst recognizes time and again how the patient's difficulties constellate his own problems, and vice versa, and

he therefore openly works not only on the patient but on himself'
(Guggenbuhl-Craig 1971, p.130).

Sedgwick (1994) views countertransference as the primary instrument of the wounded healer and makes a strong case for the therapist's
subjective involvement in the psychotherapeutic process. He refers to
homeopathic healing and the idea that 'like cures like' (Sedgewick 1994,
p.20). Jung (1929), a wounded healer himself, emphasised the mutuality
of the analytical process and suggested that the analyst is as much in the
analysis as the client. He believed that the analyst's psychological transformations could have a crucial transformative effect on the client.

Recent studies have found higher rates of childhood abuse in mental
health professionals than in other professionals (Pearlman and Saakvitne
1995). This makes sense. As a therapist, the majority of the clients I see
are creative arts therapy students or therapists and the majority suffer
from some kind of childhood trauma ranging from sexual and/or
physical abuse to abandonment issues related to an accumulation of
unmet dependency needs. As a therapist-client, I have participated in
various therapy, supervision and training groups with other 'wounded
healers' like myself. One of the positive aspects for the therapist of being
wounded and working through one's childhood injuries is the enhanced
capacity to understand and empathise with one's clients. The ability to
perceive and respond intuitively to the unconscious needs of others that
once helped the child (therapist) survive, can now be used in service of
the client (Miller 1981).

Many therapists with histories of childhood trauma have developed
'heightened capacities to be attentive to the needs of others ... including
an acute sensitivity to the affects, needs and unspoken defenses of
another' (Pearlman and Saakvitne 1995). Such therapists often bring to
the work a deep sense of commitment, compassion, and an understanding only gained through personal experience of the debilitating effects of
trauma on one's sense of self as well as the courage required to make the
long and difficult journey toward recovery. These therapists can make
excellent role models. Clients generally feel safer with a therapist who has
'been there'. As they say in Alcoholics Anonymous, someone who
doesn't just 'talk the talk' but who 'walks the walk'.

There are also potential dangers when 'like treats like'. Similarities between client and therapist can be a help or a hindrance. The threshold between self and other can become slippery when therapist and client have overlapping issues. Of course, a therapist who has the ongoing support of personal therapy and supervision will be better equipped to protect him- or herself and his or her client from unconscious re-enactments and retraumatisation. There are however challenging countertransferential issues for any therapist working with adults traumatised as children that can be exacerbated when the therapist is also recovering from traumatic experiences of his or her own.

The lack of literature dealing with 'survivor therapists' (Pearlman and Saakvitne 1995, pp.175–176) seems to reflect the profession's difficulty in acknowledging our humanity as therapists and the vulnerability and fallibility that is part of that humanity. The fact that the therapist's personality and his or her unconscious feelings, fantasies and inner state can affect the client is often overlooked in the psychoanalytic literature. This lack of attention to the special issues of survivor therapists can contribute to feelings of isolation, shame and conflict about disclosing personal material in their professional lives that may parallel the experiences they struggle with in their personal lives (Natterson and Friedman 1995; Pearlman and Saakvitne 1995; Sedgwick 1994).

Vicarious traumatisation is at times unavoidable for any therapist working with trauma and is not always an indicator of the therapist's unresolved psychological issues, but part of the reality and process of trauma therapy. Vicarious traumatization is a process through which the therapist's inner experience is deeply affected and negatively transformed through empathic engagement with the client's trauma material (McCann and Pearlman 1990). Personal memories, painful associations and strong emotions can easily be induced and/or awakened in the therapist when empathy leads to identification. Current stressful circumstances in the therapist's life can make him or her more vulnerable to being strongly impacted by his or her client's stories and feelings of loss, disconnection and pain. Life stressors can also affect the therapist's ability to perceive and work with difficult transferential and countertransferential issues. The therapist may turn to a variety of defensive strategies, some of which open him or her to further traumatisation (like dissociation). The therapist's defences will affect his or her ability to focus on his or her client's needs and may result in a traumatic re-enactment for the client.

In the complex interactive field of client and therapist, it can become difficult to discern who owns which psychic content and who is in a reactive state to whom or to what, especially when working within the music: 'Is the therapist reacting to the client's unconscious as it resonates through the music, or is the therapist's music activating the client's unconscious' (Austin 1998, p.332). The urge to resolve trauma through re-enactment is extremely compelling (Levine 1997). This compulsion to repeat or re-enact the original trauma can be looked at as an attempt to master the original damaging experience and re-establish a sense of empowerment or an attempt to remember that which has been denied or dissociated from consciousness (Freud 1938; Herman 1992; Kalsched 1996).

In the past few years, I have become very interested in what I refer to as an 'addiction to trauma'. I have witnessed this phenomenon in some of my clients. Perhaps this compulsion to go deeper and deeper into the pain is an attempt to self-cure, to finally get to the bottom of it all, to the core of the trauma. Sometimes the behaviour seems masochistic, like picking at a sore. Sometimes it seems as if the person is self-perpetrating and then self-soothing, playing two roles in what might be a traumatic re-enactment of the original victim–perpetrator drama. Returning to the 'black hole' of grief and terror over and over again might be an attempt to remain united with one's deeply wounded parent. Levine (1997) refers to this turbulent, compelling black hole as a 'trauma vortex' (Levine 1997, p.197). Drawing on Freud's early definition of trauma, he describes a breach in the protective barrier against stimuli which causes a rupture in one's psychic container:

> With the rupture, an explosive rushing out of life-energy creates a trauma vortex … it is common for traumatized individuals either to get sucked into the trauma vortex or to avoid the breach entirely by staying distanced from the region where the breach (trauma) occurred. (Levine 1997, p.197)

At some point in the retraumatisation cycle, this pull toward the 'vortex' appears to take on a life of its own. These highly activated emotional states have a biochemical component to them. The heightened arousal state can release a surge of energy that may feel exhilarating (Levine 1997; van der Kolk 1987). Some people who suffer from trauma symptoms have difficulty in accessing feelings, and intense or volatile emotional states may provide a relief from numbness and a sense of feeling alive.

When the client seems compelled continuously to re-enact and relive her trauma, the therapist has to work very slowly and sensitively, use interventions cautiously and be extremely aware of the client's feelings, sensations and non-verbal communications from moment to moment in order to prevent emotional flooding and retraumatisation. Resolution of profound injuries to one's sense of self involves a process of gradually accessing and naming the feelings that emerge, and gaining insight into the origins of the injuries. Having a context helps the client to understand the traumatic symptoms and make sense of them. Finding the meaning in the suffering is healing. A skilled, empathic therapist can guide and support the client through this rocky terrain of feelings, memories and associations and can provide her with a reparative experience.

What happens though when the wounded therapist is 'addicted to trauma'? My interest in this subject grew after I attended a few workshops and experiential classes where I observed therapists who appeared intent on providing a cathartic release for the participants and who seemed unaware of the dangers of retraumatisation. It could be that these therapists had not received adequate or sufficient psychotherapy and/or supervision. One creative arts therapy workshop I attended culminated in a kind of group vicarious retraumatisation, when a group member who was working on issues related to childhood sexual abuse went into a terrifying spontaneous regression and the whole group was affected. Afterwards, I wondered if the therapist was aware of the power inherent in the arts therapies. These so-called 'safe' therapies can easily penetrate defensive barriers and therefore need to be used responsibly, and with knowledge of the client's history, including particular strengths and vulnerabilities.

There also exists the possibility that a traumatised therapist could be attempting to heal him- or herself vicariously by healing the client. Using one's client unconsciously in an attempt to heal oneself has been described by Guggenbuhl-Craig (1971), Miller (1981) and Sedgwick (1994) among others. The therapist who has not recovered enough of him- or herself to maintain a vital connection to her feelings may unconsciously crave the drama and emotional intensity traumatic re-enactments provide. States of heightened arousal may substitute for genuine feelings of aliveness.

I know that I am affected sometimes quite deeply by my clients and I believe they are affected by me as well. So I return to the metaphor of the therapist as an instrument in constant need of tuning, an instrument that needs to be looked after and played with sensitivity. Staying in tune can be achieved by going to therapy, supervision, peer support groups and by playing music. I have also found it helpful to have family and friends I can talk to honestly and who will tell me the truth even when the mirror they hold up is not so pretty. Exercise, play and time alone to write, reflect or just be are other ways I nurture myself so that I can be present for my clients.

Case example

Vicky, a 28-year-old professional cellist, sought out music psychotherapy for what she believed was a psychosomatic illness. After a successful performance approximately two years ago, she awoke to find that she could not move her right hand. Since that episode, she had been suffering from a periodic pain in both her right hand and arm that was seriously affecting her ability to practise and perform. Vicky had been to the best doctors and physiotherapists, who found nothing wrong with her. She felt she was losing her 'musical self' and she was now convinced the problem was not in her body but in her mind. She was very ashamed of acknowledging this. Vicky described her family as 'normal'. Her mother worked full time as a high school principal and her father had his own medical practice. She had a brother three years younger who still lived at home.

Initially, Vicky was reluctant to discuss her family and only wanted to talk about her music and her physical ailment. She appeared to be very bright, serious and responsible, a person driven constantly to achieve and pursued by a harsh perfectionistic inner critic. She seemed to live in her head and spoke very quickly in a high-pitched, monotone voice seldom taking a deep breath or leaving any space for feelings to emerge. I sensed a great deal of anxiety and fragility underneath her confident manner. Vicky was interested in her dreams and usually brought at least one to each session. The majority of these were archetypal 'trauma dreams' (Kalsched 1996) with images of car crashes, wounded animals and dismembered bodies. I felt the dreams were providing us with a picture of what was happening to Vicky intrapsychically, and revealed the severe split between her mind and her instinctual self. As the therapy progressed, Vicky came more into focus as a 'parentified child' (Miller 1981) who took care of her emotionally immature and unavailable parents by 'holding herself together' and relinquishing her needs and her young, feeling self in the process.

Vicky's music was the one area of her life in which she had felt free to express her feelings. Listening to Vicky describe her situation and hearing the desperation in her voice, I was reminded of my senior year of high school when I developed vocal nodes. I remembered how devastated I felt. Like Vicky, I depended on my music (singing in my case) to provide an outlet for feelings that were otherwise too difficult and frightening to express. I had the sense that Vicky's psychosomatic symptoms were related to the shame and guilt she felt in acknowledging her feelings and the problems within her family; that it was all right to complain about physical problems but not emotional ones. Intuitively, I felt that her hand was carrying all her unresolved grief and rage. Vicky's dreams provided information about her unconscious processes, but her associations to the material remained on an intellectual level. I felt we needed to access the feelings connected to the dream images. I often use music to work with dreams. Since music and dreams speak a similar language (symbolic), and both directly access the unconscious, it is as if no translation is necessary for the music to resonate in the heart of the dream image and release its affective component.

I thought singing would be an effective way of working with Vicky because she was not identified with her voice. There was no performance pressure associated with singing and her hands would not be involved. It was a conflict-free area. Vicky had enjoyed singing in choirs during her school years but had never improvised using her voice before. During one session I introduced her to vocal holding techniques and when we stopped singing she said, 'I felt a chill, like a ghost came into me ... I've always been two people, one is independent and rational; the other is all energy and emotion ... it's like they came together for a minute.' Vocal holding techniques are especially useful when working with dissociative defences and the kind of mind–body splits so prevalent in traumatised clients (Austin 1998, 1999). The two parts that Vicky experienced coming together during the singing symbolised a moment of integration that would have to be repeated over and over again to be resolved.

The session that follows took place during our third month of working together. Vicky had just returned from a weekend with her parents. When I asked her how things went she said: 'Fine, but my hand started hurting again when I was practising on Sunday.' When I enquired further about her interactions with her family and any feelings she had experienced during the weekend, she was vague and changed the subject. She was speaking very fast and in an excited manner but with little real effect. She kept changing topics. I had the thought 'a moving target is hard to hit', and that she was defending herself against delving too deeply into any subject. At one point she mentioned a past dream she'd had and I asked her if she'd had any dreams this weekend. She reported the following: 'I am at the airport and I'm all excited watching the planes taking off. A plane takes off right in front of me but then turns to the right suddenly and crashes into a building. The plane goes up in flames and I start yelling for help. Men come out of the airport with stretchers and I go with them. There are people badly burned lying on the ground. Then I see a baby. I'm not sure if it's alive or dead. It's all shrivelled up.'

Instead of asking Vicky for her associations to the dream and/or offering any interpretations, I asked if she would like to try exploring the dream in the music, using two chords and singing. She agreed and came to the piano to sit beside me. I suggested either singing the overall feeling of the dream or an image that felt particularly meaningful to her. She wanted to focus on the image of the baby. I asked her what chords she would like and she said she wasn't sure. I played different combinations for her and she settled on A minor 9 to F major 9. We began by breathing together several times. I suggested this because breathing helps the client (and the therapist) release excess anxiety, get grounded in his/her body and begins the process of vocal attunement. It also serves as a transition state between speaking and singing. I played slowly and softly in the middle register of the piano. The tempo, dynamics, repetitious rocking rhythm, chord voicings (suspended ninths that resolved) and occasional arpeggios seemed to support her voice and create a feeling state that complemented the dream. I liked this music. It felt soothing to me, yet conveyed a particular kind of sadness mixed with longing.

Vicky began by singing 'ah-h-h', holding the tone as if stretching it out. The tone she chose and the open sound suggested a willingness to explore her feelings. I joined her immediately and we started singing in unison. She seemed comfortable with the unison, as if taking in my support and gathering strength by merging or joining with me before beginning to move on her own. She slowly began a descending melodic line, which I mirrored and harmonised with and then we returned to unison. Her singing voice was softer, breathier and had a more feeling, receptive quality than the music of her speaking voice, which was usually monotone, fast and staccato. At moments, her singing sounded frail and vulnerable to me and it seemed to give voice to her young, wounded feminine self. At one point she began an ascending melodic line and I remember thinking that she needed a firm grounding base to support this upward movement. I held a low tone while she ascended. I had an image of a little bird whose spirit had been broken but who kept trying to get off the ground. I believed the baby in the dream was her young, feeling self that was suspended somewhere between life and death. This belief was grounded in experience both professional but also personal. I had spent many years in psychotherapy working to reclaim and integrate the young dissociated feeling parts of myself. The image of the shrivelled up baby filled me with sadness and compassion.

Vicky's singing became dissonant at one point alternating between the flat five and the fifth of A minor 9, and then between the dominant seventh and the seventh of F major. She may have been influenced by my use of suspended ninths to create tension and resolution. I was playing whole steps to produce this effect, whereas she was singing half steps and creating even more tension by alternately singing tri-tones. I think that this music was reflecting her pain and perhaps her ambivalence about living. The music built and then diminished in volume and intensity as

Vicky sang descending and ascending melodic lines. I alternated between unison and harmony, sometimes mirroring and overlapping into unison and harmony again. The music felt sad to me and filled with yearning. We 'pulsed' together in unison and harmony, and the volume and intensity increased as we ascended up the scale. I felt connected to her. I noticed that when singing she utilised a vocal range of over an octave, a contrast with the fairly monotone range she spoke in. We descended again in pitch and her voice grew soft. I began playing in the high register of the piano and arpeggiating the notes in what felt like a sort of music box sound. She changed from 'ah-h' to 'hm-m-m-'; this was a more closed sound, which seemed more regressive and perhaps protective. I joined her singing. I saw that she was rocking back and forth and I matched her movement. The singing grew softer and we breathed together and came to a close. We sat in silence for a few moments when the music ended.

I then asked her what she was experiencing. She said, 'It's like we were waking up that dead baby.' She began crying and continued, 'Everyone thinks I'm the happy one and my life should be so good … I feel sad for my brother and my mother, I worry about her.' Vicky began to talk more openly about her family and how they affected her. Her father emerged as a self-centred person with severe mood swings, who could be verbally abusive at times and more loving at others. Over the weekend he was extremely critical of her playing and told her she should give up the cello and pursue another career. At the end of the session, I reflected how unsafe she must have felt growing up with such an unpredictable parent and how difficult it must have been to express herself in such a critical atmosphere. I believe the 'vocal holding' created a nurturing safe environment that enabled Vicky to dialogue with her unconscious so that she could retrieve a piece of what had been lost to her – an image from the depths and the feelings connecting her to the part of herself contained within the image.

This session was at times difficult for me. I could easily empathise with aspects of Vicky – the perfectionism and the accompanying performance anxiety, the successful persona and the fragile child underneath. I attempted to use my countertransferential feelings to understand and connect with her. I was also aware of the dangers of overidentifying with

Vicky, of losing my therapeutic stance and with it the ability to be fully present to Vicky and her experience. I reminded myself that although we had some similar wounds we were different people at different stages in the healing process. Deep breathing also helped me to tune into my own feelings and physical sensations, stay grounded in my body and maintain my boundaries.

Free associative singing

'Free associative singing' is the term I use to describe a technique that can be implemented when words enter the vocal holding process. It is similar to Freud's technique of free association (1938) in that the client is encouraged to verbalise whatever comes into her head with the expectation that by doing so she will come into contact with unconscious images, memories and associated feelings. It differs from Freud's technique in that the client is singing instead of speaking, but more significantly the therapist is also singing and contributing to the musical stream of consciousness by making active *verbal* and musical interventions. The accompaniment (two-chord holding pattern or repetitive riff) and the therapist's singing, continue to contain the client's process. However, the emphasis now is not only on 'holding' the client's emerging self and psychic contents, but on creating momentum through the music and lyrics that will propel the improvisation and the therapeutic process forward. The progression to words and the more active role taken by the therapist promotes a greater differentiation between client and therapist. When the therapist begins questioning, reframing and interpreting within the improvisational dyad, the transference and counter-transference can become much more complex. The client may experience the therapist not only as the 'good-enough' mother, but in other roles as well (figures from the client's interpersonal and intrapsychic world).

In its simplest form free associative singing involves the client singing a word or phrase and the therapist mirroring (repeating) the words and the melody back to the client. The vocal holding techniques of singing in unison, harmonising and grounding add additional support and variation. As previously stated, the consistent, repetitive two-chord pattern and the therapist's vocal support and attunement can relax defences, induce an altered state of consciousness and facilitate a creative regression in service of the self (Austin 1998, 1999). This improvisational structure continues to support the creation of a predictable secure environment that enables the traumatised client to feel safe enough to express him- or herself and gradually explore his or her inner world. However, this two-chord structure is not rigid. With the movement to words there is often a need for more variations in dynamics, tempo, voicing, arpeggiation, rhythm, accents, rests and so on. The therapist can use not only his or her voice and the lyrics, but also music to empathise with the client's experience, encourage play and further the exploration of conscious and unconscious material. It should be noted that the spontaneity and unpredictability of play and fantasy can feel chaotic and out of control for traumatised adults. Vocal holding provides a containing play space where spontaneity and creativity can be restored along with a greater sense of reality and wholeness (Dayton 1997).

Throughout the improvisation, the therapist is making critical decisions about when, how and what to sing with the client. This is especially true when the therapist moves beyond simply mirroring the client's lyrics and music and begins to provide empathic reflection, ask questions, use repetition to emphasise important words, and musically role play significant people in the client's life, as well as parts of the self as they emerge in the therapy. By taking a more active role in facilitating the therapeutic process and with the use of words, the therapist can help the client understand and make meaning out of what he or she is experiencing in the present and what he or she experienced in the past, and how these events affected his or her sense of self. Old, unrealistic self-concepts can be replaced by new, realistic ones resulting in self-acceptance and increased self-esteem.

An intervention that I use consistently and find invaluable, which I previously referred to as an 'alter ego' (Austin 1998, 1999), is a musical version of the psychodramatic 'double' (Moreno 1994). When the therapist 'doubles', he or she sings as the inner voice of the client and uses first person ('I'). Drawing on induced countertransference, empathy, intuition as well as knowledge of the client's history, he or she gives voice to feelings and thoughts the client may be experiencing but is not yet singing. When the therapist's doubling is not accurate, the client can ignore or change the words to fit his or her truth. This intervention is especially useful for clients working to integrate thinking and feeling or a mind–body split. This split can be observed in clients who can talk about events and feelings without experiencing effect and/or can express intense feelings but have no words to enable them to make meaning out of their emotional experience. Doubling offers an effective way to breathe feelings into words and supply words for feelings. In addition, the naming or labelling of unprocessed trauma material can aid in preventing uncontrolled regression and retraumatisation (Hudgins and Kiesler 1987).

Case example

Beth, a 35-year-old artist, originally came to therapy because she felt unable to assert herself in work situations and ended up feeling underpaid and undervalued. She felt her low self-esteem was the problem. As we began to work together it became apparent that Beth suffered from anxiety and depression. Sometimes this was so crippling that she had a difficult time leaving her apartment. As her story unfolded, it became clear why she had these symptoms. Beth was an only child whose parents divorced when she was seven. She always felt closer to her father even though she rarely saw him. Beth described her mother as 'intellectual' and 'strong', but unaffectionate and prone to angry outbursts. With time I learned that some of these 'angry outbursts' took the form of physical attacks on Beth with whatever was handy (a shoe, a pan, etc.) and verbal assaults. If Beth cried, the punishment was even harsher.

Beth survived by living in her own world. She would 'leave' and go someplace deep inside herself. In this inner sanctuary she would sing and rock herself and tell herself sad stories. Her art also helped her by giving her a creative emotional outlet. Even though she craved attention, receiving it was frightening because Beth associated attention with judgement and pain.

During the first year of therapy, Beth often used a sketchpad and crayons to express feelings for which she had no words. As trust in our relationship grew, we began to improvise together at the piano and on other instruments. Beth gradually began to find her voice, both literally and symbolically. When I first met her, I had noticed that she spoke very softly, and would gradually speed up her speech while simultaneously fading out at the end of a sentence. As she began to set limits with people in her life and assert her feelings and needs, her voice reflected this change. She sounded stronger and more embodied. We sometimes did breathing exercises together, which also contributed to a reduction in interpersonal anxiety and helped her stay present while speaking to others.

During the third year of our work together, we began to vocally improvise using the holding techniques. The session I will now describe began with a discussion of Beth's relationship with her close friend, Michelle. Michelle had once again disappointed Beth by cancelling plans at the last minute. When Beth told Michelle how hurt she felt and that this was an ongoing pattern in their relationship, Michelle 'exploded' and hung up the phone on her. This painful interaction led to an exploration of Beth's abandonment issues with her mother. I asked Beth if she was willing to explore her relationship with her mother in the music by singing together. She agreed and came to sit beside me at the piano (on a separate bench).

Beth said she wanted 'dark' chords and then said 'minor'. I played E minor 7 to A minor 7 in a medium to slow tempo. The voicing was 1–5 in the left hand and 3–7 in the right, to 5–1 in the left hand and 7–3 in the right. We began by breathing together and then singing in unison on 'ah'. I felt Beth was getting in touch with her resources, her inner strength and the qualities that helped her survive difficult times. Her face softened and her shoulders relaxed. Her voice became steady and grew stronger as we continued singing. She appeared to be grounding herself in her own body and feeling the support available in our connection. After a few moments she sang 'I'm not the person I was' and I mirrored the words and melody back to her. She continued 'the person you made me think I was'. Again I reflected her words and melody while matching her volume, vocal quality and phrasing. She repeated these two phrases and then sang 'I'm not ugly, mother, I'm not ugly'. She repeated this phrase and then said 'I'm not a child anymore'. I mirrored her words and joined her in harmony on the word 'child' which we held for a measure. Beth then increased the volume and intensity of her singing and doubled up the time in her phrasing, perhaps to express her excitement and/or her feelings of empowerment. She sang 'I am a woman, a strong woman, a flower, a tree'. She held 'tree' and repeated it so I was able to support this affirmation by harmonising with her.

Beth was singing in a range of less than an octave. Her melodies included many ascending fourths and fifths. My association to this music was that Beth was taking a leap and landing on solid ground. She then sang 'you didn't kill me' and I got chills. I stopped singing, although I continued to play the piano. She sang 'I'm still here', and again I did not sing. In retrospect I think I lost my voice for a moment due to countertransferential feelings. As with Vicky, Beth had issues with which I could easily identify. I too felt abandoned by my mother and nearly 'killed off' in my relationship with her. Although I had spent many years in therapy working to resolve these childhood injuries and now had a good relationship with my mother, as many of you know these kinds of deep wounds are very slow to heal.

Beth sang 'I wish I could say you're not my mother anymore. I'm my own mother'. I felt sad at this point. I also felt she was singing with a greater depth of feeling. I sang 'I feel sad' (using my countertransference and singing as her 'double'). She picked this up and sang 'I feel sad' and her voice was soft and breathy. She sang 'I never had a real mother'. I mirrored this, joining her in unison on 'mother' and then sang 'I wanted a mother' ('doubling' her again). She repeated this phrase and we sang it over and over in unison, harmony and overlapping mirroring. I moved my left hand and played lower in the bass of the piano to support the intensity of our singing. I played eighth note triplets in my right hand to match her energy when she began singing louder and fuller.

Beth then sang 'you hurt me'. Again I repeated this and we sang the phrase over and over again. It felt as if the words were sinking in deeper each time we sang them. I sang 'I won't let you hurt me anymore' ('doubling') and she repeated this and added 'I can say NO!' We sang this phrase together in unison and harmony, going up the scale melodically and building dynamically. Then she paused and I sang 'ahs' to keep 'holding' and supporting her. After a while Beth came back in and sang 'How could you not see a child so full of love?', in a voice that sounded vulnerable and childlike. I sang 'You never saw me' (singing as her double and using my knowledge of her as well as drawing on my own experience). She repeated this and went on 'You never saw my drawings ... you never saw a little girl'. I echoed her words and melody and then sang 'so I went away'. There was a brief pause and then Beth sang 'but now I'm back'. At this point in the music Beth began crying softly. I slowly brought the music to a close singing on 'oo' to soothe and comfort her. I was feeling very moved and I was also in tears. Perhaps I was soothing myself as well. Afterwards, we briefly processed what had transpired in the music. Beth said, 'You sang a lot of things I was feeling but didn't know, couldn't find the words for ... and when I heard my words sung back to me I felt validated, real ... I *have* come back, at least for today.'

Conclusion

We come into the world as helpless infants, dependent on our mothers and other caretakers to meet our physical, emotional and psychological needs; dependent on them for our very existence. When these needs are not met, when a child cries and there is no answering voice, or the sound that returns confuses or obliterates, then the ability to play, explore, learn and grow is compromised. How do we find our own sounds, movements, feelings and sensations? How do we discern our own voices and grow into our own unique identities, without a safe environment and a consistent empathic presence to hold us and let us go? We can blame our parents, but they had parents, who had parents ... The cycle of abuse, neglect and just plain unconsciousness will continue until we make an effort to stop it.

I believe that the primary healing element in music psychotherapy is the relationship. The self cannot develop without a relationship to another self. Traumatised clients have difficulty trusting and forming healthy bonds with others. Music, and vocal holding techniques in particular, provide a fluid yet stable structure, a safe dependable container for vocal play and the expression of feelings and needs. Singing together can bring about physical, emotional, psychological and spiritual connection between the client and therapist and the client and his or her core self.

Adult clients who suffer from the symptoms of childhood abuse, neglect, emotional deprivation and inadequate parenting require a method of psychotherapy that can address pre-verbal wounds and the unmet dependency needs of early childhood. Music therapy is one very effective way of working with this population. I believe that music is 'medial' (Austin 1996). It flows easily between the conscious and unconscious worlds, bringing with it feelings, images and associations from the personal and collective unconscious and a creative means of expressing them. Vocal holding techniques can induce a therapeutic regression in which early mother–child relatedness can be replicated and the client can have a reparative experience by renegotiating crucial junctures where the relationship with the primary caretaker was ruptured.

Singing, being physically based, enables a severely dissociated client to re-enter her body, to access and give voice to what was previously inexpressible. Through free associative singing, the music allows the words to become embodied and linked to feelings, so that clients can more easily heal splits between thinking, feeling and sensation.

Trauma survivors are used to feeling misunderstood, lonely and isolated. Singing can break through the walls of isolation, but this requires courage on the part of client and therapist. It takes courage for the client to work through the shame and allow him- or herself to be seen as needy and vulnerable. It takes courage for the therapist to stay present and available while companioning the client down dark, empty corridors and into rooms filled with violent and painful memories.

The music shared deepens the relationship. It also provides a safe, intimate space where the authentic voice of the client can come forward and experience empathy and understanding, and gather strength and hope in the process. In the music there is a meeting – a coming together of two realities that create a third one. In the silence, in the words, in the music, the client feels the therapist singing, 'I too have lived through such pain and believe it can be tolerated, understood and accepted. I am not afraid and I want to be here with you … now.'

Acknowledgements

For my mother, who inspired my passion for this subject, and for my clients who have helped me to learn how to help them. With thanks to *Music Therapy Perspectives* for granting permission to use material that previously appeared in my article 'In search of the self: the use of vocal holding techniques with adults traumatized as children.' (Volume 19, Issue 1)

References

Austin, D. (1986) 'The healing symbol: sound, song and psychotherapy.' Unpublished masters thesis, New York University.

Austin, D. (1991) 'The musical mirror: music therapy for the narcissistically injured.' In K.E. Bruscia (ed) *Case Studies in Music Therapy*. Phoenixville PA: Barcelona, pp.291–307.

Austin, D. (1993) 'Projection of parts of the self onto music and musical instruments.' In G.M. Rolla (ed) *Your Inner Music*. Wilmette IL: Chiron.

Austin, D. (1996) 'The role of improvised music in psychodynamic music therapy with adults.' *MusicTherapy 14*, 1, 29–43.

Austin, D. (1998) 'When the psyche sings: transference and countertransference in improvised singing with individual adults.' In K.E. Bruscia (ed) *The Dynamics of Music Psychotherapy*. Gilsum NH: Barcelona.

Austin, D. (1999) 'Vocal improvisation in analytically oriented music therapy with adults.' In T. Wigram and J. De Backer (eds) *Clinical Applications of Music Therapy in Psychiatry*. London: Jessica Kingsley Publishers.

Bowlby, J. (1969) *Attachment, Vol. 1*. New York: Basic Books.

Davies, J.M. and Frawley, M.G. (1994) *Treating the Adult Survivor of Childhood Sexual Abuse: A Psychoanalytic Perspective*. New York: Basic Books.

Dayton, T. (1997) *Heartwounds: The Impact of Unresolved Trauma and Grief on Relationships*. Deerfield Beach FL: Health Communications.

Freud, S. (1938) *An Outline of Psychoanalysis*. New York: Norton.

Gardner, H. (1994) *The Arts and Human Develpoment*. New York: Basic Books.

Guggenbuhl-Craig, A. (1971) *Power in the Helping Professions*. Dallas TX: Spring Publications.

Hegeman, E. (1995) 'Transferential issues in the psychoanalytic treatment of incest survivors.' In J.L. Alpert (ed) *Sexual Abuse Recalled: Treating Trauma in the Era of the Recovered Memory Debate*. Northvale NJ: Jason Aronson.

Herman, J.L. (1992) *Trauma and Recovery*. New York: Basic Books.

Hudgins, M.K. and Kiesler, D.J. (1987) 'Individual experiential psychotherapy: an analogue validation of the intervention module of psychodynamic doubling.' *Psychotherapy 24*, 245–255.

Jung, C.G.(1929) *Problems of Modern Psychotherapy: Volume 16 of Collected Works*. Princeton NJ: Princeton University Press.

Jung, C.G. (1947) *On the Nature of the Psyche, Volume 8 of Collected Works.* Princeton NJ: Princeton University Press.

Kalsched, D. (1996) *The Inner World of Trauma: Archetypal Defenses of the Personal Spirit.* New York: Routledge.

Keyes, L.E. (1973) *Toning: The Creative Power of the Voice.* Marina del Rey CA: DeVorss.

Levine, P.A. (1997) *Waking the Tiger: Healing Trauma.* Berkeley CA: North Atlantic Books.

McCann, I.L. and Pearlman, L.A. (1990) 'Vicarious traumatization: a contextual model for understanding the effects of trauma on helpers.' *Journal of Traumatic Stress 3*, 1, 131–149.

Mahler, M.S., Pine, F. and Bergman, A. (1975) *The Psychological Birth of the Human Infant.* New York: Basic Books.

Masterson, J.F. (1988) *The Search for the Real Self: Unmasking the Personality Disorders of our Age.* New York: Macmillan.

Miller, A. (1981) *The Drama of the Gifted Child.* New York: Basic Books.

Moreno, L. (1994) *Psychodrama.* McLean VA: American Society for Group Psychotherapy and Psychodrama.

Natterson, J.M. and Friedman, R.J. (1995) *A Primer of Clinical Intersubjectivity.* Northvale NJ: Jason Aronson.

Newham, P. (1998) *Therapeutic Voicework: Principles and Practice for the Use of Singing as a Therapy.* London: Jessica Kingsley Publishers.

Pearlman, L.A. and Saakvitne, K.W. (1995) *Trauma and the Therapist.* New York: Norton.

Sedgwick, D. (1994) *The Wounded Healer.* New York: Routledge.

Terr, L. (1990 *Too Scared to Cry: Psychic Trauma in Childhood.* New York: Basic Books.

Tomatis, A. (1991) *The Conscious Ear: My Life of Transformation Through Listening.* NewYork: Station Hill Press.

Ulman, R.B. and Brothers, D. (1988) *The Shattered Self: A Psychoanalytic Study of Trauma.* Hillsdale, NJ: Analytic Press.

Winnicott, D.W. (1965) *The Maturational Process and the Facilitating Environment.* London: Hogarth Press.

Winnicott, D.W. (1971) *Playing and Reality.* London: Routledge.

van der Kolk, B. (ed) (1987) *Psychological Trauma.* Washington DC: American Psychiatric Press.

Afterword

Julie P. Sutton

While the perspectives in this book have ranged across disciplines and continents, there has been a continuity of thinking throughout. In different ways the authors have explored the theme of music, music therapy and trauma, as told through their own and their clients' different voices and experiences. The impact of these experiences is clear and at times powerful, as is the extraordinary resilience shown by those affected by trauma. Throughout these stories and narratives a case for the particular usefulness of a contained and disciplined application of music has been argued, as is the care with which the work must be undertaken.

Like traumatic events themselves, this work is always ongoing, and future authors will draw and expand upon the work cited in this volume. As indicated in the first chapter, trauma work is not static. Descriptions of traumatic conditions will continue to be redefined, with new knowledge being added as a result of new events taking place. This observation is made all the more pertinent when traumatic incidents take place. During the course of the final preparation for this publication, a single day intruded into mass consciousness. While sharply felt at the time, the impact of the New York and Washington attacks of September 11 2001 will continue to recede further into the past for the majority of people. Unbelievably, a month later, yet another traumatic event occurred in New York, and this time a terrorist cause was absent. When an aeroplane crashed into the residential area of Queens, it not only shocked those who had witnessed the events of September 11, but also intruded into the very area where many of the rescue workers lived. It is still unknown how this later event will have added to the effects of trauma already being experienced by so many in New York. Again, the aeroplane crash will become an increasingly distant memory for those not immediately involved. This is unlikely to be the case for the people closer to the events. For these people it will always remain a part of their lives and will be intensely felt at different times during the coming years. It is to these people and those who accompany them – and others like them – that this book speaks.

Julie Sutton
Belfast
November 2001

The Contributors

Diane Austin

Diane Austin MA, ACMT is a music therapist in private practice who specialises in clinical vocal improvisation. She is a faculty member in the graduate music therapy programme at New York University, where she teaches vocal improvisation, leads music therapy groups and supervises students in the programme. She is also a doctoral candidate at NYU and is currently working to define and codify her own method of music therapy. Diane is the Director of the Music Therapy Programme for Adolescents in Foster Care at the Turtle Bay Music School. She has been published in many professional journals and texts and has lectured and taught internationally, focusing primarily on music psychotherapy and the use of the voice in the therapeutic process. A member of the Scientific Committees for both the Seventh and Eighth World Congresses of Music Therapy, she now serves on the International Committee for Clinical Practice.

Hilary Bracefield

Hilary Bracefield has MAs in both Music and English from the University of Otago, New Zealand. Since 1976 she has lectured at the University of Ulster and is currently senior lecturer and Head of Music. Her research includes aesthetics, the music of Stravinsky, popular music and aspects of music therapy. Recently she has been interviewing and studying the music of young Northern Irish classical composers, and the chapter forms a part of this research. She is active in British academic music circles, including the Council of the Royal Musical Association.

Matthew Dixon

Matthew took a degree in English at Cambridge University and then studied for three years at the Royal Academy and Royal College of Music in London. After working for several years as a baroque oboist, he trained as a music therapist at the Nordoff-Robbins Music Therapy centre in 1995. He currently works in three very different places in London: the Medical Foundation for the Care of Victims of Torture, the Regional Rehabilitation Unit (for people with brain injury) in Northwick Park Hospital, and the Nordoff-Robbins Music Therapy Centre. His MA thesis was on musical endings in music therapy and he has written a chapter in a forthcoming book on therapeutic interventions for children traumatised by violence.

Adva Frank-Schwebel

Adva Frank-Schwebel (MA, RMT) was raised in South America and lives in Israel. She has worked as a music therapist for 18 years in the fields of child psychiatry, eating disorders and emotional and interpersonal disorders with children and adults. She works in Jerusalem in private practice, teaches and supervises in the Institute for Arts Therapy in the David Yellin College in Jerusalem, and in Bar Ilan University.

Louise Lang and Una McInerney

Having trained in the UK, Louise Lang and Una McInerney have pioneered clinical work in Bosnia, with the support of the War Child organisation. With clinical experience in the UK, Louise and a colleague set up the Music Therapy Wing at the Pavarotti Music Centre, Mostar, Bosnia-Herzegovina. Louise heads this unit, which caters for children from the Mostar area and beyond. With clinical experience in Ireland and Romania, Una McInerney joined the Mostar team. She has worked with clients with a variety of needs, including orphans, refugees and those with learning difficulties. Both Una and Louise have been responsible for the further development of the music therapy service during the ongoing post-war changes in Bosnia. This is the first major presentation of the work of the Pavarotti Centre team.

Louise Lang, Una McInerney, Rosemary Monaghan, Julie P. Sutton

Louise Lang and Una McInerney were both trained in the UK, later working at the Pavarotti Music Centre in Mostar, Bosnia during the changing post-war period. Rosemary Monaghan and Julie Sutton also trained in the UK and are registered clinical supervisors with the Association of Professional Music Therapists in the UK. Rosemary is the co-ordinator for the new London Musicspace centre.

Mercédès Pavlicevic

Dr Mercédès Pavlicevic is a senior lecturer and co-director of the music therapy programme at the University of Pretoria, South Africa and research adviser at the Nordoff-Robbins Music Therapy Centre in London. She has published and lectured internationally on music therapy and is especially interested in bringing together music therapy and African healing practices.

Marie Smyth

Dr Marie Smyth is Research Fellow with INCORE (the Initiative on Conflict Resolution and Ethnicity) of the University of Ulster and the United Nations University and Project Director, Templegrove Action Research, The Cost of the Troubles Study and Community Conflict Impact on Children. In addition to her research experience and many publications relating to this, she has also been part of many advisory panels including the NI Victims' Commission, the Forum for Peace and Reconciliation (Government of the Republic of Ireland) and the Mediation Network for Northern Ireland. A Member of the British Council Committee for Northern Ireland, Dr Smyth has lectured internationally and is also a poet.

Julie P. Sutton (editor)

Julie has practised as a registered music therapist for over 18 years, working with a wide range of clients and also as a researcher and registered clinical supervisor. Her research interests include Parkinson's disease, complex speech and language impairment, Rett syndrome, psychological trauma and interpersonal processes in improvisation. She has a private practice, working regularly in Belfast, Dublin, London and for the Pavarotti Music Therapy Centre in Bosnia-Herzegovina. She has published and presented internationally and is the editor of the *British Journal of Music Therapy*. A member of several professional groups and the UK representative for the European Music Therapy Confederation, Julie completed her doctorate in 2001.

Michael Swallow

Dr Michael Swallow trained in medicine in London and qualified MB BS in 1952. He found an early interest in neurology and after postgraduate work at the National Hospital for Nervous Diseases he was appointed Consultant Neurologist to the Royal Victoria Hospital, Belfast in 1964. His lifelong interest in music started with choristerships at Westminster Abbey and Magdalen College, Oxford. In Northern Ireland he directed the Royal Victoria Hospital Choir and the Ulster Singers and has worked as an accompanist with disabled people including SHARE MUSIC and the founding of the NI Music Therapy Trust. He is a Vice President of the British Society for Music Therapy, adviser to the Association of Professional Music Therapists and sits on the Arts Therapy Board of the Council for Professions Supplementary to Medicine. He was awarded an OBE in 1995 for his contributions to arts and disability and music therapy.

Helen M. Tyler

After completing her music degree and MPhil at Reading University, Helen taught music to a wide range of children, from nursery school to A level. She then trained as a music therapist at the Nordoff-Robbins Music Therapy Centre in London. She is now Assistant Director of the Nordoff-Robbins Centre and a Senior Tutor on the training course. She has written and lectured extensively on music therapy, and has published chapters and papers in books and journals.

Ruth Walsh Stewart and David Stewart

Ruth trained as a psychodynamic music therapist in London in 1993. Since then she has worked on an individual and group basis with children and adults in the areas of special education, mental health, physical illness and disability. She has published some of her work in the *Journal of the Irish Association for Counselling and Therapy* and in the *British Journal of Music Therapy*. She is currently training as a psychoanalytic psychotherapist. Ruth is a co-founder of PossAbilities Network, a voluntary organisation which offers clinical music therapy, consultation and creative arts projects in the community.

David Stewart is a musician, therapist and trainer. He qualified as a psychodynamic music therapist from Roehampton Institute London in 1989 and in 1999 completed a masters in music therapy. David is also a qualified social worker and has worked as a child therapist in a community counselling/psychotherapy centre in north Belfast. David has published in several UK journals and has presented his work in Ireland, England, Scotland, USA and South Africa.

Subject index

abandonment, trauma of early, in psychodynamic music therapy 133–52
absence
  conflicts of 105–6
  and presence 104
abuse and trauma 25
accountants 68
action-discharge 140
acute stress disorder *see* ASD
'Adagio' (Albinoni) 203–4, 205
adrenocoticotrophin (ACTH) 50
Afghanistan 131
African drumming 155
aggression 101, 160, 163, 171–2
alcohol 74, 77
Alcoholics Anonymous 242
alone in presence of another 138
alternative health practitioners 67
amusia 45
amygdala 46, 50
anger 122, 124
annihilation, fear of 101
anxiety 31, 77, 160
apartheid 99, 102
aphasia 45
Argentina 70
artists 83
Arts Council of Northern Ireland 84
art therapy 77
Armagh, Northern Ireland 59, 60
ASD (acute stress disorder) 22–3
Association of Professional Music Therapists in the UK 213
attachment
  and separation 102–4
  theory 105
attitude, consistency of 135
autism 179

avoidance behaviours 160, 163, 169–70

'bad behaviour' 111
ballet classes 155
BBC 88
Beast in the Nursery, The (Phillips) 149
Being and Nothingness (Sartre) 186
Belfast 11, 17, 32, 59, 60, 88, 92, 213
bereavement 75, 166
birdsong 41
'bleak' and 'cold' violence 99–100
Bloody Sunday 75
Blue Danube Waltz (Strauss) 44
bodhrán 78
borderline personality disorder 193
Bosnia-Herzegovina (B-H) 15, 17, 213, 215
  music therapy service in post-war environment 153–74
  developmental level of client at time of war 161
  family situation 161–2
  issues specific to psychological trauma and 159–62
  nature of traumatic event 160–1
  other aspects of post-war life 162
boundaries 134–5, 137
brain processes
  primary and secondary 25
  see also neurology
British Army 62
By Kilbrannon Sound (Gribbin) 90

Cambodia 69–70
Catholics 61–2, 84, 85, 87
catharsis 125
Cease (Gribbin) 91
central nervous system 51
cerebral cortex 45, 46
chemists 67

child guidance 67
childhood
  making sense of violence in 108–10
  origins of violence in: psychological perspective 102–6
children's fiction 185
circle as symbol of wholeness 145–6
Citizens' Advice Bureau 67
classical music 78
clinical psychologists 67
clinical work, central issues relating to 220–5
Commonsense View of All Music, A (Blacking) 42
communication
  concrete 140
  and music 44–5
community nurses 67
community workers 68
composers in Northern Ireland 83–93
concentration problems 111
concrete communication 140
consistency of attitude 135
consistency of setting 135
consistency of time 134
control, loss of 101
Cookstown, Northern Ireland 60
coping
  emotional 49
  mechanisms 110
counselling 73
counsellors 67
country music 78
Craigavon, Northern Ireland 59
creative interaction in music therapy sessions 127–8
creativity and healing 57–81
Criminal Damages Scheme 71
Criminal Injuries Compensation Scheme 71
Croatia 153, 159
Croats 153, 154
Crossgar, Northern Ireland 90
cultural aspects
  for music therapists 158
  for translators 157–8
culture and society 57–81

and musical perspectives
  55–93
dancing 124
deaf musicians 51
deaths during the Troubles
  58–62
  rates 60, 62, 69–70
deconditioning 50
dehumanisation 74
denial 22
Denmark 91
depression 160, 163, 165–8
deprivation 60
  and early abandonment
    in psychodynamic
    music therapy
    133–52
Derry, Northern Ireland 59,
  60, 87–8
deskilling 74
deterrence 75
developmental psychology see
  infant psychology
developmental trauma and its
  relation to sound and
  music (Israel) 193–207
  clinical illustrations
    199–205
Different Drums 78
disaster and trauma 24
disempowerment 74
disorganised-disorientated
  one-year-olds (Group D)
  103
distance supervision of work
  with traumatised
  children 211–3
  beginning 214–17
    supervisees'
      experience
      214–15
    supervisors'
      experience
      215–17
  central issues relating to
    clinical work 220–5
    traumatised clients
      223–5
    working with
      translator
      221–3
  changes in supervision
    focus 217–20
    supervisees'
      experience
      217–18

supervisors'
  experience
  218–20
telephone supervision
  and long-distance
  relationship 225–8
  supervisees'
    experience
    226–7
  supervisors'
    experience
    227–8
distress 65
DJ workshops 155
doctors 67
dopamine 51
dreams 63
drug treatment 50
Drumcree, Northern Ireland
  91
drum playing 122, 125, 126,
  140–2
DSM-IV (Diagnostic and
  Statistical Manual of
  Mental Disorders) 22, 23,
  72, 111
duality of musical energy
  115
Dungannon, Northern
  Ireland 59, 60
dynamic form 35

early infancy trauma
  and idea of regression as
    curative factor 194–5
  regression and sound
    195–8
Eastern Cape, South Africa
  98
eastern European composers
  85
Edinburgh 88
Egypt 89
EMDR (Eye Movement
  Desensitisation and
  Reprocessing) 73, 77
emotional coping 49
emotional withdrawal 105
emotions
  and limbic system 46
  and music 41
empathy 105
employment 68
environment, mother as 137
epilepsy 47
eros-related violence 100
ethnomusicology 42

ethno-national conflicts 74,
  75
event axis 111
evolution 42
experiencing oneself through
  music 35
explosions 58

facilitating environment,
  encountering 140–3
fairy tales 185
faith healers 68
false self 193
family
  situation in post-war
    society of
    Bosnia-Herzegovina
    161–2
  survival strategy 31
fear
  attacks of 74
  conditioning 50
fearfulness 160
financial compensation for
  physical or
  psychological injury 71
fight or flight responses 25
folk dancing 155
folk music (Irish) 86
Follow the Horse (Gribbin) 90
football chants 124
fragmentation 115
free associative singing
  251–3
'Frère Jacques' 186
From the Besieged City
  (O'Connell) 87
frustration 115
fundamentalism 78

Gauteng clinic, South Africa
  97, 113, 114, 116
Glasgow 88
going-on-being 137
gospel music 78
GPs 67
Grace Notes (MacLaverty) 91
grief 27, 58 160
grounding 238
group music therapy 116
guilt 160
Gulf War 159

harmonising 238
harmony 41
healing and creativity 57–81

help and support for victims
    of Troubles 66–8
helplessness 65, 66, 74, 101
high alert 101
high road response to
    stimulus 48–9
hippocampus 46, 47, 49
His Eyes (Gribbin) 90
HIV/AIDS 97
holding
    environment 137
    vocal holding techniques
        236–41
homeostasis 47
hope, unconscious 141
hostile acts 99
human rights and music
    119–32
hyper arousal 111
hypnosis 77
hypothalamus 46, 47

imprisonment 58
improvisational music therapy
    111–12, 193
individual axis 111
infant psychology 26
    ego development
        (Winnicott) 30–1
    groups (Ainsworth)
        103–4
    Kleinian 26
injuries 58
    financial compensation
        for 71
insecure-ambivalent
    one-year-olds (Group C)
        103–4
insecure-avoidant
    one-year-olds (Group A)
        103–4
insomnia 111
institutionalised violence
    100, 109
interaction in music therapy
    sessions 127
Interactive Image Work 77
International Classification of
    Diseases (ICD) 72
international clinical
    perspectives 95–207
interpersonal relationships,
    difficulties in 160
intimidation 58
IRA 23, 60, 73
Irish Congress of Trade
    Unions 59

Irish Republic *see* Republic of
    Ireland
irritability 111
Isamnion Fragments (Gribbin)
    90
Israel 15
    developmental trauma
        and its relation to
        sound and music
        193–207
Italy 154

Jack B (Gribbin) 90

Kicking Down (Flood) 88
Kleinian psychology 26

Lambeg drums 78, 91
language 42
    and music 44–5
lasting effect of trauma 22
lawyers 68
learned helplessness 165
limbic system 130–1
    and emotions 46
    and memory 46–8
listening together, processes
    in 211–30
loneliness 109
Londonderry 88
loss, traumatic 75
low intensity conflict 70
low road response to stimulus
    48–9
Loyalist paramilitaries 62

Macha's Curse (Alcorn) 90
Mad Cow Songs (Gribbin) 90
major and minor trauma
    110–11
marriage counsellors 67
Medical Foundation for the
    Care of Victims of
    Torture, London
    119–20, 121, 129, 130,
    131
memory and limbic system
    46–8
'Men Behind the Wire, The'
    91
Mental Health Act 74
Micro Statistics Centre,
    University of
    Manchester 59
Middle East, conflict in 75
Middle Music School,
    Pavarotti Music Centre
    155

Millennium Award 11
mind–body
    alienation 74
    links 25
ministers 67
mirroring 238
Modena, Italy 154
Mostar, Bosnia-Herzegovina
    153–6, 159, 160, 162,
    163, 165, 169, 171,
    173, 213–16, 223
mother
    as environment 137
    –infant interaction
        136–40
        and music 120
    as object 137
movement and music 42–4
music
    act of making 127–9
    and communication 44–5
    developmental trauma
        and its relation to
        193–207
    as external pacemaker
        42–4
    and human rights
        119–32
    and movement 42–4
    in music prison (story of
        Pablo) 175–92
    and violence 120–1
    what music expresses
        124–5
    what music represents
        123–4
    see also music therapy
music therapy
    aspects of psychological
        trauma in 163–72
    example in context
        29–32
    in Northern Ireland 78–9
    practice in Bosnia 156–9
    service in postwar
        environment (Bosnia)
        153–74
    with South African
        children 97–118
    and trauma 50–1,
        110–15, 159–62
Music Therapy Department,
    Pavarotti Music Centre
    155–6
musical dysgraphia 45
musical dyslexia 45

musical vertex of analytical
    attention 35
Music Child (Nordoff and
    Robbins) 112, 114
Music for the Third Ear
    (Senstad) 175, 191
Music Ireland 83
Muslims 153, 154
myths and legends, Irish 86

narcissistic disorder 193
neurology of trauma 25,
    41–53
neuropeptides 51
neurophysiological changes
    caused by music 41
Newry and Mourne,
    Northern Ireland 59, 60
news reporting of traumatic
    events 27–8
New York
    events of 11 September
        2001 21, 27, 36,
        260–1
nightmares 63, 111
noradrenaline 49, 51
North (Gribbin) 90
Northern Ireland 11, 13, 15,
    17, 23, 26, 29, 32–3,
    57–79, 121, 215
    composers in 83–93
    use of music therapy in
        78–9
    see also Troubles, the
Northern Province, South
    Africa 98, 100
Notes on the Edge (Gribbin) 92
nose brain 47
numbing 105, 111

object, mother as 137
objectless violence 102
ocean drum 140–1
'Ode to a Nightingale'
    (Keats) 50
Of the Taín (Gribbin) 90, 91
olfactory system 47
Orangeism 78
Orange marches 91
orchestral music 78, 88–90
orphanage 104
otherness 105, 109–10

pain of contrast 141
painful memories 63
paranoid-schizoid position
    187

Parkinson's disease (PD)
    43–4
passive-aggressive violence
    101
Pavarotti Music Centre
    (PMC) 15, 153, 213
    profile of 158
    War Child and 154–5
percussion instruments 107,
    144–5, 179
performance of music 51
personnel departments 68
pessimistic world view 160
Peter Pan (Barrie) 185
pharmacists 67
physiology, effect of music on
    42–3
piano 126, 140, 141, 179
pipes 78
'plastic shamrock' Irish music
    86, 88
play 113, 136
    four stages in Winnicott's
        theory of 136–8
        stage 1: mother as
            environment
            137
        stage 2: separation
            and discovery
            of transitional
            play 137–8
        stage 3: alone in
            presence of
            another 138
        stage 4: playing
            relationship
            138
    impact of early trauma on
        capacity for 139–40
    playing alone in presence
        of someone 146–9
    symbolic 148, 149, 150
    therapy 186
    transformative experience
        and beginnings of
        144–5
Playing and Reality (Winnicott)
    136
political violence 129–31
politicians 68
post trauma responses 22–5,
    27–8
    see also PTSD
post-war society of
    Bosnia-Herzegovina
    family situation 161–2
    impact of 159

powerlessness 31
presence and absence 104
pre-symbolic experience of
    music 35–6
Pretoria 97
priests 67
primary brain processes 25
primary love 143
prison visiting 60
programme music 123
projection 105
protective mechanisms 33–4
Protestants 61–2, 78, 84, 87,
    88, 90
proto-conversation 42
psychiatrist 67
psychodynamic music therapy
    134–6
    deprivation and early
        abandonment in
        133–52
psychological buffer zone
    109
psycho-social trauma 110
psychotic children 188
psychotropic drugs to 'treat'
    trauma 74
PTSD (post traumatic stress
    disorder) 22, 23, 71, 72,
    111

racial conflicts 74, 75
rage 65, 115
random violence 100
rap music 121
recovery 77
Red Riding Hood 185
regression 163, 168–9
    as curative factor in early
        infancy trauma
        194–5
    early infancy trauma,
        sound and 195–8
regressive behaviours 160
rejection 105
relational violence 102
relationship
    counsellors 67
    playing 138
Relief of Derry, The symphony
    (Davey) 87
religion 60–2
Remembrance Day bombing,
    Northern Ireland 29–30
Republic of Ireland 84, 86
    working with trauma of
        early abandonment

and deprivation in psychodynamic music therapy 133–52
Republican paramilitaries 62
retaliation 75
retraumatisation 245
rhinencephalon (nose brain) 47
rhythmical stimuli, responses to 42
rhythms of body, effect of music on 42–3
'Ricochet' (Zilkić) 12
Rising (Flood) 88
rock school 155
Romania 133, 141, 151
Russia 74

safety, loss of 25–6, 31, 36, 66, 74
St Patrick's Night 88
Salvador 69–70
Samaritans 67
Sash, The 90
SAS 73
school 107
    welfare, support through 67
Schools' Music Programme, Pavarotti Music Centre 155
Scotland 91
Scottish bagpipes 78
secondary brain processes 25
secrecy and trauma 31
securely-attached one-year-olds (Group B) 103–4, 106
self, sense of 130, 136
self-esteem, poor 105, 160
self-help groups 67
self-medication 77
separation
    and attachment 102–4
    discovery of transitional play 137–8
Serbian army 153
Serbs 153, 154
serotonin 51
setting, consistency of 135
shell shock 25
shock and trauma 22, 24–5, 27
shootings 58
siege of Derry (1689) 87
silence

to storytelling 178–84
and trauma 31, 34
singing, free associative 251–3
sleep problems 64, 74, 77
Snaidhm an Ghrà (The True Lover's Knot) 89
social relations 130
social security agencies 67
social workers 67
society and culture 57–81
solicitors 68
Sonorities Festival of Twentieth Century Music 89
sound
    developmental trauma and its relation to 193–207
    early infancy trauma, regression and 195–8
South Africa 14, 42
    music therapy with South African children 97–118
space 137
speech, development of 42
splitting 105
spontaneous music making 112
Stanford Orchestra, California 90
storytelling 73–4
    from silence to 178–84
Strabane, Northern Ireland 60
stress 110
    disorders 49
stuckness 140
'Sunday Bloody Sunday' (U2) 91
supervision 211–3
support
    perspective 209–59
    through school welfare 67
survival 36
    mechanisms 101
survivors of violence 101, 112
symbolic play 148, 149, 150

Taliban 131
Tavistock model 111
teachers 67, 107

telephone supervision and long-distance relationship 225–8
terrorism 27
thanatos-related violence 100
tiger story 181, 185
time, consistency of 134
torture 130
transformation 115
transformational circle 150
transformative experience and beginnings of play 144–5
transitional objects 138
transitional play, separation and discovery of 137–8
transitional space 137
Transkei 98
translators 157–8
    cultural aspects for 157–8
    working with 157, 221–3
'Trap, The' (Jerry) 29
trauma 11–13
    biological basis of brain's response to 48–9
    concept of 71
    in context 21–39
    context of therapist's stance 32–7
    contextualising multidisciplinary attitudes to 24–9
    contextualising definitions of 22–4
    distance supervision of work with traumatised children 211–3
    of early abandonment and deprivation in psychodynamic music therapy 133–52
    early infancy, and idea of regression as curative factor 194–5
    giving trauma a voice 234–6
    impact of, on capacity for play 139–40
    and music and music therapy 50–1, 110–15, 159–62
        aspects of psychological

trauma in
163–72
nature of traumatic event
160–1
perspectives 29–53
traumatised clients
223–5
treating traumatic effect
of violence 129–30
wounded healer's
perspective 231–59
Tribe (Gribbin) 91
Trinity College, Dublin 85
triune brain 46
Troubles, the (Northern
Ireland) 13–14, 33, 57,
121
comparison with other
conflicts 69–70
composers in 83–93
effects of 62–6
help and support for
victims of 66–8
overview of human
impact of 57–8
and use of music therapy
78–9
political, social and
cultural factors 71–7
when did deaths occur?
58
where did deaths occur?
59–60
trust, lack of 65–6, 74
Tswana 98
tuberculosis 97
Turkey 70

Uileann pipes (Irish) 78
Ulster see Northern Ireland;
Troubles, the
Ulster Processional 89
Ulster Youth Orchestra 88
unborn child, effect of music
on 42
unconscious hope 141
undamaged self behind
apparent disability
130–1
Unionism (Ireland) 78
United Kingdom 84, 213
music and human rights
in 119–32
in music prison (story of
Pablo) 175–92
period 1: from
silence to

storytelling
178–84
period 2: tigers and
torture 185–90

Valium 50
Venda people, South Africa
42
video sessions 108
Vietnam 22, 72, 159
vibro-acoustic therapy (VAT)
51
vicarious traumatisation 243
victimisation, recovering
power after 57–81
victims of violence 101, 112
and the Troubles 59
characteristics 60
creativity of 76
violence
and music 120–1
and trauma 25, 33–4,
58, 71, 98
nature of, individual and
collective 99–102
origins in childhood:
psychological
perspective 102–6
absence and
presence 104
attachment and
separation
102–4
conflicts of absence
105–6
making sense of
violence in
childhood
108–10
treating traumatic effect
of 129–30
VK/D3 77
vocal holding techniques
236–41
voluntary organisations 68,
72

Wanting, Not Wanting
(Gardner) 88, 89
war
developmental level of
client at time of 161
and trauma 24, 25, 31,
32
War Child and Pavarotti
Music Centre 154–5
War Child Netherlands 155

Washington attack, 11
September 2001 260
Where the Wild Things Are
(Sendak) 185
wild animal music 180–1
withdrawal 160
Women in Music
Commissioning Fund
award 92
World War I 25
World War II 159
wound and trauma 22
wounded healer 231–59
case examples 246–51,
253–6
free associative singing
251–3
giving trauma a voice
234–6
vocal holding techniques
236–41

Xhosa 97–8

'Yesterday' (Beatles) 204, 205
Yugoslavia, former 153, 155
Yugoslavian National Army
153